A
MANUAL ON EXAMINATION
OF
LOUISIANA LAND TITLES

by

JOSEPH KENTON BAILEY

THE INDUSTRIES PUBLISHING CO., INC.

NEW ORLEANS, LA.

1942

NOTICE

In response to our many requests for Bailey's LOUISIANA LAND TITLES, *Claitor's* contracted for this exact photo reprint of the original edition. We will very much appreciate the reader's report of corrections, and suggestions for improvement and additions, as it is our intention to publish a supplement or a revised edition at a later date.

Dedication

To the legal profession which I trust will derive some benefit from a perusal and use of this work.

The Author

TABLE OF CONTENTS I

TABLE OF CONTENTS

TABLE OF CONTENTS   III

EXAMINING TITLES TO LAND IN LOUISIANA
CHAPTER I
General Observations

In Louisiana all allodial titles, as in other states of the Union, have their inception in the sovereign.

Divestiture of title from the sovereign is governed by the laws of that sovereign. A State can in no manner prescribe any rules or effect any changes bearing on the primary disposal of the public land by the United States (1) but once the title is divested from the United States to the individual it is governed by the laws of the State in which the land is situated.

Acquisition by the individual from the sovereign takes various forms; grants and purchases from foreign governments prior to the Louisiana purchase; patents and grants from the United States, and purchases from the state.

Primarily, title to real property is acquired by the individual by one of two means: by purchase and by inheritance, though there are several other means of such acquisitions, as by donation inter vivos and by prescription acquirendi causa, though the latter can never be the foundation of a title from the sovereign; (2) and the former only in a few instances, as for example by the United States to the States and grants to railroads and perhaps homestead entries, although these last two are properly speaking onerous donations and not real donations.

Through a wise system of law, known as the Civil Law, which has prevailed in Louisiana from its earliest settlement, continued and strengthened by legislative enactments and by jurisprudence establishing rules of property, titles to land in Louisiana can

1—Irvin v Marshall, 61 U. S. (20 Howard) 558
2—Jordan v Barrett, et al, U. S. (4 Howards), 185

be said to be as safe and free from doubt as is human-
ly possible. Because of these laws the title examiner
in Louisiana is not vexed by the perplexities, refine-
ments and subtle distinctions involved in titles under
the common law system of land tenure and of devise
and descent. This satisfactory condition is due in the
main to those equitable and clear provisions of our
Civil Code which guide, control and establish the
rights of the individual in his relations with his fellow
man.

The chief of these provisions, as affecting land
titles are:

        Ownership
        Inheritance, with the subdivisions of
            Descent
            Forced heirship
            Wills and testaments
        Community rights of spouses
        Recordation and registration and their effect
            on the rights and claims of third par-
            ties.
        Prescription
            Both acquirendi and liberandi.

The Courts, in their interpretation of the codal
provisions have consistently sought to adhere to the
principles laid down by the Code and to adjudicate in
strict accordance with its spirit.

A very important fact to be noted as affecting
the security of titles in this State, is the unvarying
policy of both the legislative and the judicial branches to discourage attacks on titles to land. Thus numerous laws which have as their purpose the quieting
of the rights of title holders who have acquired in
good faith, have been enacted, while the courts, by
a long line of decisions have given the widest scope to

those laws, going to the extreme in upholding titles as against adverse claims.

Thus they have held that no parol evidence will be admitted to contest title, although the contestants are the original parties to the transaction and even though the rights of third parties are not affected. So parol evidence is not admitted to show a sale was intended for a mortgage, though vendor remained in possession; (1) nor to show fraud in agent who purchased in his own name; (2) nor to prove fraudulent violation of parol mandate to purchase: (2) nor as to parties to the instrument, heirs, not forced ones, to show simulation; (3) nor to prove claim to property acquired by agent with funds stolen from principal (4).

All of the above rules of property were established on the broad ground that security of land titles cannot be jeopardized by parol evidence.

The codal articles on the subject are:

C. C. Art. 2275. Every transfer of immovable property must be in writing, but if a verbal sale, or other disposition of such property be made, it shall be good against the vendee, who confesses it when interrogated on oath provided actual delivery has been made of the property thus sold.

C. C. Art. 2276. Parol evidence against or beyond acts. Neither shall parol evidence be admitted against or beyond what is contained in the acts, nor on what may

1—Franklin v Sewall, 110 La., 292; 147 La. 1035;160 La. 152;
    Johnson v Johnson, 191 La. 416.
2—Perrault v Perrault, 32 A.635; Scurto v LeBlanc, 191 L.145, 152
3—Herbert v Lege, 29 A.511; Schrock v Bolding et al. 171 L.938
4—Hackenburg v Gartsa, av 30 A.898; Scurto v LeBlanc, 191 L. 145, 152
See also Heis v Cronan, 12 A.213; Passadue v Connolly, 10 R.66; Succ.
    Curtis 110 L.1070

have been said before, or at the time of making them, or since. (1)

So a completed act of sale precludes parol evidence as to previous offers and conditions thereof; but even where such offer and conditions are written but where the act is obviously incomplete parol evidence admissable to show actual contract. (2)

There is one exception to the principle that parol evidence will not be admitted to upset title to real estate, which exception is embodied in Article 2230 of the Civil Code, as amended by Act 5 of 1884, which provides:

Counter letters can have no effect against creditors or bona fide purchasers; they are valid as against all others but forced heirs shall have the same right to annul absolutely and by parol evidence the simulated contracts of those from whom they inherit and shall not be restricted to the legitime.

Prior to the enactment of Act 5, 1884, forced heirs were restricted to their legitime. (3)

This exception has been held by the courts to very narrow limits they holding that it is only in those cases in which the property had been held by an ancestor in his own name and the transfer made by him to another, could the forced heirs attack the transfer as simulated (4)

In a suit by forced heirs to annul a sale made by an ancestor to a coheir of an immovable for a price recited in the act as being paid in cash, it has been decided that parol evidence is permissible to show the real consideration was the obligation undertaken by

1—Halmeel v Moore, 194, L.504; Guaranty B. & L. Co., v Hunter, 173 L.502; Cook v Parkerson, 16 L.130; Glover v Abney, 160 L. 182
2—Davies v. Bierce 114 L.668
3—Succ. Block 137 L.302, Carter v Loeb 177 L.447
4—Eberle v Eberle 161 L.313

the co-heir to support ancestor and his wife during their natural lives. In other words, that there was a real consideration though not the one recited in the act and that therefore the transfer was not a simulated one (1)

There is of course the exception of gross fraud, although it has been held that it is not in every case that fraud will invalidate a title as when both parties to the contract have entered into conspiracy to defraud others, neither party may sue to annul the contract (2)

This rule (inadmissibility of parol evidence) does not apply, on the other hand, to parties whose interest are affected by a fraudulent or simulated transfer of real property, but who took no part in the transaction (3)

It is true that the most dangerous links in a chain of title are those involving the rights of minors and community interest, but this fact arises not from any obscurity or lack of uniformity in the laws governing those rights and their alienation or in the judicial interpretation thereof, but principally from a failure to properly comply with those laws in an attempt at alienation, which failures are frequently due entirely to attempted short cuts dictated by expediency or haste.

The probate proceedings which are a necessary part of such a link puts the examiner upon his guard and it is only necessary for him to critically examine the proceedings to ascertain whether or not the minors rights have been properly protected and that the alienation thereof has been carried out in the form

1—Landry v Landry 40 A.229
2—Ackerman v Peters 113 L.156
3—Telle v Fish 34 A. 1243

and manner prescribed by law. This does not necessarily mean that these proceedings and alienations should have been executed in a slavish adherence to every letter of the law. A substantial compliance with the law is all that is called for in any case.

Of course the minor who has not been brought into the proceedings at all, or where the alienation of his interest has not been carried out in accordance with the requirements laid down by law, or in other words whose rights have been ignored, has not been divested of those rights.

This subject will be hereafter discussed in detail and at greater length under the proper heading.

The ignoring of the minor's rights as outlined above constitutes the real doubt in any link in any title where minor's rights are involved, but it is one which is inseparable from land titles.

Community interests are far less dangerous and any doubtful alienation may be cured at far less expense and with greater certainty than a defect in the case of a minor.

In addition, prescription liberandi causa gives further strength, stability, security and validity to titles in which doubtful links occur.

Other strong factors which contribute to the validity of titles are the laws governing constructive notice, registration and recordation.

In Louisiana the registration or recording of all instruments and claims affecting real property is absolutely necessary and when so registered or recorded is notice to the world. The mere depositing, filing, and the endorsement of such filing thereon, by the recorder of an act makes it a part of the records of

See "defects and their Cures" in this volume

the office and affects third parties even before the actual recording thereof (1)

The provision of the Civil Code governing this requirement (Article 2254) reads:

> It shall be the duty of the recorder to endorse on the back of each act deposited with him the time it was received by him, and to record the same without delay in the order in which they were received; and such acts shall have effect against third persons only from the date of their being deposited in the office of parish recorders.

This notice is effective as to third parties even in those cases where the description contained in an act is erroneous, (2) so the vendee in an act of sale is protected (3).

A corollary to this is the principle that nothing that is not recorded or registered is binding on anyone save the parties to the transaction; hence a claim not of record is not binding on third parties; (4) even though those parties have other notice. (5)

Other articles of the Civil Code on the same subject, read:

> Art. 2246. Sales or exchange of immovable property by instruments made under private signature are valid against bona fide purchasers and creditors only from the day on which they are registered in the manner prescribed by law.

> Art. 2262. In the parish of Orleans, acts, whether they are passed before a notary public or otherwise, shall have no effect against

1—Way v Levy 41 A.454
2—Albert Hansen Lr. Co., v Baldwin Lumber Co., 80 L.849
3—Payne v Paney 29 A.116
4—Schniedau v N. O. Land Co., 132 L.273
5—McDuffie v Walker 125 L.152

third persons, but from the date of their being deposited in the office of the register of conveyances.

Art. 2264. No notarial act concerning immovable property shall have any effect against third persons, until the same shall have been deposited in the office of the parish recorder or register of conveyance of the parish where such immovable is situated. (1)

Art. 2265. All sales of immovable property made by the sheriff or other officer, by virtue of any execution or other order of court; all marriage contracts made within this state tending in anywise to convey, transfer, assure or effect the estate of the parties, or being intended to ascertain the dotal rights of the wife, or that her marriage portion is liable to some reserves or stipulated to be paraphernal or extra dotal property; and all final judgments affecting immovable property shall be recorded in the parish where the immovable property is situated.

Incidently, prior to the enactment of the last clause in above article in re judgments of courts, such judgments did not have to be recorded to have effect against third parties, (2) it being deemed that such courts were courts of record and their judgment were notice to the world.

Art. 2266. All sales, contracts and judgments affecting immovable property which shall not be so recorded shall be utterly null and void, except as between the parties themselves. The recording may be made at any

1—Schniedau v Land Co. 132 L.273 McDuffie v Walker 125 L.152
2—Brewer v Bright 130 L.491

time, but shall only affect third persons from the time of the recording. The recording shall have effect from the time when the act is deposited n the proper office and indorsed by the proper officer.

In matters of titles to immovable property no other notice than registry can prove knowledge, that is, knowledge acquired de hors the recorder's office is not binding on third parties; (1) and though a sale be a bona fide one, it will not prime a judicial mortgage if the latter has been recorded prior to the sale, (2) and so an adjudication of succession property at auc- is good against previous unrecorded sales (3)

There are two exceptions to this principle:
Certain servitudes.
Prescription acquirendi causa.

Of the first class, the servitudes established by law, Civil Code Chapter 3, such as passage and right of way, walls, fences and ditches in common etc., continuous and apparent servitudes (C. C. 765) and those mentioned in Article 769, namely, "If the owner of two estates, between which there exists an apparent sign of servitude, sell one of those estates, and if the deed of sale be silent respecting the servitude, the same shall continue to exist actively or passively in favor of or upon the estate which has been sold", do not need recordation or registry to have effect against third persons.

No claim or notice of title is required in the prescription of thirty years, nor will the recording of a sale of the property involved interrupt prescription (4)

As stated before there were at one time another

1—Boyer v Sheriff, 30 A.660; Gee v Clark, 42 A.920
2—Baker v Atkins, 107 L.490; Schnidau v N. O. Land Co., 132, L.173
3—McDuffie v Walker, 125 L.157
4—Kinnison, Wall La. App. 146 Sou. 371

exception to the rule discussed above, namely judgments affecting real property such as judgment sending heirs in possession. In Brewer v Bright 130 L. 491, the court, citing other decisions, held that registry of titles by descent is unnecessary to affect third persons. The court said that there was no law requiring it, but this is no longer true as may be noted in the citation of Article 2265 given above.

It may be said, by way of comment, that fraudulent conveyances, with the exceptions noted above, are not protected by these laws, hence a sale of one's property by another, without the owner's knowledge or consent, expressed or implied (as where the pretended owner forged the real owner's signature), is not a sale and would not be binding on him, even if recorded by the purchaser. This on the principle that there was no sale. Article 2252 Revised Civil Code.

But in this, as in all other cases, thirty years' prescription coupled with corporeal possession, would defeat the owner's claim, also ten years prescription where purchaser was in good faith.

CLASSES OF TITLES

There are three classes of titles.

1st—Those titles in which all the requirements and formalities of law have been met not only in the last link but in all.

These need neither ratification nor confirmation, nor the invoking of prescription to render them perfect valid titles.

2nd—Those titles, though they lack some of the formalities required by law, or in which defects may be urged against them, are not open to attack because the law and the jurisprudence have declared that such informalities or defects not sufficient to defeat title, such as certain minor irregularities in proceedings leading up to a sale by the sheriff, executor, administrator etc; the courts holding in numerous instances that the judgment and the sale thereunder protects the purchaser in good faith.

3rd—Those titles in which the defects have been cured by prescription.

In the first two classes title is good against the world even before prescription period has run.

Under the plan adopted here, an endeavor has been made to set out all the formalities and requirements of law required to place a title in the first class mentioned above, and then to discuss the effect as to its validity, a lack of such formalities and requirements would have in a title; and finally to point out and suggest the means and methods of curing such defects for the purpose of placing the title in at least the second, if not the first class.

The author's purpose is to assist the examiner in his work by bringing together for ready reference the principles of law involved in each muniment of title, and, as a ready means to that end the plan has been adopted of proceeding as if a title, the chain of which contained all the links by which property could be acquired, was being examined, that is, beginning with a patent and ending with the link which exhausted every means or method by which a title could have been acquired.

For convenience and ready reference, all of the methods of acquiring title to real property have been set out in sequence and each is taken up and discussed fully from the standpoint of the substantive law as well as the jurisprudence.

A point the examiner should keep sharply in mind that the validity of a title in any given link is determined by the law as it existed at the time of the transaction and not by subsequent laws which change or modify the former law without at the same time quieting transactions based on the previous statute, as far example; Article 1753 of the Revised Civil Code has been repealed by Act 238 of 1918, but the latter act does not contain any provision for the quieting or ratifying transaction, violative of that Article.

This naturally is important as a title which may be valid under existing laws may not be so under a previous law in force at the date of the transaction, unless the legislature has enacted specific ratifying statutes, as it has done in several instances, such as recent acts quieting sales of minors' interest improperly divested.

In the examination of titles to land, the examiner may do the abstract work himself, or that work may be done by an abstracter, who may or may not be a lawyer, but in either case a careful, clear and accurate take off should be made to enable the examiner to have every essential element in each link before him for study and analysis at his leisure. In no other way can the conscientious examiner give an honest and correct opinion on the title under examination.

In addition to this, these notes or abstracts, when properly prepared and filed, form a valuable reference on all future occasions in any lawyer's office. The more perfect an abstract is, whether made by the examiner or by someone else, the more useful it may become in any future controversy or attack.

Reverting to the above declaration that even if the abstract is made by the examiner himself, it should be full, accurate and complete, it may be said that many lawyers, noted in the profession as being careful and conscientious title examiners, do not make such an abstract, but examine each link as they reach it in abstracting, confining their notes to such items as they deem important, unless they find that there is a serious defect in the link, or deem it necessary to make further study of the point involved. Notwithstanding this fact, such a form of examination is not commendable, because of the danger of an unintentional overlooking of a vital element, a danger that is ever present, be the examiner ever so experienced, able and careful.

In a recent case, involving valuable lands, the defendant suffered very serious and extensive losses simply because one of the links in the title omitted a vitally essential fact and it seemed no effort was made to obtain the information before acceptance of title. The attorneys who had examined the title for the parties were experienced, skilled practitioners, thoroughly familiar with title work, especially of that character so there is no justification in a belief that the error was due to lack of skill, experience or knowledge. It is therefore fair to presume that there had been an oversight, and while it cannot be stated as a positive fact, the case has all the appearance of a "running examination" of the title. In any event the incident brings attention sharply to the necessity of an examination in which the abstract is made with full attention to a complete and careful take off of the links, undisturbed, without that distraction necessarily present where the examiner attempts to pass on the validity of each link as he progresses.

With all due deference to practitioners who have followed such a system with satisfaction to themselves, it cannot be claimed that it is in accord with modern practices of scientific methods and efficiency in all other lines of work.

However successful such methods of title examination have been in the past, the enormous increase of values in land in recent years, partially due to the rapid development of all lines of business in Louisiana and greatly to the oil and mineral development in the state, these methods have no place in the office of a lawyer who assumes the responsibility of passing on a title which may be the base upon which large financial transactions depend.

Certainly the young practitioner who enters the field of land title examination must recognize his responsibilities in undertaking this work and prepare himself to carry on his labors with such care and correctness and attention to vital details involved, as to preclude, as far as possible, any chance of error which may be charged to a lack of knowledge, diligence or skill on his part.

Notwithstanding the special nature of title examination there has not been in the past, with a few exceptions, which exceptions have been rather sketchy and incomplete, any attempt to give the lawyer a comprehensive outline of the laws which affect titles to real property, the essential elements of which constitutes a good title, or a digest of the jurisprudence which have established rules of property; or to set up guide posts by which he may check his opinions.

So vast is the subject and so complex is the task that it must be with great diffidence and misgiving that an author, however experienced or skilled he may be, attempts the work.

However the recognized need of some compilation of this character and the usefulness to the examiner of a book which would bring together in one volume the laws and jurisprudence affecting titles to real property and point out the dangers and pitfalls to be avoided in passing upon such titles, serves at once as an excuse and an apology for the author's temerity in undertaking such compilation.

At the outset the hopelessness of attempting to cover in one or even a dozen volumes, the subject in such a manner and so completely that an examiner can feel sure of finding therein an answer to every question however presented and in whatever shape, is recognized, but it is hoped that in this volume the examiner will find guidance and assistance in solving most if not all of the problems with which he is confronted in almost any title.

The author has in view two objectives: first to give the examiner the law and the jurisprudence applicable to titles in concrete form so as to enable him to decide whether or not the elements, constituting a link, meet the requirements called for in a valid title; and second, to decide whether or not such elements constitute a defective link or a good link. The latter task is the most difficult, because a link or a title in which all the elements conform to the requirements of the law and the jurisprudence, requires on the part of the examiner only a knowledge of that law and that jurisprudence. It is when a link or title fails to so conform in varying degrees that the examiner is confronted with the necessity of a decision which throws upon him a grave responsibility. Unfortunately he will be confronted with many of these problems in the course of his labors. Careless and inefficient confection of acts, omissions and errors in probate proceedings, irregularities in execution of Judgments, and in general, acts and facts which create doubt and misgivings, force upon the examiner

the necessity of acting as counsel for plantiff as well
as for defendant, and finally as judge in the controversy, with full realization that his judgment may
be, after an expensive trial, reversed by the courts.

It is of course impossible to include here more
than a small list of such border line cases, but it is
hoped that such as they are, they will aid the examiner and facilitate the solving of many of his problems.

As a further aid and relief in many cases the examiner has in this volume a complete list of the leading cases which constitute the jurisprudence on the
subject, the uniformity of which gives to titles in this
state full security against attack save in such cases
as are founded upon substantial ground.

As another answer to harassing perplexing questions the examiner has at hand the prescriptive laws,
which consistently supported by our courts, furnish
him with a magic wand which waved with certainty,
banishes from furrowed brows the wrinkles implanted
there by otherwise insurmountable difficulties.

While this work covers the whole range of title
examination whether in the country or in the cities,
titles to country property present problems never encountered in city titles, and vice versa and for illustration we note some.

In the cities (especially New Orleans) the long established origin of titles, the many links in the chain
and the continuous and notorious physical possesssion
of the property, renders unnecessary any examination
beyond a period of sixty years the time sufficient to
establish prescription against the world, including
minors, except in rare cases.

In the country an examination should be extended
to the original grant from the sovereign, as there

can be no question of prescription unless the sovereign has been legally divested of ownership.

Again, in the cities, descriptions, boundaries and the quantity of land involved, have greater importance than they do in the country. Pavings, alleys, restrictions and servitudes also have an importance that is negligible in the country.

There are other differences which will be referred to hereafter.

The plan adopted for the proper treatment of the subject of this volume consists of an analysis in separate chapters, of every link which may be found in a chain of title, beginning with grants, patents etc, from the governments of Spain, France, the United States and the State of Louisiana, every element in each link being presented and examined, with the law and the jurisprudence governing same, with proper reference to the statutes and the decisions of the courts on the particular subject.

Then follows, in other chapters, examples of omissions, irregular and illegal factors, comments as to their effect on the validity of the title, with references to the jurisprudence of the State which support the conclusions reached. Also, suggestions as to the cure of such defects as may be pointed out, by operation of estoppel, prescription and other factors.

These series of chapters are followed by chapters in which the laws and jurisprudence by which estoppels, prescription etc, serve as curatives, are analyzed and discussed.

Separate chapters are devoted to subjects which require special treatment because they cannot properly form part of the chapters on each link, although they vitally affect such links, such as adoption of children, appeals, clerks of courts substituted service, community of acquets and gains, divorce, etc.

Descriptions, maps, boundaries, surveys, both in the country and in the cities are fully explained and commented upon in other chapters.

Finally an index has been carefully prepared, designed to the end that the examiner may readily and quickly find in any part of the book the exact place where the point in which he is interested, as well as the articles of the Code, the Statutes and the Reports of the Courts affecting same, is discussed, analyzed and examined. As an example: "Witnesses" will not only be found under that heading but also under "Estoppel," "Sales", "Wills" and any other document or instrument in which witnesses are required, under the appropriate head.

The author may seem to be somewhat prolix in that some of the most elementary legal principles have been discussed and analyzed at length but the reason for this is two fold. First, even the most experienced lawyer is sometimes at a loss momentarily, when confronted with some question involving the most elementary principle of law, necessitating a research perhaps of considerable length. Should he be faced with such a situation while examining a title, he should promptly find his answer in this volume. Second, the author found it advisable and convenient to omit no principle however elementary, from discussion for fear that some jurisprudence of extreme importance in titles might be omitted with serious injury to the value of the book.

CHAPTER II

Methods By Which Real Property Is Acquired And Which Form Muniments Of Title.

As a prelude to the following it will be useful to learn what ownership is and what the Civil Code defines ownership to be, how it distinguishes it and regulates its acquirement.

So it defines ownership as the right by which a thing belongs to some one in particular to the exclusion of all other persons, (1) and declares that the ownership of a thing is vested in him who has the immediate dominion over it and not in him who has a mere beneficiary right to it, (2), which ownership continues though there has been a perpetual servitude established. (3) ownership is perfect when it is perpetual and when the thing is unincumbered with any real right towards any other person than the owner. (4) The effect is that perfect ownership gives the right to use, to enjoy and to dispose of one's property in the most unlimited manner, provided it is not used in any way prohibited by law or ordinances. (5)

The Code further declares it is the essence of the right of ownership that it cannot exist in two persons for the whole of the same thing; but they may be owners of the same thing in common and each for the part he may have therein. (6)

A sale whereby the vendee is unconditionally bound for the price while the vendor remains the exclusive owner of the thing sold until the sale price is fully paid, finds no sanction in our law. (7)

1—R. C. C. 488
2—R. C. C. 489
3—Cotton Exchange v Board of Assessors, 37 A.425
4—R.'C. C. 490
5—R. C. C. 491
6—R. C. C. 494
7—Barber Asph. Co.,v St. Louis Cyp. Co., 121 L.152;
      Thomas v Werlein 181 L.110

The ownership of things or property is acquired by inheritance, either legal or testamentary, by the effect of obligation and by the operation of law.[1]

Namely by succession, purchase, exchange etc., and by prescription.

As it has been seen title to real property may be acquired by various methods which methods have been arranged in order for better analysis and discussion. In this order voluntary transactions are placed in one class, while other transfers of ownership, such as sales under execution etc. which are by their nature not voluntary on the part of the owners, are placed in another class.

Various methods of acquisition will be found in both of these classes although they may partake of the same nature, as for example, sale or purchase. A change of ownership may be made by a voluntary act or it may be made under execution, so the sale affecting that change may be either voluntary or forced.

Title may be acquired from the sovereign and, although it is usually purchased, because of its peculiar nature it has been placed in an order by itself; or as has been said, it may be acquired by purchase or by donation, intervivos or mortis causa; it may be by inheritance; or it may be acquired by prescription acquirendi causa; therefore the order adopted separates the method as of classes.

1—R. C. C. 870

CHAPTER III

Change Of Ownership

Change of ownership of real property occurs in three forms.

Voluntary transfer.

Involuntary or forced transfer.

Inheritance.

The inheritance form strictly construed belongs to the second class, because the change of ownership brought about by death is involuntary, since it takes place without consent of the owner, but for convenience it is placed in a class by itself for purposes of discussion.

In each of these cases different laws and the judicial interpretation thereof govern and determine the validity or otherwise, of each link forming part of the chain of title.

Voluntary Transfer

This is the most common form of change of ownership and present the least difficult of the many questions which require correct answers by the examiner before he may safely approve a title.

Omitting for the moment the first link, which is the divestiture of the sovereign's ownership, as this will be discussed in a subsequent chapter, the elements of any voluntary transfer may be listed as follows:

The parties thereto.

The right and power of the transferer to make a transfer and the extent of that right and power.

The instrument by which the transfer is made

The form in which the transfer is made.

The rights of the parties to the transfer under
the instrument.

The rights of third parties contra to the parties
to the instrument.

The correct or incorrect execution of the intent
of the parties.

A voluntary transfer involves:

A sale (purchase)

A Donation

A Dation en paiement

A dedication

A counter letter

An exchange

A Partition

A redemption of a tax sale

A renunciation

A recission

A vente a remere

Involuntary Or Forced Divestiture

Involuntary or forced divestiture occur in the
following cases:

In the enforcement of an order or judgment
of court, such as sheriffs' sales under a fieri
facias, or other writs; to pay debts of a succession, or otherwise settle a succession; ....to
effect a partition; and the enforcement of
specific performances; in banqruptcy, receiverships etc.

Transfer of a minor's or interdict's property.

Sale by a Trustee of property placed in his
possession under a trust.

In the exercise of eminent domain

By Tax sale.

These are called involuntary or forced transfers

because the owner's consent is not a prerequisite.

The validity of these transfers is affected by the following elements:

The jurisdiction of the court, where the transfer is made under authority of a court.

The legality of the proceedings resulting in the transfer.

The proper execution of the judgment or order of court, where there is one.

The powers and authority of the Trustee under the terms of the instrument creating the trust and the laws governing trusts.

The power and authority of the corporation exercising the right of eminent domain.

The legality and correctness of the assessment and sale of the property for taxes.

Inheritance

This form connotes:

The death of the owner.

A judgment of court having jurisdiction of the sucession or the minor.

The legality and correctness of the proceedings by which a minor's interest are divested.

The right and capacity of the transferee under the laws of inheritance in intestate estates.

The right and capacity of the transferee to take under the terms of the will in testate estates.

The proper formation of the will and the validity of its provision as affected by the inheritance laws of the state.

Reverting to the subject of voluntary transfers, the first element listed is that of the parties.

There must be of course two parties, the transferer and transferee. Either or both parties may act through another and there must be on the one part an intention to transfer and on the other in intention to accept the transfer. This intention must be evidenced by the transfer in writing, though the transferee may in certain cases evidence his intention to accept by other means.

The Right And Power Of The Owner To Make A Transfer And The Extent Of That Right

No voluntary transfer can be made by any other than a person who is sui juris. There are two classes of owners who are sui juris-natural persons and corporations. (1) In general a person is sui juris who is above the age of twenty one, or who has been fully emancipated according to law, and who is of sound mind. Prior to 1921, married women were not, in respect to their property, sui juris, but under statutes enacted in that year (2) the disabilities of married women were removed so that now, in regard to her own property (not community) she is sui juris.

A minor above the age of 18 who has been emancipated by court (3) or by marriage (4) may dispose of his property without restraint.

The extent of an owner's right and power is affected by the terms and conditions of his acquisition; and as regard community property, by any change in his marital status, such as the death of his spouse, divorce or separation.

It is also affected by the legal claims of third parties arising out of liens, mortgages, servitudes, restrictions and other limitations imposed or placed

1—Articles 24, 25, 433 R. C. C.
2—Acts 33 and 44 1921 E. S.
3—Articles 385 to 387 R. C. C.
4—Articles 379 to 382 R. C. C.

on the property by the owner or by operation of law. (1)

A corporation's right and power are affected by all of the elements set forth in the foregoing paragraphs, with the exception of course of the marital status; and are further affected by the powers and limitations conferred or imposed by its articles of incorporation.

The Instrument By Which The Transfer Is Effected

It may be an authentic act, an act under private signature or by a private written agreement, unacknowledged.

The force and effect of these various acts are fully set out in the Civil Code (2)

The Form In Which The Transfer Is Made

Under this heading come donations, exchanges, retrocessions partitions, dation en paiements and sales. Each form is governed by the laws applicable to it.

Rights Of The Parties To The Instruments

In the main this covers the right of the owner or vendor to be paid the purchase price, if a sale, or to an annullment of the contract if the price is so inadequate as to give rise to an action of lesion beyond moiety (3) or for error, fraud, violence or menace (4). In other forms of transfer the transferer has the right of obtaining a performance of the obligations entered into by the other party, or to annul the contract.

The rights of the transferee are to be put into possession of the exact property transfered free from encumbrances or claims, unless otherwise provided in the contract and to the free and peaceful possession thereof.

1—R. C. C. Articles 2444, 2445 and 2446
2—R. C. C. Articles 2440, 2441 and 2442
3—R. C. C. Articles 1860 to 1881
4—R. C. C. Article 1881

Rights Of Third Parties, Contra To The Parties To The Instrument

Such rights are usually those which are evidenced by recorded claims, such as liens, privileges and mortgages, servitudes and restrictions but also include certain inchoate rights granted by law to the State and its political subdivisions, such as franchise taxes in the case of corporations, right of eminent domain etc.

The Correct Or Incorrect Execution Of The Intent Of The Parties

This has reference generally to the amount and location of the property, the description thereof, proper inclusion of the conditions under whch the transfer is made and finally to clerical errors occurring in the instrument.

All of the above remarks apply to all forms of change of ownership such as donations, exchanges, retrocessions, partitions, dation en paiements, etc, with such exceptions and additions as are provided for by the law in each case and which will be more fully discussed in the following chapters.

Involuntary Or Forced Divestiture

Involuntary or forced divestitures are of such varied classes and are so complex in their elements that the discussion of them must be deferred to those chapters which are devoted to a detailed recital of those elements vital to their validity.

However, it may be said here that in those cases where the involuntary divestiture arises out of an order or judgment of court, the jurisdiction and power of the court issuing, the petitions, citations trial and rendering of judgments; the execution of those judgments are important elements upon which rests the validity of the transfer.

In sales made by trustees under created trusts, the instrument by which the trust is created and the law of trust estates, are the chief sources to be examined.

Tax sales are subject to so many technicalities that any attempt to discuss the laws governing such sales would be too great a task and entail too much space to be discussed here. The subject is exhaustively treated in another chapter.

Inheritance

This form too is subject to so many technicalities and contain so many angles that to attempt to summarize them would be a waste of time and would to no advantage, as at this point more than a summary would be impossible and the chapters devoted to the subject will cover it completely.

CHAPTER IV

Patents, Grants And Purchasers from the Sovereign.

From Foreign Government, i. e. French and Spanish. Also English.

No attempt can be made to give here in minute detail the formalities and requisites of a French or Spanish grant.

In the main, it can be said that such a grant required the signature of the King or his Procurator General and the land had to be surveyed and segregated from the public domain.

Grants in various forms were made by the French and Spanish governments, even by the latter during the period from 1800 to 1803, when France and not Spain was the sovereign, the latter having been by a secret treaty signed October 1, 1800, retroceded Louisiana to the French.

The American government, by its treaty stipulations with France, agreed to respect the grants made by the former sovereigns (Spain and France) and, as a preliminary measure, Congress by various Acts, the first of which was dated March 2, 1805, organized Boards of Commissioners to investigate these claims. Acts of a similar character was passed March 3, 1811, April 25, 1812 and April 12, 1814. The latter Act confirmed titles under incomplete French or Spanish grants made prior to Dec. 20, 1803 and having definite location. It did not confirm any French or Spanish claim unsupported by written evidence of title.

In the Orleans and Louisiana Territories (which for a short period were separated) the Commissioners had the power of deciding finally on all claims not exceeding one league of land, but for claims of greater extent, they had to refer back to Congress the result of their investigations and report their opinions. Congress thereupon confirmed or rejected the claim.

June 22, 1860, Congress, by an act for the final adjustment of claims in Louisiana, constituted the Receiver and the Register of the Land office a commission to pass upon and decide claims under written grants, but not on those claimed by reason of settlement, or those derived from grants from the Spanish government during the years 1800 to 1803.

By Act of March 2, 1867 and of June 10, 1877, Congress gave recognition to the latter claims.

It is impossible, of course, to undertake to detail the thousand of private claims which have been made and confirmed or which are now awaiting confirmation.

The claims referred to above were three in number.

The first class were those persons or their legal representatives who, on the first day of October, 1800 were residents of the territory and had obtained from Spain or France respectively, during the time said governments had been in actual possession of the duly registered warrants or orders of survey for lands lying within said territory and which were on that date actually cultivated by said person or persons for his or their use, and said persons were head of a family and above the age of 21 years.

The second class were those above the age of twenty one years, who had, prior to the 20th of December 1803, with the permission of some Spanish officer, and in conformity with the laws and customs and usuages of the Spanish government, actually settled on said land.

The third class were those who possessed prior to October 1, 1800 legal French or Spanish grants made and completed prior to that date.

The first and second classes were required to make proof that they possessed the land in accordance with the prerequisites stated above, before their claims could be confirmed by the commissioners, but those of the third class needed only to prove up their claims by the grants themselves.

All classes had to register their claims under penalty of nullity.

The above provisions are contained in the Act of Congress covering the subject (1).

For a very informative and interesting discussion of the whole subject matter, the reader is referred to the case of the Board of Directors v N. O. Land Co., reported in the 132 L.42. which is too lengthy to be included here.

For the examiner's benefit the following sources of information are listed.

The Laws relating to the Public Lands. Appendix, 1827

U. S. Statutes at Large, after 1804.

Instructions to Commissioners September 3, 1866 and November 14, 1806.

American State Papers Volume 2. "Public Lands"

Louisiana Digests under the title "Public Lands— Colonial Grants and Concessions IV.   ,

The General Land Office may also be called upon for information in specific cases.

Lands Acquired From The United States

All public land in Louisiana, upon its admission to the Union belonged to the United States and the State retained no title to any public land, except the

1 2—Statutes at Large, p. 324

lands within the tidewater of the sea and bays and beds of navigable waters as well as the beds of all bayous, lagoons, lakes and bays, (1) hence the State acquired title only from the United States (2).

Some public lands have been acquired by individuals directly from the United States under various Acts of Congress (A partial list of which is to be found at the end of this chapter), while some have been acquired indirectly from the United States through the State.

Lands acquired directly from the United States are by means of public land sales, pre-emption, homestead, military warrants etc. See list at end of chapter.

In the case of public land sales, the land is first required to be surveyed, advertised and then exposed for sale at public auction.

Thereafter the land is open to private entry, if not sold at the public auction, at a price fixed by the government. (3)

Entry is affected by written application to the Register of the Land Office containing a full description of the land to be entered, to which the Register of the Land Office affixes a certificate to the effect that the land is open to entry and fixing the price. The application is then taken to the Receiver of Pub-Moneys to whom the payment is made. Two receipts are issued, one kept by the entryman and the other is presented to the Register of Land Office who thereupon issues a certificate of purchase (4). It is upon this certificate that the patent issues.

Preemption entry. A preemption entry is a for-

1—State v Sweet Lake Land & Oil Co. 164 L.240
2—Act 258 of 1910
3—Rev. U. S. Stat. paragraph 2353 et seq.
4—U. S. Comp. Statutes, 2245 et seq.

mal declaration made to the proper officer describing the land settled upon and reciting intention to claim same under the provisions of the Act and within twelve months thereafter the entryman must make proof of settlement and payment. This applies only to surveyed lands subject to entry. By another Act of Congress the claimant of unsurveyed lands was permitted to file his claim and declaratory statement within three months from the date the land was officially surveyed. Laws on this subject were passed as early as 1803 (1).

A preemption entry differs from the public land sale entry in this: it gives the applicant the preference in the purchase of the land settled upon.

The certificate of purchase issued in the case of publc land sales, conferred an equitable title and is property and the owner may transfer it, devise or otherwise dispose of his rights thereunder prior to issuance of patent, and when the patent did issue it would be issued to the entryman or his heirs or assignees.

It, however, is always liable to be defeated as the government could, until issuance of the patent withdraw the land from public sale.

The preemption entry on the contrary confers no title, even equitable. It represents merely a prior right to purchase under certain conditions. It is not even heritable, but if the entryman should die before he has established his claim, his heirs could perfect it. (2)

It may be said that a patent regularly issued by the government is the best and only perfect title, subject however to be defeated by a superior title, that is a patent previously issued to another entry

1—U. S. Statutes at Large, 418
2—Burgess v Gray 16 Howard, 48; Yosemite Valley Case 15 Wall 72

man by the government, which on occasions has occurred. Hence where it is found that the actual patent has never been issued, the examiner should require its issuance in order to put at rest any question as to the validity of the entry.

In passing upon a patent it is always advisable to examine the particular Act of Congress (or the State) under which it is issued and to note whether or not it has been issued in proper form, i e., in case of a United States Patent that it is signed in the name of the President, by himself, or by his secretary appointed for that purpose, sealed with the seal of the General Land Office and countersigned by the Recorder. This is sacramental. Where the patent has been issued by the State, it must be issued in accordance with the laws governing the entry of the land.

Homesteads: Entries under the homestead laws are governed by the provisions of the various Acts of Congress and all the requirements of the law must be complied with by the homesteader.

The applicant must file with the Register of the District Land Office an application designating the tract desired to be entered to which must be attached an affidavit setting forth that he is the head of a family and intends to use the land for settlement, cultivation and continuous occupation as a home by him for a period of five years. (1)

Upon filing of the application the Recorder issues duplicate homestead receipts one of which is delivered to the homesteader and the other forwarded to the General Land Office.

Homestead right is the right given to every person who is the head of a family, or who has arrived

1—12 Stat. U. S. 392

at the age of twenty one, and is a citizen of the
United States, or has filed his declaration of intention of becoming a citizen of the United States, in
accordance with the naturalization laws of the country. (1)

No certificate is issued until the expiration of
five years and until proof has been made that all the
requirements of the law have been complied with.

No title and no rights are required by the entryman, prior to the issuance of the patent, other
than a preemption right.

The homesteader in making final proof must
take an oath that he has sold no part of the land, except for church, cemetery or school purposes or for
a right of way of a railroad.

The amount of land that may be homesteaded is
limited to 160 acres. The claim is not heritable, but
the heirs may complete by complying with the conditions, the law giving them the benefit of their ancestor's residence on the land. (2)

Townsites, Bounties and Donations: It will be
necessary for the examiner to refer to the various
Acts of Congress, providing for the disposition of
lands under these different classes of land grants.
They would occupy too much space to be set out in
full.

Railroad Grants: Until 1862 all grants made by
Congress for the benefit of railroads were made
through the state, the state holding title until all
the conditions laid down had been met, whereupon
the state conveyed to the railroad.

When made direct to the railroad the grants were
in praesenti and was the conveyance itself. Where
grant was made of unsurveyed land, title was com-

1—General Land Office, Circular No. 541, 1924
2—81 Rev. Stat. U. S. par. 2288; 82 Rev. Stat. U. S. 2291

plete in the railroad when lands were surveyed and the official plat filed in the General Land Office.

It is impossible to give a full list of these grants The various act of Congress covering the subject should be examined for further information.

Land Grants To The State

Swamp Lands: Among the earliest of grants by the Federal government to the State, were the swamp land grants. (1) The grant was in aid of drainage and applied only to Louisiana but was followed by other acts making grants to other states.

The Louisiana grant vested the fee in the State upon approval of the selections made by the Secretary of the Interior.

School Lands: Congress as early as 1806 and 1843 granted to the State, in line with its declared policy of encouraging education, every sixteenth section of the public domains, needing only survey to vest title in the State. In cases where the sixteenth section had been, in whole or in part, included in private claims the state could select the equivalent of such sections in other unreserved lands. (2)

In addition to the sixteenth sections referred to above, the State received by acts of Congress, two townships or 46080 acres of land in aid of higher education, seminaries and universities. (3) Congress also donated to the State 30,000 acres for each senator and representative in Congress from the State, Louisiana receiving a total of 210,000 acres. (4) This donation was in aid of colleges to be instituted by the State to further agriculture and mechanics.

This grant was in the form of land scrip which

1—Act of March 2, 1849, Chap. 87
2—U. S. v Morrison 240 U. S. 205
3—Acts April 21, 1806; March 3, 1811; March 3, 1827
4—Act July 2, 1862

the state had the right to dispose of, its assignees having the right to locate to the amount of acreage specified upon any public land subject to private entry in any state in the Union, or tender same in payment of pre-emptions and in commutting homestead entries.

Internal Improvement Grants: Congress also, from time to time, granted large tracts of the public domain to the states in aid of the development of the country.

The Acts themselves were in conveyances in praesenti and constituted a fee simple in the state. Where the land was unlocated of course title did not pass to any particular tract, but when the land was located and surveyed, title of tract related back to the grant. (1)

In one Act Congress granted 500,000 acres to the state for such purposes. (Sept. 4th 1841)

Public Highways: In 1866, Congress granted a right of way for the construction of public roads over public lands not reserved for public use. (2)

The principal laws under which the agricultural lands in Louisiana have been disposed of by the United States to the individual are as follows: Cash and credit sales; (3) repealed as to credit sales; (4) Military Warrants; (5) Pre-emption; (6) Enlarged Homesteads; (7) Homesteads; (8) Grazing Homesteads; (9) Reclamation Homesteads; (10) Isolated Tracts. (11)

1—U. S. v Porchman; 7 Peters 51 U. S.; U. S. v Brooks, 10 Howard
    442; R. R. Co. v U. S. 92 U. S. 733
2—14 Statutes at Large 253
3—2 Statutes at Large 15
4—3 Statutes at Large 576
5—Compiled Statutes Sec. 2414 to 2416
6—5 Statutes at Large 453
7—35 Statutes at Large 630
8—12 Statutes at Large 392
9—39 Statutes at Large 362
10—32 Statutes at Large 388
11—Compiled Statutes 2455
In general Compiled Statutes (1901) Sects. 220 to 2490; also U. S.
    C. A. Tit. 43

All irregularities in an entry are cured by a pre-scription of six years. (1)

Lands Acquired From The State

Divestiture of title from the State is by means of sales, grants and homestead.

Following are the statutes affecting divestiture of the State's title to public lands.

R. S. 1322; 2916 to 1930 both inclusive; 1936-39-40-41-42 to 2949; 2951-2-3-7-8-9-60-62-66-76-7; 2970 to 2975; 2981-2-3.

Acts: 248 of 1852; 247 of 1855; 166 of 1858; 124 of 1862; 38 of 1870; 21 of 1871; 104 of 1871.... 75 of 1880; 12 and 57 of 1884; 21 and 107 of 1886; 76 and 104 of 1888; 97, 152, 43, 74 of 1890; 43 of 1892; 40 of 1896; 66, 87, and 195 of 1898; 123, 124, 125, 177, 217 of 1902; 86 of 1904; 86 and 185 of 1906; 85, 215, 216 of 1908; 6, 158, 247, 269 and 301 of 1910; 62, 217 and 246 of 1912; 258 and 283 of 1914: 213 of 1918; 143 and 151 of 1920; 11 of 1921 E. S.; 316 of 1926; 184 and 230 of 1928; 172 and 233 of 1932; 11 and 15 of 1936; 235 of 1938.

R. S. 1322 and Acts 5 and 42 of 1877; 158 of 1910; 168 of 1894; 123 of 1912 and 151 of 1920 cover the sixteenth school sections.

Acts 97 of 1890; 74 of 1892; and 215 of 1908 are acts turning over lands to the levee districts.

In 1880, the State, through the Governor, made a contract with Samuel McEnery, for the recovery of land from the United States and in payment of his services he was to receive land script to the extent of fifty percent of the land recovered; said script to apply either to the land recovered or to other public lands belonging to the state. (2) There were consider-

1—Act 62 of 1912
2—Act 23, 1880

able litigation over the legality of this script but was finally held that they were valid. (1)

The Legislature of 1928 further validated this scrip by providing that if the holders of this scrip made prior to 1930, a payment of $1.50 per acre, their title to the land acquired through such scrip would be confirmed. (2)

The Lanier Certificates of Purchase: Lanier, Register of the State land office issued certificates of purchase but failed to turn over the purchase money to the State Treasury, hence the certificates of purchase were pronounced void, on the ground that Act 75 of 1880 provides that all monies received from the sale of public lands should be paid over to the Treasurer.   Hence the courts took the view that the patents issued on the Lanier certificates were void for the reason that the purchasers failed to comply with the above provision; that if they paid it to Lanier the Register, they did so at their own risk and hence the State was not estopped from cancelling the patent certificate issued by Lanier. (3)

It would therefore be necessary in examining a title based on a Lanier certificate of purchase to ascertain whether or not duplicate patents issued and that payments for the land were covered into the State Treasury in accordance with Act 75 of 1880.

It is needless to say that patents and grants from the State, as well as purchases, have to be in strict accord with the statutory provisions.

Levee Boards: In addition to the disposing of public lands to individuals by way of sales, homestead, etc., the State has turned over to the Levee

1—State er rel. Mcnery v Nichols, 42 A. 209
2—Act 88 of 1928
3—Cordill v Quaker Realty Co., 139 L.133 ; Linder v Roth, 11 Orleans
    App. 301; State ex Rel. Duggan v Crandell, 144 L.22

Boards of the State, for levee purposes, two classes of land.

    1st—Lands forfeited or sold to the State for taxes. (1)

    2nd—Those lands received from the United States known as swamp lands. (2)

In these class of cases, while they do not come strictly under a discussion of patents, it is important that certain facts be developed as affecting titles derived from the State and therefore they are included in this chapter.

It is important for the examiner to note in these cases that the land involved is not located in the bed of a navigable stream, and also that it does not involve meanderings of streams, as both of these classes of lands have been the cause of considerable litigation and it would be advisable for the examiner to refer to decisions of the federal and state courts in the Caddo cases as well as other decisions affecting title to such lands. (3)

As to the first class of cases the validity of the tax title in the State should be investigated with the same care as would be used in other tax sales. It is axiomatic that the State can, no more than the individual, sell what it does not own and a title defective as to the individual is defective as to the State.

The constitutional prescription however operates in favor of the state as it does in favor of the individual.

Another important fact connected with these titles is that in a large number of cases, titles from the levee boards were found defective for want of proper

1—Act 97, 1890; 5, 1877; 74, 1892, 215, 1908
2—Act 97 of 1890; 74 of 1892; 125 of 1902
3—McDade v Caplis, 154 L1019; Palmer Co. v Wilkinson, 141 L.874; Bruning v N. O., 165 L.511; Acadia-Vermilion Rice Irr. Co. v Miller, 178 L. 954

signatures, only one officer of the Board signing where the statute required two. However the courts have decided that a transfer of land by the State to levee districts not insufficient because not signed by both Auditor and Register, (1) and such defects in titles prior to 1926 were cured by an act of the Legislature. (2)

A question was raised at one time as to the right of the State to sell school lands, but it has been settled in the affirmative. (3)

The grants of land to the State by the Acts of Congress were grants in praesenti (4) and therefore required no further action to be taken by Congress, but title did not pass to the state until and unless such lands were surveyed (5), which is another way of saying that the land had to be identified and segregated to vest the title in the State.

The Florida parishes, of Washington, St. Tammany, Tangipahoa, St. Helena and Livingston, were acquired by the United States from Spain and the same recognition was given by the treaty under which the transfer was made, as was given under the Louisiana Purchase to the grants made by Spain and England and provisions were made by various Acts of Congress, (6) recognized grants made in those parishes by both Spain and the English.

1—Barnett v State Mineral Board, 193 L.1055
2—Act 316, 1926
3—Cooper v Howard, 18 Howard, 173; State v Joyce 261 Fed. 123
4—Hartigan v Weaver, 126 L.492
5—Elme v Foote, 129 L.978
6—Acts Congress, March 3, 1819; April 5, 1912; May 8, 1822
    Boatner v Ventress, 8 Martin (N. S.), 644 March 27, 1804

CHAPTER V

Examining A Title

It will now be assumed that the title to be examined has its inception in the sovereign and therefore the examination must be started from the divestiture at that point.

A colonial grant or concession: There were two classes of these grants or concessions.

1st—Grants in writing from the French or Spanish governments.

2nd—Inchoate or incomplete grants from the same source.

In the first class of grants there were no Congressional action necessary, as the United States agreed to recognize all grants made by the two governments. (1) It will therefore only be necessary to identify the land, title to which is under examination with the original foreign grant, to be assured that divestiture from the sovereign is complete and that therefore prescription began to run as to that sovereign. Provided of course that such a grant has been registered in accordance with the statutory requirements.

In the second class of grants were a number issued by Spain between 1800 and 1803 as the defacto government (notwithstanding the retrocession to France), in addition to other unconfirmed grants. A great many of these grants have been confirmed by Congress. A check should be made where necessary to establish that the title being examined has been confirmed by Congress.

There were what might be called a third class of cases, which, although issued by both French and

1—U. S. v Perchman, 7 Peters, 51 ; Soulard v U. S. 4 Peters, 511

the Spanish government officials or claimed under certain certificates issued by such officials, were in fact invalid on the grounds, either that the officers issuing them were not authorized to do so, or that they were issued by the respective officials after the government had changed, in the one case, after the cession by France to Spain and in the other after the retrocession by Spain to France had occurred. (1)

Grants From The United States: At the outset it will be necessary for the examiner to decide by what method, that is, under what class of legislation the patent was issued, viz; whether entry preemption, homestead, military, etc., as each of these classes is governed by different laws.

A list of the principal acts have been given, but there are numerous other acts of Congress in individual cases, either original or ratifying or confirming attempted entries, but their number is too great to be detailed here.

The patent is prima facie evidence of title. The certificate is not, but when the patent issues on it, the title reverts to the date of the certificate of purchase as it does likewise in preemption or homestead. (2)

The purchaser need not look beyond the patent to ascertain whether or not it has been regularly issued to one entitled to it, but he is charged with notice of any defects apparent on the face of the patent. (3)

It is important that the examiner make sure that the patent is in proper form, i. e, that it is issued in the name of the President and signed either by himself or by his duly appointed secretary, sealed with

1—Foster v Neibson 2 Peters (U. S.) 253
2—Starks v Starr, 6 Wall. 402
3—U. S. v Land Grant Co., 21 Fed. 19

the seal of the General Land Office and counter-signed by the Recorder.

The identity of the property must be established and its description and measurements must correspond with the patent.

A correct survey is essential as prescription cannot run until the land is segregated from the public domain.

The patent should have been registered in the United States Land Office and in the parish where the land is situated although it has been held that the latter registration is not necessary, but it is the best practice. (1)

In most of the parishes a record of every entry may be found. This record contains the date, name of entryman, location and description of every entry in the parish, and a notation as to the issuance of a patent.

It is to be remarked that, while a patent is prima facie evidence that all the formalities have been observed and that the requirements of the laws have been complied with, the sovereign can, no more than the individual, transfer what it does not own, consequently a patent may be attacked on the ground that the land covered by it has already been patented to another.

However possession in good faith, as evidenced by the patent and prescription liberandi, will operate to sustain title as in all other cases. Even prescription acquirendi causa may be applicable as the government in such a case has been divested of ownership.

The foregoing applies equally to patents, entries, grants and purchases from the State, viz it is important to ascertain whether or not the formalities

1—McQuenn v Flasdick 135 L.698; 150 L.108

and requirements of the law have been compiled with; that there has been proper survey, issuance of patent and possession.

Grants from the State: In addition to the requirements outlined above, as the State is the second owner in the title, it is necessary that it be ascertained that the State itself has complied with the terms of the grant from the United States; that it has accepted the grant in accordance with the terms of the law; that it has not divested itself of title by a patent, sale or grant to another.

All of these facts can be ascertained by proper inquiry and research of the original grants from the United States and the Records of the Register of the Land Office at Baton Rouge, La.

CHAPTER VI

Of Voluntary Transfers

As changes in ownership most frequently take place in voluntary transfers of immovable property through purchase and sale, the latter will be the first of these changes to be discussed.

As this is a sale it is in order to look to the articles of the Civil Code for a definition of sale and for the rules governing them.

In all cases where no special provision is made under the present title, the contract of a sale is subjected to the general rules established under the title: Of Conventional obligations. (1)

The contract of sale is an agreement by which one gives a thing for a price in current money and the other gives the price in order to have the thing itself. Three circumstances concur to the perfection of the contract, to-wit: the thing sold, the price and the consent. (2)

The form of the instrument is of little importance, the legal effect thereof that must be considered. (3)

All sales of immovables shall be made by authentic act or under private signature. Except as provided for in Article 2275, every verbal sale of immovables shall be null, as well for third persons as for the contracting parties themselves and the testimonial proof of it shall not be admitted. (4) (Article 2275 provides that a verbal sale shall be good against the vendor as well as against the vendee who confesses it when interrogated on oath, provided actual delivery has been made).

1—R. C. C. 2438
2—R. C. C. 2439
3—Thompson v Duson, 40 A.712; State v Wiless, 104 L.134
4—R. C. C. 2440

An act under private signature acknowledged by the party against whom it is adduced, or legally held to be acknowledged, has the same credit as an authentic act. (1)

The Civil Code further prescribes as to who may buy or sell All persons may buy and sell, except those interdicted by law. (2) In effect only those who are sui juris may buy or sell.

A contract or sale between husband and wife can take place only in the three following cases. 1. When one of the spouses makes a transfer of property to the other who is judicially separated from him or her in payment of his rights or her rights. 2 When the transfer made by the husband to the wife, even though not separated, has a legitimate cause, as the replacing of her dotal or other effects alienated. 3 When the wife makes a transfer of property to her husband in payment of a sum promised him as a dowry. Saving in these three cases to the heirs of the contracting parties, their rights, if there exists an indirect advantage. (3) A sale from husband to wife during marriage in any other than the above cases, is an absolute nullity. (4) This is true even if the sale is made to an interposed person who in turn sells to the spouse. (5) Succession and other public and judicial sales are excepted from this prohibition. (6)

There are other transfers which are prohibited by law because of the relationship existing between the parties, such as public officers connected with courts of justice, such as judges, advocates, attor-

1—R. C. C. 2441
2—R. C. C. 2445
3—R. C. C. 2446; Loranger v Citizens Nat'l. Bank; 162 L.1054
4—Rush v Flanders, 107 L.548
5—Securities Co. v Talbot, 49 A.1402
6—Hugnet v Bates, 32 A.454; Brewer v Brewer. 145 L.835

neys, clerks and sheriffs, who cannot purchase litigious rights which fall under the jurisdiction of the tribunal in which they exercise their functions, under penalty of nullity (1), though this nullity is relative and a civil action is necessary to enforce this right. (2) Which amounts to this. Such a transfer is not ipso facto null and void.

Executors and administrators cannot purchase the property of the succession which they administer unless they be heirs; (3) or partner. (4)

A tutor may not sell or buy from his ward. (5)

The Code also provides what things may or may not be sold.

The sale of a thing belonging to another person is null. (6)

The thing claimed as the property of the claimant cannot be alienated pending the action, so as to prejudice his right, nor shall it be lawful for debtors or third possessors of property subject to a mortgage of any kind to transfer or alienate such property pending an action to enforce the mortgage and any transfer or alienation made in contraventon of the provsions of the article, shall have no effect as against plaintiff in such pending action. (7)

As a corollary to the above an act of the Legislature passed in 1904 and as a modification thereof, provided that the pendency of an action in court affecting title or asserting a mortgage or lien upon immovable property, shall not be construed or considered as notice to third persons not parties to such suit,

1—R. C. C. 1447; Huck v Johnson, 114 L.781
2—Saint v Martel, 122 L.93
3—R. C. C. 1146; Succ. Hawthorne, 158 L.637
    Aronstein v Irwin. 49 A.1478
4—Savary v Williams, 15 A.250
5—R. C. C. 337, Smith v Krause & Managan, 125, L.703; 192 L.593
6—R. C. C.2452
7—R . C. C. 2453

unless a notice of pendency of such action shall have been made, filed or registered in compliance with the act which prescribed the manner in which notice should be made and registered. (1)

The succession of a living person cannot be sold. (2)

As been said the most frequent transfer of property is a purchase and sale by and between persons sui juris and as a preliminary to a discussion of this form, a list is here made of the elements which should be checked in the act.

Character of the instrument (Authentic act etc)

The officer before whom the act is executed.

Date of the instrument

Parties

Marital statii

Declaratory and conveying clauses

Warranty and subrogation thereof

Vendee

Description of property conveyed

Acquisition thereof

Consideration

Certificates (Conveyance, Mortgage, United States, Paving)

Stipulations, servitudes, restrictions and other limitation of full ownership and other clauses.

Tax researches

Witnesses

Signatures

Registration.

Character of the instrument: The transfer may be by authentic act, by an act under private signature

1—Act 22, 1904
2—R. C. C. 2454: Succ. Brand, 166 L.880

duly acknowledge or by a mere instrument in writing.

In Louisiana the authentic act is preferred because of numerous advantages, the principal one being that it is full proof in itself of its contents, though of course, it may be attacked by third parties but never by the parties themselves.

The Codal definition of an authentic act reads: The authentic act, as relates to contracts is that which has been executed before a notary public, or other officer authorized to execute such functions in presence of two witness, aged at least fourteen years, or of three witnessess, if the party is blind. If a party does not know how to sign, the notary must cause him to affix his mark to the instrument. (1)

All proces verbals of sale of succession property signed by sheriff or other person making the same, by the purchaser and two witnesses, are authentic act. (2) So also are all sheriff's and constables sales in execution sales. (3)

Acts before ambassadors, consuls, vice consuls are authentic Acts. (4)

Louisiana Commissioners in other states have the powers of a notary public, (5) but acknowledgments before such an officer must conform with Article 2234 (R.C.C.) to render same authentic. (6)

A mere acknowledgment before a notary and two witnesses does not convert an act under private signature into an authentic act. (7) It must conform to the requirements of Article 2234. (8) See form of acknowledgement on page 50.

1—R. C. C. 2234, Act 171, 1920
2—R. C. C. 2234
3—R. S. 1455
4—Act 164, 1898
5—R. S. 597; Act 117, 1894
6—Leibe v Hebertsmith. 39 A.1050
7—Baker v Baker, 125 L.974
8—R. C. 2234

The authentic act is full proof of the agreement contained in it against the contracting parties and their heirs, unless it be declared and proved a forgery. (1) But the Supreme Court has interpreted this article as not binding on forced heirs. (2)

Acts under private signature: Little need be said on this subject. A deed under private signature is rather a poor link in a chain of title, even if properly acknowledged, because of its liability of loss and its failure to contain within itself proof of those requirements essential to a marketable title. In any event, it is advisable that acts under private signature where they are properly acknowledged be deposited in the archives of a notary public where ever possible.

An act not authentic through incompetence or incapacity of the officer, or through defect of form, avails as a private writing if it be signed by the parties. (3)

The Supreme Court has held that an act not signed by the notary is not an authentic act. (4)

The following is a form of acknowledgment which has been accepted by the bar as complying with the codal requirements of an authentic act.

State of

Parish (County) of

Before me the undersigned authority personally came and appeared   personally known to me, who executed the above and foregoing act of in my presence and in the presence of the undersigned witnesses, and who declared to me, notary, in the presence of the said witnesses, that he has executed the said act for the uses and purposes therein set forth.

1—R. C. C. 2236
2—Font et al v Land & Inv. Co., 47 A.272
3—R. C. C. 2235, 10 L.304
4—West La. Bank v Dawson, 154 L.830

In witness whereof the said appearer, witnesses and I notary, have hereunto signed on this day of 19

Signatures.

Officer before whom executed: All authentic acts must be passed before a notary public, duly commissioned and qualified and residing in the parish where the act is executed. The powers and duties of notaries are set forth in Sections 6285 to 6306 inclusive Dart's Revised Statutes and need not be detailed here. An act passed before a de facto notary, that is, one who has not been properly commissioned or qualified is a valid act. (1)

To this rule above ennunciated there are exceptions as in the case of sales made by sheriff's and constables, as has been noted.

Formerly acts affecting property in Louisiana executed outside of the state, had to be passed before a commissioner duly appointed for the state in which such act was passed, but in 1896 (amended in 1918) an act was passed authorizing notaries public in other states, to perform the same functions as a notary public in this State; and it was declared therein that any and all acts that shall be passed before any notary public and two witnesses in the District of Columbia or any State of the United States or in foreign countries before any commissioned officer of the army or navy of the United States of America serving there in, shall be authentic acts and shall have the same force and effect as if passed before a notary public in Louisiana. (2)

The Legislature in 1894 authorized all ambassadors, ministers charge d'affaires, secretaries of legations, consul generals, consuls vice consuls and com-

1—Liberman v Liberman, 47 Ann. 153; Davenport v Davenport, 116 L.1029
2—Acts 140, 1896 and 192, 1918

mercial agents of the United States in any foreign land, to act as commissioners and perform the duties of a notary and provided that such certifications should have the force and effect of an authentic act. (1)

No provision seems to have been made in regard to attestations and acknowledgments made or taken before notaries or other officials of foreign countries but the Supreme Court on one occasion declared: When an official in Germany (a police official in a town in that country) certifies to the genuineness of the signatures to a power of attorney and the American Vice Consul certifies to the signature and seal of that officer, and his capacity and authority to make the acknowledgment, the signatures to the power must be held proved. (2)

The clerks of court in Louisiana are ex-offico, notaries and hence their acts have the same validity as other notarial acts.

Date of the Instrument: The date is of course of great importance, as its omission would undoubtedly destroy its value as an authentic act and would otherwise create confusion and doubt. (3)

Parties: In an act of this character they may be any of the following classes of parties.
1. An owner who has never married.
2. A corporation.
3. A married owner.
4. An owner who acts through an agent (This includes corporations)
5. A minor who is emancipated.
6. A purchaser who has the status of any of the foregoing classes.

1—Sections 602 and 603 as amended by Act 34, 1894
2—Werner v Marx, 113 La. 1002
3—Livingston v Dick, 1 Ann. 328

7.   A purchaser who is a minor or has been interdicted
who is represented by his tutor or curator authorized to make the purchase on behalf of the ward by
court having jurisdiction over his person.

All, with the exception of the secondly, fifthly
and seventhly named parties must be o fthe full age
of majority, or in case of the case of the emancipated
minor sui juris through judicial proceedings or by
marriage. If through the latter he must be above the
age of eighteen years.

Each class involves questions the   answers   to
which affects the title.

An owner who has never married. Beyond the
question of age and mental capacity this class presents no difficulty. Whether man or   woman   the
rights and powers are the same.

A corporation: A corporation being an intellect-
ual entity, its status as a sui juris is governed by its
articles of incorporation and the laws governing corporations, hence an inquiry into those articles is necessary for the purpose of ascertaining its legal existence
and its rights and powers.

The whole subject is of such a broad scope that
it has been deemed best to discuss it in a separate
chapter, but insofar as the examination of a sale by
or to a corporation, the following points are emphasized.

1.   Its legal incorporation
2.   Its power of owning and alienating real property
3.   The manner in which its property may be alienated
      and through what officer or officers
4.   The actual manner in which that authority is ex-
      ercised

A corporation must be organized in strict accordance with the laws of its domicile.   The laws govern-

ing Louisiana corporations will be found fully discussed in the chapter on that subject.

A corporation organized for profit may purchase' and sell real property incidental to and acquired in the course of its business without consent of its stockholders but it may not do so to an extent which would amount to a change of business not authorized by its charter. Corporations organized to deal in real estate are, of course, excepted from this rule. Non profit corporations may not buy or sell real property except on the authorization of its stockholders or members.

In every case an examination of the act of incorparation should be made to ascertain whether or not it is properly incorporated, although the examiner is not called upon to do more than assure himself that the laws has been fairly complied with and a certificate of the Secretary of State that its charter has been registered in his office and that the corporation is authorized to do business should be insisted upon, although the issuance of the certificate is not proof of the legality of the incorporation.

The requirements of an act purporting to be a sale by or from a corporation are:

1. Its charter name and the appearance of the proper officer designated in the resolution of the board of directors or stockholders to sign on behalf of the corporation.

2. A duly certified copy of the resolution, signed by the proper officers, passed by the board of directors or the stock holders, authorizing the sale, price terms, etc., and sealed with the corporate seal, should be affixed to the act, unless this authority is expressly conferred on an officer by the charter itself.

At one period the courts held that a resolution of

the directors not bearing the seal of the corporation was not an authentic act and therefore could not be the basis of a foreclosure, (1) but by an act passed 1928, (2) the use of a seal even where it has one is not necessary to the validity of the act.

The resolution should agree in every particular, in description, price terms and conditions upon which the sale or purchase was made, with those in the act.

In all other respects the requirements of an authentic act as set out in chapter six should be met.

There is a class of sales made by corporations that are not in the ordinary course of business, that is, the sales made by liquidators of a corporation in process of liquidation. Sales of this character are not very frequent, most corporations being liquidated through the courts and sales made under court orders.

Such a transfer calls for an examination of the proceedings leading up to the appointment of the liquidators, but as the chapter on corporations fully discusses these formalities, the examiner is referred to that chapter.

It will be necesary, however, that proper evidence of the payment of all debts of the corporation be produced. The certificate of the Secretary of State certifying to the final dissolution of the corporation is the best evidence of the settlement of all claims against the corporation.

Sales by municipal corporations are governed by their charter provisions, hence no general discussion can be had of such in this chapter, such sales being specially discussed in another chapter.

By a married man: Community property can only be transferred by the husband without the sig-

1—Interstate Trust & Banking Co. v Powell Bros., 126 L.22
2—Section 12, Sub-section II (a), Act 250, 1928

nature of the wife, or her heirs, during the actual existence of the marriage. As he acts in these cases as head of the community it necessarily follows that he ceases to be such upon the dissolution of the marriage either by death or separation or divorce. The extent of his right to alienate is therefore fixed by his marital status which should be established in the act of sale. The subject is more fully discussed in the sub section immediately following under that head.

The vender should be of the full age of majority, or fully emancipated by judgment of court, or by marriage. In the event of a judicial emancipation a proper reference to the proceedings should be included in the act, and such proceedings examined. If the emancipation results from marriage, the examiner should satisfy himself that the vendor has reached the age of eighteen.

As the emancipation of minors has an important bearing on the alienation of his real property by a minor a separate chapter covering the statutes and jurisprudence anent emancipation has been included in this work.

By a married woman: Prior to 1921 a married woman could not alienate, grant, mortgage or acquire, either by gratuitous or incumbered title, unless authorized by her husband, nor could she give security for him, but in that year and subsequent years all of her disabilities have been removed and her status is that of an unmarried woman, except insofar as community property is concerned, (1) except that if under the age of eighteen years, she does not come under the provisions of the act. (2)

A married woman may, since that year sell or

1—Acts 33, 1921; 34, 1921; 283, 1928
2—Sec. 4, Act 283, 1928

mortgage her separate property without the authority of her husband, but unless the examiner is thoroughly convinced by reason of the manner in which she acquired (by inheritance etc), if the husband has not also signed the act, he should require a ratification of the sale by the husband, or by his joining with the wife in executing the act by which she alienates, mortgages or leases the property.

There is another class of titles in which title to property has been placed in the name of the wife (without reference to its character) or in the joint names of both husband and wife.

Insuch cases both should join in act affecting title.

Marital Status. Information as to the marital status of a party to any act of alienation, mortgage etc., is of vital improtance in any examination of a title for the reason that without it ownership of the property involved is left in the gravest doubt. Nor can the true situation be ascertained, unless the declaration containd in the act be specific and fully detailed. Naturally a declaration "had never married" would be sufficient, but the phrase "married" or "married to Miss Alice Brown", would not for the reason that the party might have been married more than once and the property might have been acquired during the community of the previous marriage, and the examiner would be at a loss to determine to which community it belonged.

The declaration of marital status should specifically state whether or not the party has ever been married, number of times; name or names of wife or wives; whether or not wife is living and residing with him, ; if wife or wives are dead, date of deaths; if divorced from any of them, or judicially separated, name of court and docket number and date.

There is a situation which has seldom received the attention of examiners because probably it is one which will occur very infrequently, but as this work is an attempt to present possible defects which occur in a title, it is here mentioned as a matter of precaution.

A married couple may have been married but once, but at one time a judicial separation had been pronounced, thereafter followed by a reconciliation, hence from a matrimonial stand point the marriage still exists, but the community status has entirely changed, so that the simple declaration in the act that the vendor had been "married but once and then to Alice Brown", it would not disclose the true situation from the standpoint of the property as the the separation put an end to the community and the reconciliation did not revive it, (1) so that, unless there had been a settlement of the community affairs in which the property involved had fallen to the husband, he would only own an undivided half interest in it. This may and probably will seem a highly improbable situation but it is distinctly a possibility and as such is mentioned here for the consideration of the reader.

An owner who acts through an agent: If one of the parties is represented by an attorney in fact, especially the vendor, a written power of attorney should be attached to the act and should be authenticated. (2)

This is a most important point in the link of a title, as while there is no precise form necessary the power must be in writing (3) and must be special and specific and contain all the grants necessary to carry out the powers to be exercised, such as the power to

1—R. C. C. 155; Succ. LeBesque, 137 L.567
2—Denegre v Fairfax, 52 L.1260; Ardell v Heirs Martinez, 6 L.A.150
3—Perrault v Perrault, 32 A.635; Hakenberg v Gastkamp, 30 A.898; Scurto v LeBlanc, 191 L.152

sell and convey, to warrant and to subrogate purchaser to vendor's rights and actions of warranty (although since 1924 both warranty and subrogation thereof runs with the land (1) and hence an omission from the power would not affect title); terms and conditions; and to receive and receipt for the price, notes, if any, etc.

It should also contain a full description of the land conveyed which should agree with the description in the act and in vendor's title.

A general power of attorney granting an agent authority to sell the principal's property without describing the land in detail will be valid, but it must be specific enough to leave no doubt as to what land is to be conveyed, such as "all lands owned by me in the parish of Orleans" or Jefferson parish etc., as the case may be. (2) The date of such power should be recent enough to justify a belief that it is still in force and effect, although under certain conditions the time is of no importance. The power may also be general as to the terms and conditions and leave these to the discretion of the agent. (3)

Corporations are always represented by their officers and authorized agents and their powers are discussed under the chapter entitled "Corporations"

A minor who is emancipated: The chapter entitled "Emancipation" covers this subject thoroughly so there is no need to elaborate upon it at this point.

A purchaser who has the status of any of the parties to the act heretofore discussed; A properly executed act should conform to the following requirements as to a vendee.

1—Act 116, 1924
2—R. C. C. 2996-7
3—Hecker v Dreaux. 9 Orleans App. 339

Full name, not the initials alone. (This applies to all parties to an act)

A declaration that will establish that he is above the age of majority or otherwise.

His marital status.

Acceptance of the transfer and acknowledgment of delivery. A purchaser who is a minor, or has been interdicted, who is represented by his tutor, or curator under order of court.

Cases of purchases by minors and interdicts are of infrequent occurrence. They occur under one of two circumstances. In the one case the purchase is made under an order of court for the benefit of the ward. The fact that the purchaser is a minor or interdict does not affect the title because no one except the minor or interdict can attack it. The vendor could not under the provisions of the Civil Code (1) and the minor could not sell the property and thereafter attack his own title. If a sale was made under order of court such a sale would repair and cure an illegal purchase.

In the other case of a purchase by a minor, the purchase is made on behalf of the minor by his living parents who have used either the minor's funds or their own. In the former case no sale could thereafter be attacked on the ground that the purchase made by the parents was illegal and void. If made by the parents with their own funds, it in reality would amount to a donation and open to all the objections which can be urged against such a transaction.

Warranty and subrogation of warranty: Since 1924 both clauses are superfluous in an act. Prior to that date subrogation of warranty did not run with the land, but since then it does, (2) even in those cases

1—R. C. C. 1791, Roe v Caldwell, 145 L.853
2—Act 116, 1924

where warranty has been expressly excluded. (1)

Warranty always ran with the land, (2) hence the express warranty contained usually in act is unnecessary but its omission would upset a tradition that has almost the force of law.

Our courts have held that where a sale is made by several vendors, without the specific mention of the portion or share sold by each vendor the warranty is binding on all. (3) Thus, in a sale by a parent and children, the parent's interest having been inherited from a predeceased son, the general warranty of all parties would prevent the children from claiming the share of the parent, in the event of the latter's remarriage under article 1753, which article though has been repealed. (4)

Description: In general two forms of description are followed in Louisiana, one of which is based on the rectangular method and is principally used in describing rural lands and the other on the lot and block system which is best adapted to urban property. The examiner should be familiar with both systems as frequently, outside of New Orleans, the first system is followed in the description of lots or plots located in small towns and subdivisions and examiners outside of New Orleans and other large cities are often called upon to pass on the lot and block descriptions.

For the convenience of those who are not familiar with both systems, there is included in this work a chapter on both the rectangular and the lot and block systems.

For a proper description, under either system,

1—Act 116, 1924; R. C. C. 2503
2—R. C. C. 2501, 2, 3
3—Jeanin v Bowman Tessier Orleans App. Dig. 153; Schultz v Ryan, 131 L.78
4—Act 238, 1918

certain factors must be included therein. These factors are:

Sufficient identification of the property, both as to what is intended to be conveyed and as to the property to which the vendor had title.

Location: By this is meant the property's actual physical situation not only as to adjacent properties, but its location within well established boundaries, such as municipalities and blocks therein, whose boundaries of record in the public records, or in subdivisions outside of such municipalities which have been surveyed and platted and such survey placed on record in the office of the parish recorder by means of official maps, in accordance with law.

Where the property is located outside of above mentioned municipalities, subdivisions etc., the description must contain a reference to the proper land district, range, township, and section in which it is situated.

Accurate measurements: This factor finds its greatest importance in parcels of land, such as lots in city blocks, or plots containing a few acres, or less in rural regions. The Supreme Court has said that the expression "more or less" means no more than "about" and its use in a description in a title may not extend the boundaries so as to include other lands adjacent to the property sold. (1) In other words, its use merely refers to the accuracy of the measurements as given in the act and not to the amount of land conveyed.

A description by metes and bounds, however, prevails over a recital of acreage or measurements. (2) but a definite reference to an established survey or plat

1—Nichols v Adams, 9 A.107; Pierce v Lefort, 197 L.1
2—Merigny v Nivet, 2 L.498; Hunter v Forrest, 188 L.441

is controlling over all other descriptions in the instrument. (1)

In titles derived from old colonial grants, the expression "so many arpents front by the usual depth" is often found, this because these grants often and in fact generally did, run forty arpents in depth, but it also often hapened that "double" concessions or grants were made; that is these concessions ran either in the original grants, or by subsequent one, eighty arpents in depth, and were called "double concessions" or even triple depths. Hence the description in these cases should specifically call for forty, eighty or more arpents in depth, if the purchase is intended for the whole tract, as the expression "usual depth" will not suffice to include the larger depths, even if the vendor's title is referred to in the acquisition.

In cities of over fifty thousand inhabitants the description should contain the square and lot numbers as given by the official map. (2)

Maps and surveys: An examiner should never approve or accept a description until he has had the opportunity of checking it with an official plat of survey. If such is not available, either as annexed to the act under examination or to another link in the title, he should require that one should be made. This is also true where the date of the survey is so old as to suggest possible changes or encroachments. This is equally true where the map or plan does not show location of improvements and fences or where the property is not tied in with the corner of the block in cities and subdivisions, or with well established starting points in the case of rural property.

In all cases outside the parish of Orleans, the

1—Miliken v Muines, 12 L.539; Littleberg v Coleman, 1 La. App. 651
2—Act 106, 1916

survey should have been or should be officially recorded in the parish where property is located. (1) In
the parish of Orleans, the City Engineer's office contains what purports to be official maps of all property
in the city, but it is not official as they are made
from surveys made by private surveyors and no attempt has been made to check their accuracy, nor are
they complete or up to date, as until recently, surveyors were not obliged to furnish that office with
a duplicate of their certificate of survey, but it is
now obligatory upon them to do so, where a new
sub-division is opened (2).

Acquisition: This is of vital importance in those
cases where the description is ambiguous or faulty,
as the usual expression "being the same property acquired" etc., may be the means of clearing up and
validating an otherwise defective title.

Conveying clause: The conveying clause should
contain such language as will leave no doubt as to the
character of the transaction.

Consideration: The consideration should be certain and sufficient in amount to avoid risk of lesion
beyond moiety. It should be for an amount in current money.   This clause in notarial acts should contain, in addition to the amount of the purchase price
an acknowledgment of the receipt of the cash portion
of the purchase price.

Where the sale or transaction is on terms, the
usual mortgage and other clauses follow, but these
subjects are not reviewed here as they properly belong
to the chapter on Liens, Privilges and Mortgages to be
found in this volume.

1—Act 51, 1930
2—Ord. 8665 C. C. S., New Orleans

Certificates:. There are certain certificates usually found attached to acts of transfer which are of the greatest assistance in determining the validity of the title and relieve the examiner to a considerable extent of tedious researches which otherwise would have to be made by him, to insure that the property is free of all encumbrances and that it has not been previously alienated by the present owner or by former owners.

These certificates are known as the conveyance and mortgage certificates, tax researches and United State Court certificates. In the city of New Orleans there are in addition two other certificates, one of which is issued by the Recorder of Mortgages and the other by the paving department of the City. The first is the recordation ordinances, if any, adopted by the City, as affecting the property conveyed, and the other shows in detail the charges for paving due by the same property. (1) The same certificates are authorized to be issued by the paving authorities in each town or city where paving has been done. (2)

Some of the above mentioned certificates are required by law to be produced, but they may be waived; others are authorized by law; and all have been found to be of such advantage that their production either at the time of the act, or subsequently, where they have been omitted, is a routine requirement.

Conveyance certificates: The production of this certificate is a notarial duty in the City of New Orleans required by the Revised Statutes (3) and the Register of Conveyance of Orleans parish must issue same whenever requested and he is responsible for the correctness thereof. Outside Orleans parish, recorders are

1—Act 338. 1936
2—Act 116. 1938
3—R. S. 2528

neither required nor authorized to issue these certificates. It is a common practice among attorneys to obtain a conveyance certificate from the Recorder of the parish wherein property conveyed is situated, but that official cannot be held on his official bond for any errors. (1) Some recorders will issue such a certificate under their official seal, but others will not.

In such a case the examiner must make his own research and many examiners conscientiously make such a research themselves in all parishes, except the parish of Orleans. Title companies and oil companies invariably require their abstracters to make this research.

A conveyance certificate should contain the names of all known owners, including the surviving spouse and all heirs whether those heirs have survived the decedent or not; also the name of purchasers at tax sales, although the property has been redeemed unless such redemption was made before the constitutional period of redemption expired. See the sub-title on tax sale redemption following.

All names should be checked carefully and any variation, either in spelling or in the addition or omission of the Christian names of the parties carefully noted. It frequently occurs in Louisiana that a person may purchase a piece of property in a name which reflects a foreign origin, such as "Jean", or "Giacomo", or "Santiago" and sell the property by an anglicized form of the same, such as "John", "James" etc. Or he may buy simply as John Smith and sell as John Edward Smith or vice versa. The maiden name of the wife as well as the name of her husband should be given, and where a doubt exists as to the paraphernality of the property, the certifi-

1—Norton v Enos, 158 L.423

cate should contain the names of both husband and wife, that is, it should be asked in both names.

The description in the certificates should exactly check with the description by which it was acquired, without reference to the description by which it is sold or mortgaged. This to enable the examiner to check any "sales out."

The acquisition data given for each owner should be the original one (as there may have been several sales and reacquisitions by the same party, as in the case of homesteads etc), unless proper certificates were attached to the last transfer.

All of the foregoing apply equally to the research when made by the examiner or abstracter.

Finally the certificate should be dated and signed by the proper official; until more recently it has been the practice to have these certificates dated as of the date of the transfer, or of registration or recordation, but it is better practice to have them dated the day after the registration or recordation, so as remove any doubt as to the registration or recordation of an alienation or encumbrance between the day of execution and the hour of actual registration or recordation.

Mortgage certificates: All notaries and other officials, such as sheriff, etc., acting as such, are by law obliged to obtain a mortgage certificate before making a transfer (1). The parties may waive the production of such a certificate. The officer issuing this certificate is obliged to issue it upon request and is liable under his bond for any errors in it.

All that has been said in regard to conveyance

1—R. C. C. 3364

certificates in reference to names, descriptions dates etc., applies to the mortgage certificate.

All recorded liens, privileges, mortgages etc., should appear on the certificate, unless cancelled previously, but it is pertinent to mention here, as a caution to the examiner, three possible encumbrances fatal to a clear title.

The first is the lien and privilege, in the case of a corporation arising out of an unpaid franchise tax. Under the statute, this is an inchoate lien and may not appear on the certificate unless the Collector of Revenue has recorded his suit. (1) Also inheritance tax unless succession has been opened and tax paid, or prescription run, income and social security taxes. Also the liens of Mechanics and Material Men.

The second encumbrance arises under the following circumstances. If a purchaser acquires in one act several pieces of property and assumes payment of mortgages placed on one of the pieces by his vendor, or by a previous vendor and assumed by the purchaser's vendor, each and every other piece purchased, though not otherwise encumbered, becomes burdened with such assumed mortgages. Unless the property conveyed is one of those properties originally mortgaged, the assumption will not appear on the certificate. (2)

The third source of danger lies in the fact that a vendor may rescind a sale for nonpayment of the purchase price, although the notes and mortgages given for the purchase price have all prescribed, and recover the property free of any alienations or mortgages subsequently made or placed thereon. (3)

1—State v J. Bodenger Realty Co., 195 L.1014
2—Citizens Bank v Cuny. 38 A.860; Scionnaux v Waguespack, 32 A.283
3—See Chap XV this volume

Tax Researches

All officers acting in the capacity of notary public, including sheriffs, are required by law to see that taxes due and unpaid for three years prior to the date of the transfer are paid. (1)

Proof of this fact is usually made in the form of a research or certificate by the tax collecting authority who is obliged to issue it, showing what taxes are paid and what are due and for what years.

In the parishes outside the parish of Orleans, the sheriff who ex officio tax collector issues this certificate but it is confined to three years. In the City of New Orleans, one certificate is issued by the State Tax Collector covering state taxes; and one certificate is issued by the City Treasurer.

Up to the year 1936, both researches covered a period running from 1877 to the date of issue but by an amendment to the city charter the city researches do not now go beyond ten years prior to the date of issue. (2) This presents a problem to the examiner because such a certificate does not give a true picture of the title from the tax standpoint. To illustrate: The present would be vendor might have acquired the property in 1928, but he failed to pay the taxes for 1927 assessed in the name of the former owner from whom he acquired it and it was sold in that owner's name in 1930. The tax research issued in 1941 would not show the sale in 1930. Nor would the conveyance certificate show such a sale unless it was taken out in the former owner's name.

In the country parishes, the examiner or abstracter should run the tax rolls himself, unless he

1—R. C. C. 2561; Act 70, 1898; 108, 1924; Act 110, 1938
2—Act 116, 1936

has made a personal search of the conveyance office index in the name of each owner.

Evidence of the payments of municipal taxes outside of New Orleans should be obtained from the proper official collector thereof.

Paving Certificates

Prior to 1938 no paving certificates were issued by the City of New Orleans, or any other municipality. In New Orleans as stated the ordinance authorizing the paving in any particular street was recorded in Mortgage Office prior to start of the paving itself. This had the effect of impressing a lien upon the property facing the street and upon property facing the cross streets for a distance of one hundred and fifty feet each way. When the amount due by each lot had been figured out by the city authorities, bills in the names of then recorded owners were made, bound in a book and filed in the mortgage office and operated as a lien on each individual property. The Recorder of Mortgages was not obliged by law to report these liens, consequently it required a personal search by the abstracter or examiner. This search was rendered difficult by reason of the fact that the owner against whom the lien was recorded may have long since parted with the ownership, so that the index did not reflect the present owner's name. The searcher was therefore obliged to leaf over the lien book covering the square in which his property was located. He then had to apply to the Paving Department of the City for the amount of paving charges due.

However, the Recorder of Mortgages is obligated by a separate certificate to show by number all paving ordinances which affect the property described in the certificate.

By an act in 1938 all paving authorities throughout the State are required to issue a certificate, when requested, covering such property, amounts paid and due on same. (1)

United States Court Certificates

No certificates from the United States Courts are now required nor does a research of the records of said Courts need to be made for the reason that judgments of the federal court have to be recorded in the parish in which the property is situated, in order to operate as a lien on it. Under various acts of Congress (2) such judgments are to have effect or priority only when so recorded. The act as amended provides that its provisions would not apply unless and until the State concerned should authorize the judgments and decrees of federal court to be registered, recorded, docketed, indexed and otherwise conform to the rules and requirements of the act. At that time (1888) the laws of Louisiana did not so authorize recordation of federal judgments and decrees in accordance with the above but in 1916 the state legislature passed an act which gave the same force and effect to federal judgments when recorded as to judgments of our own courts (3).

This removed the necessity of obtaining such certificates insofar as judgments were concerned, but left open the question as to Federal Tax Liens. In other words, as the state act did not include such liens in the act above referred to, the federal act did

1—Act 116, 1938.
2—Act August 1, 1888, c729, Sl, 25, U. S. Stat. 357; March 3, 1911 c231, s291, 36 Stat. 1167; Aug. 17, 1912; c300 37 Stat. 311, now embodied in title 28, F. C. A.
3—Act 133, 1916

not operate so as to require recordation. In 1924 the Legislature passed an act which gave the above mentioned liens the same force and effect as liens under the state laws (1).

There is one phase of the matter which has been the cause of considerable controversy among members of the Bar. The point involved is this: Do judgments and liens rendered or imposed upon defendants prior to 1924 when the enabling act was passed by the State, come within the provisions of the federal enactments, so as to require recordation or are they vested rights which may not be impaired by subsequent legislation? There being no jurisprudence on the subject it is a matter of individual opinion. Some examiners hold the statutes applied to all judgments and liens and therefore no certificates are required, while others hold otherwise, insofar as judgments and liens existing prior to 1924 and require such certificates if the property was acquired by the vendor prior to 1924, but require no certificates if the property has been acquired since that date. The reasoning behind this practice is difficult to figure out. An owner may not have acquired a piece of property prior to 1924, but a judgment may have been rendered against him, or a government lien imposed upon him prior to that date and under the doctrine outlined above either being a vested right need not have been recorded in the parish where the property is situated but attaches immediately to the property.

Other examiners take the safe plan of requiring certificates in all instances.

In so far as federal judgments in favor of in-

1—Act 7, 1924
See U. S. v Kendall, 263 Fed. 126; Also notes following Sec. 812, Title 28, FCA.

dividuals that is not the government itself, the theory anent vested rights, is academic because prescription would bar recovery under those judgments after 1924 but prescription not running against the Federal government, the point is of importance, but in that case it would seem that certificates should be obtained in all cases.

Servitudes, Restrictions and Other Clauses

These subjects require too great an elaboration to be given much space and the examiner is referred to the chapter on those subjects.

Closing Clauses: These clauses are merely formal declarations that the whole act was executed in the presence of the parties, notary and witnesses in the notary's office so require little comment.

The law requires that all acts before a notary be passed in his office, but the Courts have declared that this is merely directory (1).

Signatures: All parties, witnesses and notary public should sign the act and a check should be made to insure that the names agree with those set out in the act.

Witnesses: The names of the witnesses should be carefully checked and taken off, not merely noted in the abstract that they had signed, because it may be found that he or she had or might have had an interest in the property conveyed, such as a husband wife or an heir. In any doubt as to the validity of the title by reason of such a claim it would be removed by his or her participation as a witness. Estoppel would undoubtedly operate.

Authentic acts should be witnessed by two witnesses or by three witnesses if the party thereto is blind.

1—Desonier v Hebert. La. Appeal, reporter, No. 177, Folio 423, citing R. S. 2494.

If a party cannot sign the notary should cause him to make his mark (1). An act with less than the required number of witnesses is not an authentic act. (2)

Registration and Recordation: The act should have been registered or recorded and the date thereof noted for comparison with the date of the instrument.

The law and the jurisprudence anent registration and recordation has been made the subject of a chapter in this work.

Auction Or Public Sales

The sales discussed are those authorized by the owner of the property, those made by officers of justice being treated separately in the appropriate chapters.

The Civil Code after having defined a public sale lays down rules governing such sales, thus: The sale by auction is that which takes place when the thing is offered publicly to be sold to whoever will give the highest price; (3) the sale by auction, whether made at the will of the seller, or by direction of law, is subjected to the rules hereafter mentioned; (4) it can not be made directly by the seller himself, but must be made through the ministry of a public officer, appointed for that purpose; (5) this officer, after having received in writing from the seller the conditions of the sale, must proclaim them in a loud and audible voice and afterwards propose that a bid shall be made for the property thus offered; (6) (authority to sell at

1—R. C. C. 2234
2—Marie v Cauchoix, 11 Martin (O. S.) 243; Savenet v LtBritton, 8
    Martin (N. S.) 502; Thomas v Kean, 10 Rob. 80
3—R. C. C. Art. 2601
4—R. C. C. Art. 2604
5—R. C. C. Art. 2605
6—R. C. C. Art. 2606

public auction must be in writing) (1) This adjudication is the completion of the sale; the purchaser becomes the owner of the article adjudged. (2)

The auctioneer's proces verbal is evidence of the sale and no act under private signature is necessary to perfect it. (3)

It is however, the universal practice for formal deed to be executed by authentic act by the auctioneer, and if the seller or sellers do not join in this act all the formalities prescribed by law must be checked, especially the written authority to sell; and the proper advertisement of the sale.

The proces verbal of the adjudication, signed by the officer making the sale, should be attached to the act. The marital status, as well as the ages of the parties, if not mentioned in the act, should be obtained in the form of affidavits or other evidence and attached to the act.

Where the seller or sellers are parties to the authentic act it is unnecessary to check or question the regularity of the public sale, as such appearance of the parties constitutes a ratification of the sale and in fact constitutes a deed direct from them to the purchaser. In all other respects the act, whether by the officer, or by the parties, should comply with all the requisites of the usual act of sale previously discussed.

The Sale A La Folle Enchere

This sale is covered by one article of the Civil Code (4) and the article reads: In all cases of sale by auction, if the person to whom the adjudication is made, does not pay the price at the time required . . .

1—3 L.459; 8 Rob. 102; 8 Ann. 283; Silverstein v Koppel, 166 L.1075
2—R. C. C. Art. 2608
3—Bibin v Winchester, 7 L.460; Lafiton v Dorin, 12 Ann. 164
4—R. C. C. 211

the seller, at the end of ten days, and after the customary notices, may again expose to public sale the thing sold, as if the first adjudication had never been made, and if at the second crying the thing is adjudged for a smaller price than that which had been offered by the person to whom the first adjudication was made, the latter shall remain debtor to the vendor for the deficiency and for all expenses incurred subsequent to the first sale. But if a higher price is offered for the thing than for which it was first adjudged the first purchaser has no claim for the excess.

The conditions of sale must be the same as in the first sale in order to hold a bidder liable. (1) Should the bidder not comply with the conditions of the sale, such as making a deposit, the seller may re-offer the same day without re-advertising. (2)

1—Labauve v McCabe, 33 A.183
2—Art 689, C. P. N. O. Mutual Ins. Co. v Ruddock & Railey, 22 A.44

CHAPTER VII

Donation Inter Vivos

The donation discussed in this chapter is the donation inter vivos, the Donation Morti Causa being discussed in a chapter forming part of the division of this book devoted to involuntary transfers.

A donation inter vios is the poorest form of title known to our law because it is open to attack from several sources, such as the donor's heirs on the ground that it is an infringement of their legitime; (1) or on the ground that the donation composed all of donor's property. In addition it may be revoked on several grounds which are not apparent on the face of the donation, such as ingratitude of the donee, non performance of the conditions laid upon the donee etc. An act of donation is not a title translative of property for the reason that the purchaser from the donee would not be a purchaser in legal good faith. (2) A donation of all the donor's property (3) may be revoked at any time by the donor, prescription not running against the action to annul. (4) The forced heirs may, in order to protect their legitime, contest, by parol evidence, the recitals in ancestor's deed. (5).

In view of the fact, however, that a donation inter vivos may, under certain circumstances, such as the existence of facts dehors the act which have been or may be established, which facts effectually put at rest any doubts as to the validity of the donation, be considered as a good link in the chain of title, the articles of the code governing donations inter vivos are herewith summarized: A donation which strips

1—R. C. C. Art 1517, Boone v Carroll, 35 A. 281; Kerwin v Hibernia Ins. Co., 35 A.33
2—Jenkins v Swan, 131 L.749; Beaulieu v Monin, 50 A.732
3—R. C. C. Art. 1497
4—116 L.101
5—Boone v Carroll, 35 A.281; Kerwin v Hibernia Ins. Co. 35 A.33

the donor of his entire property is null and void; (1) there are three kinds of donations, the donation purely gratuitous, the onerous donation, or that which is burdened with charges by the donor, and the remunerative donation, or that the object of which is to recompense the donee for services rendered; (2) the onerous donation is not a real donation if the value of the object given does not clearly exceed that of of the charges on the donee; (3) the remunerative donation is not a real donation if the value of the services should be little inferior to that of the gift; (4) in such cases the rules peculiar to donations inter vivos do not apply to the two donations above mentioned; (5) a donation inter vivos can comprehend only the present property of the donor. As to future property it shall be null as to that; (6) every donation inter vivos made on conditions the execution of which depends on the will of the donor is null (7).

The courts held at one time that donations made by unmarried person without forced heirs, could not be set aside or reduced as an infringement of their legitime by children of a subsequent marriage (8) but this decision was reversed by subsequent decision. (9)

No feigned delivery of immovables shall have effect against third persons; (10) a donation inter vivos is binding on the donor only from the day of its being accepted in precise terms; (11) donations are liable

1—R. C. C. Art 1497
2—R. C. C. Art. 1523
3—R. C. C. Art. 1524
4—R. C. C. Art. 1525
5—R. C. C. Art. 1526
6—R. C. C. Art. 1528
7—R. C. C. Art. 1529
8—Grasser v Blank, 110 L.493
9—Guidry v Caire, 181 L.895
10—R. C. C. Art. 1540; Baker v Baker; 125 L. 969; Latour v Guillory, 130 L. 570
11—R. C. C. Art. 1559

to be revoked or dissolved on account of the ingratitude cf the donee; nonfulfilment of the eventual conditions which suspend their consummation, or the non performance of the conditions imposed on the donee; the revocation on account of ingratitude can take place only in the case the donee has attempted to take the life of the donor, if he has been guilty toward him of cruel treatment, crimes or grevious injuries, or if he has refused him food when in distress; (1) this revocation affects neither the alienation by the donee, nor the mortgages, nor the real encumbrances he may have laid on the thing given, provided such transactions were anterior to the bringing of the suit for revocation; (2) in the event of revocation on account of the non execution of conditions, the property shall return to the donor free of all encumbrances or mortgages created by the donee, and the donor shall have all the rights against third possessors that he would have against the donee himself (3).

While Article 1478, as amended by Act 87 of 1871 declares that a donation inter vivos is irrevocable, it has been shown that it is revocable under certain conditions and in certain events.

There are another class of donations inter vivos which are governed by the rules prescribed in Chapters 8 and 9 of Title II, Book III of the Civil Code, that is donations by and between married persons before and after marriage, and by others to the parties to the marriage.

Such donations, that is, the donations made inter vivos, though by marriage contract to the husband

1—R. C. C. Art. 1560
2—R. C. C. Art 1562
3—R. C. C. Art. 1568

and wife, or either of them, are subject to the general rules prescribed for donations made under that title. It cannot take effect for the benefit of children not yet born. (1)

Fathers, mothers, other ascendants, collateral relatives of either of the parties to the marriage and even strangers, may give the whole or the part of the property they shall leave on the day of their decease, both for the benefit of the parties, and for that of the children born of their marriage, in case the donor survives the donee, such a donation, though made for the benefit of the parties to the marriage, or for one of them, is always, in case of survivorship of the donor, presumed to be made for the benefit of the children or descendents to proceed from that marriage; (2) a donation in the form specified in the preceeding article is irrevocable only in this sense that the donor can no longer dispose of the objects comprised in the donation on a gratuitous title, unless it be for moderate sums by way of recompense or otherwise. The donor retains until death the full liberty of selling and mortgaging unless he has formally barred himself from this right. (3)

Donations made by marriage contract cannot be declared void on pretense of want of acceptance; (4) and every donation in favor of marriage falls if the marriage does not take place; (5) married persons may by marriage contract, make to each other reciprocally, what donations they think proper under the following modifications; (6) donations intervivos made between married persons by marriage contract shall

1—R. C. C. Art. 1734
2—R. C. C. Art. 1735
3—R. C. C. Art. 1736
4—R. C. C. Art. 1739
5—R. C. C. Art. 1740
6—R. C. C. Art 1743

not be deemed to be done on the condition of the survivorship of the donee, if that condition be not formally expressed, and they are subject to all the rules
prescribed for those kind of donations; (1) a donation
of the property in future or of property present and
in future made between married persons by marriage
contract, whether simple or reciprocal, shall be subject to the rules established in the preceding chapter
with regard to similar donations made to them by
a third person, except that it shall not be transmis-
sive to the children, the issue of the marriage, in
case of death of the donee before the donor; (2) one of
the married couple may, either by marriage contract
or during the marriage, give to the other in full
property, all that he or she might give to a stranger,
(but an excessive donation by the husband to the
wife (or reverse) may be reduced to disposable portion.) (3) all donations made between married persons
during the marriage, though termed inter vivos, shall
always be revocable. The revocation may be made
by the wife without her being authorized to that
effect by the husband or by a court of justice; (4) (C.
C. 1749 must be construed with C. C. 3478 and so
must be held to mean that such interspousal donations shall always be revocable save as against third
possessors who can plead ten years prescription) (5);
subsequent birth of children do not automatically revoke these donations, provided they do not exceed
the legitime; (6) a married person who contracts a second marriage, having children by the former one,
can give to the other spouse, either by donation or

1—R. C. C. Art. 1744
2—R. C. C. Art. 1745
3—R. C. C. Art. 1746; Succ. of Moore, 40 A.531; Carroll
    v Cockerham, 38 A.813
4—R. C. C. Art. 1749
5—Leverett v Loeb. 117 L.310
6—R. C. C. Art. 1750

by last will and testament, in full property or its usufruct, not exceeding one third of his or her property; (1) if a person who marries a second time, has children by the previous marriage, he or she can not dispose of the property bequeathed to him or her by the deceased spouse or which came to him or her from a brother or sister of any of the children which remain. This property becomes by the second marriage, the property of the children of the preceding marriage and the spouse who marries again only has the usufruct of it; (2) (donations made by one of the spouses to the other before marriage comes within the purview of Article 1753; and this applies to inherited as well as donated property); (3) (This article was repealed by the legislature); (4) husbands and wives cannot give to each other directly or indirectly beyond what is permitted by these articles. All donations disguised or made to persons interposed shall be null and void; (5) (disguised donations made in evasion of this article are absolutely null and void, not merely reducible to the disposable portion) (6) (This applies only to donations between husbands and wives. Such a donation made between others are not as to forced heirs null by reason of being disguised). (7) (which simply means that donations to others may be reduced to the legitime): all donations made by one of the married parties to the child or children of the other party by a former marriage, or to relations to whom the other party is a presumptive heir on the day of donation, although the latter may not

1—R. C. C. Art. 1752
2—R. C. C. Art. 1753
3—Didlake v Cappel, 116 L.844
4—Act 238, 1918
5—R. C. C. Art, 1754

survive the relation who is the donee, shall be deemed to be made to persons interposed. (1)

It is sacramental that the act of donation shall be passed before a notary public and two witnesses; (2) and a donation made under private signature is null and void. (3) All donations must be accepted in writing by the donee either in the act of donation or in a separate act (4) and both the donation and the acceptance, if made separately, must be recorded within the time prescribed for mortgages in a separate book kept for that purpose by the Recorder of Mortagages. (5)

1—R. C. C. Art 1755
2—R. C. C. 1536
3—Foote v Lafaye, 115 L.1089; Baker v Baker, 125 L.969
4—R. C. C. 1540
5—R. C. C. Art. 1554

CHAPTER VIII

Dation En Paiement

An act of dation en paiement, if authentic in form, should comply with all the formalities prescribed by law for that form, as well as with the rules regarding dates, official, parties, marital status, description, certificates etc., hereinbefore discussed in the chapter on sales.

An act of dation en paiement may also be executed under private signature, subject of course, to all the objections inherent in that form of transfer.

Practically in all cases where the consideration for the transfer is anything other than money (except in exchanges) it constitutes a giving in payment.

Even in such extreme cases as the transfer of real estate by a subscriber to a corporation organized for the purpose of purchasing the very property transferred, and the consideration therefor being a certain number of shares of the capital stock of such corporation, there is clearly a dation en paiement, because there is always in such cases, an obligation which has been incurred by the transferer, by reason of his subscription to the stock; and on the other hand, the corporation has contracted to purchase the property.

Again, during the recent depression, building and loan associations offered to and did accept their own stock in payment of property held by them. These transactions do not constitute a dation en paiement on their face, but in reality they do for the reason that under the law, these corporations have the obligation, under certain limitations, of permitting any holder of their stock, to surrender their stock and withdraw the amount represented by that stock, hence in accepting the stock in lieu of cash, these corporations were merely giving the property in liquidation of their obligation. This obligation is made more evident by jurisprudence which has declared that the capital stock of homestead companies amounts to nothing more than a deposit (1).

The Civil Code defines a dation en paiement as an act by which the debtor gives a thing in payment to the creditor who is willing to receive it in payment of a sum which is due; (2) (the necessary essentials are an existing debt, just valuation and delivery; (3) and a fixed price; (4) giving in payment differs from an ordinary contract of sale in this, that the latter is perfect by the mere consent of the parties, even before delivery, while the giving in payment is made only on delivery; (5) (delivery is essential, (6) but where the vendee acknowledges by implication, or expressly as in an act of sale, the delivery is deemed accomplished; (7) this difference gives rise to another in the effect of these contracts, in cases of insolvency of the debtor. He may, though insolvent, lawfully sell for the price which is paid to him, but he may not give in payment to one creditor to the prejudice of the others anything other than the sum of money due; (8) (a dation en paiement by an insolvent debtor to one of his creditor, is fraudulent and may

1—Succ D'Anna, 6 L.App.142; Dimitry v Shreveport Mut. Life Assn., 167 L.685

2—R. C. C. Art. 2655

3—Peoples Nat. Bank v Voorhies, 134 L.303

4—Lovell v Payne, 30 A.511; Webster v Harman, 148 L.1093

5—R. C. C. Art. 2656

6—Hughes v Mattes, 104 L.223; Pugh y Hunter, 150 L.275; Turner v Young, 5 La. App. 425

7—Jaubert v Quilter, 48 A. 244; Wells v Blackman, 121 L.413

8—R. C. C. Art. 2658

be set aside) (1) except in this respect a dation en paiement is subject to all the rules which govern the ordinary contract of sale. (2)

An exception to the rule that an insolvent debtor cannot give in payment anything other than money to one creditor to the prejudice of another, is found in the dation en paiement which a husband makes to his wife in payment of her legal claim against him whether she has a mortgage or not. His insolvency is no obstacle to such a transaction, even on the eve of bankruptcy, (3) and is not subject to the revocatory action. (4)

The wife, if such a transaction is attacked, has the burden of proving the bona fides thereof.

1—Simon Gregory v H. & C. Newman. 50 A.338; Lovell v Payne 30 A.511; Lumber Co. v Manufacturing Co., 49 A.74; Newman v Mahoney, 44 A. 424
2—R. C. C. Art. 2659
3—R. C. Art. 2446; La. Digest v Marriage Par. 850; Pons v M. V. R. R., 122 L.170
4—Thompson & Co. v Freeman, 34 A.095

CHAPTER IX

Dedications

An individual never acquires property by dedication: it is strictly a donation made to the public for the public use.

Nevertheless, as it is an alienation as well as a donation, it is necessary to inquire into the principles governing the subject, when the owner, who made the dedication, attempts to revoke it and to sell the property free of such dedication; also as it affects title to the extent that it restricts the use of the whole or part of the property.

A dedication once made or legally held to have been made, may not be revoked, except in extreme case, nor is it subject to any of the ordinary rules governing rights of property.

The Civil Code is silent on the specific subject, the nearest reference to it being Article 765 wherein it is provided that the public, through the parish may acquire the use of property for a highway, but this is in the nature of a servitude and not a dedication.

A dedication, strictly speaking, is the act of an individual owner of property who sets aside a certain part of his property for public use, whether that public be composed of every individual who may use the place dedicated, such as a road or street, or certain individuals to whose special use the land dedicated is restricted.

There is a slight difference between a dedication in which the owner actually parts with the fee simple and a dedication in which the fee is retained, but in either case, once the public or that part of the public to whom the use is restricted, has availed itself of the dedication, the distinction is lost and whether it is considered as a servitude or a dedication the owner cannot recall it.

The usual occasions of dedications are road, streets and public squares.

The most frequent kind of dedications are those additions to towns and cities known as "sub-divisions" in which the owner of a large tract of land subdivides it into town lots or plots and lays out streets and squares, the first for passage way of the general public and the second for the recreation of such persons as may reside in the sub-division.

If the dedication has been made in express terms, either in a public act, or on the plat of survey usually made in such cases and the plat recorded, there exists no difficulty in arriving at a conclusion on the subject; and should any lots be sold, the owner is barred from ever revoking the dedication, (1) nor can there be any reversion of the fee to the owner, provided he does not reacquire all of the property in the tract, (2) in which case confusion would destroy the dedication, but this is not so where the streets have been opened and used for passage way by the general public, residents or otherwise (3) nor where the municipal authorities have accepted the dedication on behalf of the public. (4)

Where the owner of the original tract who has established a street, alley or otherwise dedicated a portion of the property to use of the public or the purchasers of the plots, has sold all the property abutting on the street, alley or other place dedicated though he may not have parted with the fee to such

1—Sarpy v Municipality, No. 2 9 A.597
2—La. Ice Co. v N. O., 47 A.217
3—Leland University v N. O., 47 A.100
4—Ibid 1, 2, 3.

dedicated places, he may not recover the land, title thereto adhering to the owners of the adjacent or abutting property, in proportion to the extent of their ownership. (1)

While the Civil Code contains nothing on the subject, the legislature and the courts have established well defined rules by which the examiner may be guided.

An intention to dedicate property to public use must be clearly established but such intention may be shown by deed, words or acts. (2)

The selling of lots with reference to plat with roadways and streets marked thereon, constitutes a dedication by intent of such streets and roadways in rural as well as urban communities, (3) and it has been held that where sales have been made in accordance with the plat, the grantee could not be deprived of a right of passage over the streets, even though the Police Jury had agreed to a cancellation of the dedication. (4)

In all cases it is the intent of the owner which must be sought, but once that intent has been made plain enough to induce others to act thereon, he is without power to recall or revoke the dedication. (5)

1—Wilkie v Wormsby, 178 L.141
2—Kenner v Kito, 141 L.76
3—Iseringhausen v Larcade, 147 L.515
4—Iseringhausen v Larcade, 153 L.976
5—N. O. v N. O. & Carr Land Co., 131 L.1092; Flournoy v Breard, 116 L.224

CHAPTER X

Counter Letters

In a strict sense counter letters do not constitute title, but practically they do, as they prove title in the true owner and when produced bind all, except bona fide purchasers from and creditors of the party in whose name the property stands, but even these are bound if and from the time the counter letter is registered in the Conveyance office. (1)

The Civil Code provides that counter letters are valid against all others except bona fide purchasers and creditors, but that forced heirs shall have the same right to annul absolutely and by parol evidence, the simulated contracts of those from whom they inherit and that they shall not be restricted to the legitime. (2)

That right is confined to forced heirs and forced heirs only; and even as to those they are restricted to an attack on a simulated transfer made by their ancestor of property standing in his name prior to the transaction complained of. (3)

Answers to facts and figures have been held the equivalent of a counter letter. (4) But such answers would not affect bona fide purchasers and creditors acquiring rights prior to such answers.

Conveyance and mortgage certificates should be required where the counter letter has not been registered, in the name of the party signing such a letter and his heirs (if he has died since acquiring the property for which the counter letter was issued), and even when registered, where the registration

1—Eberle v Eberle, 161 L. 313
2—R. C. C. Art. 2239
3—Eberle v Eberle, 161 L. 313
4—Bilgery v Ferguson, 80 A.30; Crozier v Ragan, S. A.154

of the property and the counter letter are not simultaneous.

Counter letters not registered are always to be viewed with suspicion and the circumstances surrounding their issue should be carefully checked.

CHAPTER XI

Exchange

An exchange, in all respects except one, amounts to two sales, since each party purchases and each party sells. The exception is that the considerations are things or rather real property instead of money. Therefore such an act requires the same careful examination as an act of sale and should conform as to date, official, parties marital statii, certificates, description etc., as required in the latter act.

The Civil Code itself declares that an exchange is a contract by which the parties to the contract give to one and another one thing for another, whatever it may be, except money, for in that case it would be a sale; (1) and it takes place by the bare consent of the parties; (2) and finally that all the other provisions relative to a contract of sale apply to the contract of exchange. And in this last contract each of the parties is individually considered as vendor and vendee. (3) An act by which A conveys to M a certain lot in consideration of another specified lot, but which act does not convey said lot to A is not an exchange. (4)

1—R. C. C. Art. 2660
2—R. C. C. Art. 2661
3—R. C. C. Art. 2667
4—Preston v Keene, 14 Peters (U. S.) 133

CHAPTER XII

Partitions In Kind Among Owners Of Full Age

Only those partitions which are of the above character, are voluntary and therefore this discussion is confined to those kind of partitions.

The subject is one which may be dismissed with the briefest comments, as owners in division possess the same rights, the same obligations and the same restrictions as individual owners, except that one owner cannot resist the demand of his co-owners for a partition, except under certain conditions, as no one can be compelled to hold property with another, unless that the contrary has been agreed upon; any one has the right to demand the division of a thing held in common by the action of parties (1). A testator may limit the right of partition among his heirs and legatees to five years, or to the happening of a certain condition, but if that condition does not happen within five years or five years have elapsed since the death of the testator, each heir may sue for a partition. (2) The legislation of 1920 and 1938 creating trust estates, (3) have modified the fore going provisions and in fact specifically repeals them insofar as the purposes of the acts are concerned, but at the outside the owners' rights are only suspended for a longer period of time than is provided in the articles of the Code, so that in examining a partition the examiner's decision as to its validity would be governed by the instrument creating the trust, provided there were such an instrument.

Co-owners may not stipulate that there never shall be a partition of a succession or of a thing held

1—R. C. C. Art. 1289
2—R. C. C. Art. 1299, 1300
3—Acts 107, 1920 and 81 of 1938

in common Such a stipulation would be void and of no effect. (1)

To effect a partition it is not always necessary to execute a formal act of partition, as a sale or sales which would effect a partition amounts to a partition. (2)

As to the regular act of partition itself, the requirements prescribed in another chapter for an act of sale should have been complied with.

Property held in common by minors and major co-owners may be partitioned in kind, without the forming of lots by experts or drawing therefor where major owners consent and court authorizes same on advice of a family meeting. (3)

But the foregoing applies only to partitions made by consent, where a judicial partition has been decreed, the property must be divided into lots of equal or near equal value and lots drawn by chance and not selected by the co-proprietors. (4)

1—R. C. C. Art. 1297
2—Stone v Jefferson, 200 Southern Report 461
3—Act 15, 1918; Washington v Smith, 156 L.902; Levy v Levy, 180 L.77
4—Jefferson Lake Oil Co. v Langridge, 182 L.57

CHAPTER XIII
Redemption of Property Sold For Taxes

A redemption of a property sold for taxes prior to the elapse of the redemption period (One year up to November 8, 1932 and three years since that date) (1) is, strictly speaking, not a voluntary act, as the tax debtor can compel such a redemption, but any redemption made after such redemption periods, is in fact a sale, as the title has become vested in the tax purchaser and the tax debtor is without the power to compel redemption. Hence any transfer of this character should be accompanied with all the certificates, researches prescribed for an act of sale, as well as by the declarations of marital status etc.

Any declaration of the parties as to the act being a redemption is of no avail against adverse interests.

Of course where this redemption period has been suspended by reason of the provisions of the law, such as "the property shall be redeemable at any time during one year (or three as the case may be) from the recordation of the tax sale." or by other causes, the right would still exist in the tax debtor and the redemption of the property from the tax sale still enforceable, the property could still be redeemed free of all alienations, mortgages, liens etc., but as this would involve research dehors the records and creates doubt, the examiner should require the usual proofs.

It is to be noted that the period of redemption runs from the "date of recordation of the tax sale, which is the date tax deed is actually transcribed in the conveyance records rather than when it was filed and indorsed by the Registrar. (2)

1—Const. 3921. Art. 10. Sec. 11. amended by Act 147, 1932
2—McLeod v Hoover, 159 L.244

In 1934 (1) the Legislature authorized the redemption of property adjudicated to the State or to any of its political subdivisions (except the city of New Orleans) upon payment of the taxes for the year for which it was adjudicated and the cancellation of all taxes subsequent thereto. In 1935 (2) another act was passed including New Orleans in its provisions.

In the case of the State taxes, the redemption presented no difficulties for the reason that the State always sells property for delinquent taxes in the year following that for which the taxes are delinquent, but in case of the City of New Orleans a different situation arose due to the fact that the City never sold property for delinquent taxes until the constitutional prescriptive period of three years had nearly elapsed, so that the property was not sold for delinquent taxes say for the year 1931, until 1934, consequently the taxes for the years 1932, 1933 and 1934, had accrued at the time of the actual date of adjudication.

A tax debtor applied to the courts for a mandamus directed to the Tax Collector for the City of New Orleans compelling the City to cancel all taxes subsequent to the year for which it was adjudicated to the City as well as the taxes accruing after the actual date of adjudication.

The court held that dues for the years subsequent to the date of adjudication should be cancelled, but not for the years between the year for which it was adjudicated and the date of the actual adjudication. (3)

In 1936 another act was passed permitting the redemption of property sold to the State or its political subdivisions for taxes and the annulling of all

1—Act 161, 1934
2—Act 14 of 1935, 4 E. S.
3—Tulane Homestead Association v Montgomery, 185 L.777

taxes "assessed and levied prior to and subsequent to the year for which the adjudication was made to the State or its political subdivisions and subsequent to the date of adjudication and up to and including the year in which the redemption was made".

This Act insofar as the above provision was concerned was declared unconstitutional. (1)

In checking the payment of taxes on a property title to which is being examined it will be necessary to ascertain definitely that no cancellation has been made of taxes due for the years between the year for which the property was adjudicated and the year in which it was actually adjudicated.

An Act validating all redemptions made under the provisions of Act 161 of 1934 and subsequent acts was passed 1940, (2) but this act could not validate those redemptions which had been declared unconstitutional by the courts.

The above acts permitted the tax debtor, his heirs, legatees and creditors to redeem under their provisions, but said nothing in reference to the widow but it has been decided that she may. (3)

1—Chess &Wymond Co. v Grace, 188 L. 129
2—Act 256, 1930
3—Woods v Register Land Office, 189 L. 69

CHAPTER XIV

Renunciations

There are three classes of renunciations.

1. Renunciation by widow of her community rights.
2. Renunciation by heir.
3. Renunciation of a real right, such as a servitude.

Each class is governed by different rules and while the first two cases occur only in case of death, they are included here because they are voluntary alienation and are to be analyzed both from the standpoint of the essentials of the instrument by which they are executed; and from the capacity of the renouncer to renounce and the effect flowing from the renunciation.

Renunciation by a widow: As the renunciation by the widow has for its purpose release from her personal liability for community debts, its validity is of little importance in an examination of title to community property, but where it has been successfully attacked by the creditors, her own separate property might become involved and the title thereto clouded.

The provisions of the Civil Code grants the widow the right of renouncing (1) but at the same time provide that in the event of so renouncing she loses every sort of right to the effects of the partnership or community of gains, (2) even though there is a residue after payment of all debts; in other words places her in the position of a stranger as regards the succession (3).

The Civil Code requires the renunciation of the widow to be made before a notary or a parish record-

1—R. C. C. Art. 2410
2—R. C. C. Art. 2411
3—Spencer v Scott. 46 A.1209

er and two witnesses, but a judicial renunciation has been deemed valid (1).

Renunciation by the heir: All the rules relating to acceptance and renunciation are applicable to testamentary as well as to intestate successions (2); a succession can be renounced only under the same circumstances in which it can be legally accepted (3); it must be express by public act before a notary public and two witnesses (4); but it may be renounced by a judicial declaration (5); a married woman cannot renounce an inheritance unless she be duly authorized by her husband, or by the judge (6); the latter, however, is inoperative since the enactment of the so called emancipation of women laws (7); if the heir renounces he loses all right to the succession just as in the case of a widow renouncing (8).

The renunciation by the heir may have three different objectives:

1. Release of personal liability for the debts of the succession.
2. For the benefit of all of the heirs.
3. For the benefit of a particular heir, or heirs.

Release from personal liability: All the rules which have been specified in the preceding pages as to a renunciation by the wife including the instrument of renunciation, apply to the heir who renounces for the purpose of releasing himself from liability for the debts of the succession.

For the benefit of all the heirs: All of the articles of the Revised Civil Code concerning acceptance and renunciation contained in Title IV, Chapter 6,

1—Union Nat'l Bank v Chopin 46 A.635
2—R. C. Art. 976
3—R. C. C. Art. 1015
4—R. C. C. Art. 1017
5—Vide 1 above
6—R. C. C. 1019
7—Dart's Rev. State. S. S. 2169, 2173
8—R. C. C. Art. 1021

Sections 1, 2, 3 and 4 apply to this character of renunciation. As to the effect of this renunciation the reader is referred to the chapter entitled, "Inheritance"

In favor of a particular heir or heirs: this, in effect, is not a renunciation but is a donation, as it connotes acceptance and is so denominated by the Code; the donation, sale or assignment which one of the co-heirs makes of rights of inheritance, either to a stranger, or to his co-heirs, is considered on his part, an acceptance of the inheritance; the same may be said (1) of the renunciation, even if gratuitious which is made by one of the heirs in favor of one or more of the co-heirs; and (2), of the renunciation, which he makes in favor of all of his co-heirs, when he receives the price thereof. And the transfer of a succession to the widow in community made by the legal heir, is an act of heirship . . . it is an acceptance of the succession pure and simple. (3) In determining the nature and effects of an act, motives of the parties must be considered. Abandonment of an heir's portion of a succession in favor of another, not with the intention of renouncing generally, but only of transferring his rights, is to be regarded not as a renunciation, but a transfer by the party so abandoning (4).

The principle above enunciated that it is the motive rather than the language of an act of this character which must be considered has been generally followed by our courts, thus 1. That Article 1003 of the Code referred only to renunciations in favor of less than all the co-heirs; 2, that love and affection is not considered a "price" within the meaning of the

1—R. C. C. A-t. 1002
2—R. C. C. Art. 1003
3—Sanford v Toadvine, 15 Ann. 170
4—Reed v Crocker 12 Ann. 436

same article, though made in favor of all the heirs indiscriminately 3. An instrument whereby two heirs, in consideration of love and affection and kind treatment, renounced, relinquished, assigned, transferred and set over all interest in the succession to the only other heir, held a renunciation and not an acceptance and donation (1). Again it was held; that an heir's renunciation in favor of her coheir in conformity with the intention of the de cujus, will be upheld as such rather than as a donation (2).

Thus it will be seen that what may seem to be a renunciation in one case may be a donation in another and vice versa, so an examiner must interpret each act for himself.

There is no doubt, however, that in principle a renunciation which does not partake of a complete abandonment of all rights of the heir in the succession with no evidence of the exercise of ownership, is a donation.

Incidently it must be assumed that in those cases where the widow renounces her rights in community property in favor of the heirs, it is a donation, not a real renunciation, as she does not inherit such rights but is already vested with them.

Renunciation of a real right: Real rights are impressed with all the rules affecting immovables and a renunciation of such a right is one of the muniments of a title and must contain the essentials required to constitute a good link. An examination must therefore involve the marital status of the renouncer; alienations and encumbrances, etc., to the extent that they are applicable to the particular act

1—Aurienne v Olivet 153 L. 451
2—In re Haaf 52 Ann. 249

of renunciation. The renunciation made without moneyed or other actual consideration amounts to a donation and hence is subject to the defects of such an act.

CHAPTER XV
Rescissions

Voluntary rescissions only are here discussed. Judicial rescission form the subject of another chapter.

The dissolving condition is that which when accomplished operates the revocation of the obligation placing matters in the same state as though the obligation had not existed; it does not suspend the execution of the obligation: it only obliges the creditor to restore what has been received in case the event provided for in the condition takes place (1). If the buyer does not pay the price the seller may sue for the dissolution of the sale. It necessarily follows that in order to rescind the sale, the seller must make a tender and restore that portion of the purchase price which has been paid in cash (2) (the vendor must return the the portion of the price paid with interest from date of the payment and must pay for improvements. The vendee must return the property and pay rent. (3)

Vendor may sue for a rescission even after an unsuccessful suit to obtain payment (4); nor does the prescription of the note bar the action (5); and sale may be rescinded and property returned though it passed into the hands of third parties (6); the vendor by sale unrecorded can rescind as to subsequent mortgage (7); where a sale of real estate is judically dissolved for nonpayment of price, the property returns to the vendor free from all mortgages, legal as well as judicial. (8)

The foregoing rules and principles seem to contem-

1—R. C. C. 2045
2—R. C. C. Art. 2561
3—School Directors v Anderson, 28 A.739
4—Canal Bank v Copeland 15 L. 79
5—Templeman v Pegues, 24 A.537
6—Prudential Sav. Home Soc. v Langermann 156 L. 76
7—Johnson v Bloodworth, 12 A.699; Ragsdale v Ragsdale, 105 L.395
8—Adler v Adler, 126 L.472

plate an application only in judicial rescissions, but are given here for the reason that many of them are equally applicable to voluntary rescissions and must be complied with in the latter cases under penalty of nullity. Thus, when in a voluntary rescission there has been no return of the purchase price with interest, but the return made only in satisfaction of the unpaid portion of the price, it comes back burdened with the mortgages and privileges to which it has been subjected in the vendee's hands (1).

On the other hand, a suit is not necessary to free the property from liens and mortgages or other encumbrance for the reason that a party may do voluntarily what he may be forced to do by suit (2); and a voluntary dissolution is ex necessitate (3), even by the surviving spouse (4).

A voluntary rescission act should conform to all essentials of an act of sale. Although theoretically mortgage and conveyance certificates are not required because no alienation or mortgage is impressed upon the property to the prejudice of the vendor, there are conditions in which this is not true, one of which has been pointed out above, another being that if the right of rescission has prescribed (which is ten years from date right accrued) the property does not return free of encumbrance etc (5).

The marital status is also important because a change in that status may have occurred and the signatures of the heirs, or of the former wife, if there has been a divorce, is advisable.

1—Wilmont v Steamer Ouachita Belle, 32 A, 607;
      Hunter v Buckner 29 A.607
2—Swan v Gayle, 24 A. 498
3—Chreiten v Richarlson, 6 A.2
4—Shields v Lafon 7 A. 25
5—Hamilton v Bank 39 A. 934

CHAPTER XVI

Vente A Remere

Not much comment is necessary in these cases, as the examiner has only to see that the formalities required in the usual act of sale have been complied with, certificates etc., attached and that the act on its face established a real vente a remere had been intended and finally that the time prescribed therein for redemption has elapsed. Beyond the record, however, he must establish clearly that the purchaser had gone into possession and continued therein, as actual possession is the one test by which to determine whether it it a real sale with a right of redemption, or another contract (1).

The Civil Code has defined a vente a remere and laid down rigid rules governing same, thus: The right of redemption is an agreement or paction by which the vendors reserves to himself the power of taking back the thing sold by returning the price paid for it (2); (There must be a stipulation for a return of the price) (3). It has been considered a conditional sale containing a suspensive condition. (4) The price must be sufficient and possession must follow, or the instrument may be held as pignorative. (5)

The right of redemption cannot be reserved for a time exceeding ten years. If a term exceeding that has been stipulated in the agreement, it shall be reduced to the term of ten years (6); the time fixed for the redemption must be rigorously observed; it cannot be prolonged by the judge (7) if that right has not

1—Latoilais v Breaux 154 L. 1006
2—R. C. C. Art. 2567
3—Downes v Scott, 3 A. 279 ; Jackson v Lemle 35 A. 855
4—Forsdick v Schall, 99 U. S. 235
5—Howe v Powell 40 A. 307
6—R. C. C. Art. 2568
7—R. C. C. Art. 2569

been exercised he cannot exercise it afterwards and the purchaser becomes irrevocably possessed of the thing (1) (in which event it is not necessary that the purchaser have the failure to redeem judicially declared to become the owner) (2) the delay runs against any person, not excepting minors (3). The vendor having sold a thing with the power of redemption may exercise that right against a second purchaser, even in case such right should not have been mentioned in the second sale (4); the person having purchased an estate under a condition of redemption, is entitled to all rights possessed by the vendor; he may prescribe against the true owner as well as against those having claims or mortgages on the thing sold (5) (which seems to mean that a purchase under the condition of redemption has all the rights of any other vendee, except as to the right of redemption which is reserved). When a vendor recovers the possession of his inheritance by virtue of the power of redemption, he recovers it free from any mortgage or incumbrance created by the purchaser, provided such possession be recovered within ten years as provided by Article 2568. If, after the expiration of ten years, the vendor recovers his estate with the consent of the purchaser, the estate remains liable for every mortgage and incumbrance laid upon it by the purchaser. (6)

In the case as stated above, the vendor, after failure to redeem within the ten years, is in no better position as regards incumbrances than an ordinary purchaser.

1—R. C. C. Art. 2570
2—Levy v Ward 32 A. 784
3—R. C. C. Art. 2571
4—R. C. C. Art. 2572
5—R. C. C. Art 2573
6—R. C. C. Art. 2587

A sale with a right of redemption is never the less a sale. After lapse of period of redemption, conveyance is complete and absolute as though right had never been retained (1).

Want of delivery constitutes a simulation and not a vent a remere (2).

A redeemable sale of real estate where vendor apparantly remains in possession and the price is vile, will be considered a mortgage (3).

The title of a purchaser in good faith, who purchases from a vendee in a sale which had become absolute by non exercise of the right of redemption, is secure against attack from original vendor or his creditors, on the ground that the act was a mortgage (4).

1—Harples v Citizens Bank 51 A. 511
2—Boone v Pelechet 13 A. 203
3—Eames v Woodson, 120 L.1031
4—Broussard v West, 47 A.1033

CHAPTER XVII

Alienations By The State, Its Political Sub-divisions And Its Agencies

Though the acquisition of property by the State, its subdivisions and agencies, and the alienation there of, constitute different links in a title and therefore should be the subject of different chapters, both the acquisition and the alienation will be examined and analyzed together in this chapter because there are certain factors which can not be included in the general plan of the work, which is an analysis of alienations rather than that of acquisitions, so for a better understanding of the subject they are examined side by side.

As heretofore stated there are three classes of governmental owners and possessors of property.

1. The State itself
2. Its political sub-divisions such as parishes and municipalities.
3. Its governmental agencies, such as school boards, levee boards, drainage, irrigation and levee districts, penitentiary board, and numerous boards and commissions and bodies, which in some way and at some point, perform or exercise governmental functions and powers as agents of the State.

It is impossible to enumerate in detail each and every one of such agents, including as they do, the departments of the state as well as divisions which function as an arm of the state.

The State acquires ownership of real property by:

1. Virtue of its sovereignty.
2. Grants from the Federal Government.

3. Tax Sales
4. Donations inter vivos and mortis causa.
5. Purchase
6. (escheat)
7. Eminent Domain

BY REASON OF SOVEREIGNTY

The property so acquired included such as were acquired and used by the former sovereign for strictly governmental purposes, and particularly the land covered by the tides, the sea shore, etc. (1).

An Act of 1910 declares that the waters of, and in all bayous, lagoons, lakes and bays and the beds thereof, within the borders of the state, not at present under the direct ownership of any person, firm or corporation, to be the property of the state (2). It further declares that the act is not retroactive insofar as acquisitions prior to its passage were concerned. The provisions of this act are not applicable to land which has become dry because of subsidence of the waters so as to form part of its shores (3).

Grants From The Federal Government.

These grants are fully covered in the chapter in which patents are discussed, so no further space will be devoted here to the subject.

Tax Sales

There are and have been no constitutional provisions for the adjudicating of tax property to the state in the event that no private bidder at the tax sale are found, such adjudications being authorized only by legislative enactments (4). Adjudications to the state have the same force and effect and are subject to

1—Morgan v Nogodish et al 40 A.426
2—Act 258 1910
8—State v Standard Oil Co. 164 L.834
4—Act 170 1890; 815 1910; 235 1928

the same defects which may be urged against a tax sale to a private bidder. A chapter on tax sales has been incorporated in this work so anything that might be said here would be mere repetition.

Donations Inter Vivos and Mortis Causa.

These donations are governed by the same laws which govern transfers of this character as between individuals, and as those laws have been discussed in other chapters, further comment is unnecessary.

Purchase.

The above remarks apply in the case of purchase, except it may be added that the authority to accept (in donations) and to acquire in purchases, are solely vested in Legislature. No official or agency of the state can legally act except under and within the limits of such authority.

Inheritance (Escheat)

The successions of persons who die without heirs, or which are not claimed by those having a right to them, belong to the State (1). In defect of lawful relations, or of a surviving husband or wife, or acknowledged child, the successions escheats to the State (2).

To paraphrase the foregoing it may be said that the State inherits only in the event that there are no existing heirs, or that those of the blood who might inherit were it not for certain circumstances, are barred (3).

The State must not only allege, but prove that the owner died without leaving anyone who could, under the law, inherit (4).

1—R. C. C. 485; Succ. Gravier 125 L.733
2—R. C. C. 929
3—Leyre v Pasco 5 Rob. 9; Succ. Manger, 12 Rob. 584
4—Succ. Herdman, 154 L.477

A natural brother or/and a natural sister, of a natural child, who dies leaving neither children nor parents, will, to the exclusion of the State, inherit from the deceased (1).

The State does, however, inherit to the exclusion of a natural child duly acknowledged, but who was an adulterous bastard (2); and to the exclusion of the adulterous collaterals of an adulterous bastard (3).

It also excludes a legitimate child of an acknowledged natural child from the inheritance of a grandfather's succession, because representation takes place only in legal successions (4), the father in this case, if he had lived to inherit would have been an irregular heir.

Where all of the heirs have renounced the State takes, not as an heir but by virtue of its sovereignty by which it may appropriate all property without a master found within its territory (5).

The principles hereinabove set forth have application only to the State's acquisition, as it never gets corporeal possession or actual title to such property for the reason, that such property must be reduced to cash in the succession in which found, and the proceeds thereof turned over to the State (6)·

Eminent Domain.

The State's sovereignty carries with it, the right of eminent domain, but it is rarely exercised by the State itself directly and never without a specific purpose.

The right is mainly exercised through the States agencies, such as levee boards, drainage commission-

1—Laclotte v Labarre 11 L.179
2—Fletcher v Decoudreau 11 A.59
3—Succ. Townsend 40 A.66
4—Hawkins v Williams 146 L.529
5—State v Ames, 23 A.69
6—R. C. C., 1196, 1204 ; Succ. Herdman, 154 L.477

ers, parishes, municipalities, or through certain corporations organized for certain public operations, as for instance, railroads, telegraph and telephone companies, etc.

The first law of society being that the general interest is superior to that of the individual, every individual who possess under the protection of the laws, any particular property, is obliged to yield it to the community, whenever it becomes necessary for the general use (1).

Expropriation proceedings do not have to be brought at the domicile of the owner. They may be brought in the parish where the property is situated (2).

The owner of the thing needed for general use, may be divested of the property by the authority of law (3).

For the validity of the actual appropriation, it is not requisite that it be preceded by the expropriation proceedings (4).

There are only three essential allegations in the proceedings: 1. That the land sought to be expropriated is actually needed for public use; 2. That the actual amount is needed; 3. That the owner has been offered a fair amount for the property and that he has refused.

The examiner must be certain that a fee simple and not a servitude was not obtained by the expropriating authority.

The regularity of the proceedings as to jurisdiction. citation, trial, judgment, signing, etc., should be checked.

1—R. C. C. 2626
2—Iberia St. M. etc. v Morgan's L. & T. R. R. 129 L. 497
3—R. C. C. 2627
4—Ouchita Parish School Bd. v Clark 1 Sou. Report. 2 S.54

Public utility corporations have been granted such powers by numerous statutes by the legislature (1). A partial list is to be found at the bottom of this page.

Acquisitions By State Political Sub-Divisions.

The term, political sub-division. is here used to denote only such subdivisions (Parishes and Municipalities), because, while other subdivisions such as levee, school boards, drainage, etc., commissions, are strictly speaking, political subdivisions, they are restricted in their functioning to narrow confines, administrative in their nature with only such powers as are necessary for the single purpose for which they are created. On the other hand, parishes and municipalities have legislative as well as administrative powers limited only by their geographical area and by the statutes creating them and by their charters in the case of a municipality.

Parishes and Municipalities may acquire property by:

1. Purchase.

2. Donations, inter vivos and mortis causa.

3. Eminent Domain.

Municipalities may also acquire property at tax sales where there are no bidders (2).

Both corporations have the right to acquire property by purchase or by expropriation for parochial and municipal and local purpose, strictly public in their nature, only under the authority granted by the law. This authority may be direct or may arise by inference where the acquisition is necessary in carrying out the purpose for which it is required (3).

1—R. S. Arts. 1478, 1493; Acts 39, 1906; 73, 1902
    111 1900; 208 1906; 117 1886.
2—State ex Rel. City of N. O. 112 L.408
3—Sec. 6, Art. 14, Const. 1921; Avery v Police Jury, 12 A.554

Donations Inter Vivos and Mortis Causa.

No comment is necessary in view of what has already been said regarding these acquisitions.

The act by which the acquisition is accomplished should be in the authentic form and contain all essentials of an act of that character. There should also be attached to it a certified copy of the ordinance with the seal authorizing the acquisition passed in accordance with the formalities prescribed by the legislature in such cases.

It would require several volumes were any attempt be made to list the legislative acts creating such political sub-divisions and to point out in detail all of the law covering these transactions. The examiner must resort to the particular statute concerned in each case.

Governmental Agencies.

The number of these agencies, which include institutions of higher learning, penitentiaries, elymosynary institutions, experiment farms, drainage, navigation, sewerage and water commissions, levee and school boards and other boards and agencies, is so great that a list can find no place herein. So also would be a list of the legislative acts creating them.

As a summary, it may be said that such powers as they possess of acquiring or alienating property are granted them by the legislative acts creating them. In general these powers are confined to the acquiring of property necessary in carrying out the purposes for which they were created. In some instances these agencies may not either acquire or alienate property except by sanction of the legislature. The examiner must perforce resort to the act itself to ascertain the exact powers that have been granted in each case.

There are two of such agencies which require particular mention and discussion for the reason that they both acquire and alienate property under different conditions and from different sources and possess power not possessed by other agencies.

These agencies are:

1. Levee Boards.
2. School Boards.

Levee Boards

There are no constitutional provisions contained in any constitution prior to that of 1921 as regards levee boards and no powers granted except inferentially; and all such boards have been organized by legislative enactments, the constitutionality of which have been affirmed, through questioned (1).

Levee Boards acquired by:

1. Grants from the State.
2. Expropriation. (Eminent Domain).

Grants From The State.

Grants have been made from time to time, either by a general grant or by special acts to particular boards. An act of 1862 (2), was one such general grant, but its language gave rise to some doubt as to whether or not the grant of such lands were in praesenti, or merely a grant of the proceeds, hence in titles to these lands sold by the levee boards, it was argued, should be issued by the State and not by the Levee Boards, but it has been finally decided that title vested in the board (3).

A list of the acts granting lands to the levee boards are enumerated in the foot notes at the bottom of this page (4).

1—Minor v Daspit 38 A. 323
2—Act 124, 1862
3—Ellerbe v Grace 162 L.846
4—Acts 97, 1890; 74, 1892; 125, 1902

These grants were of two classes of property:

1. Lands adjudicated to the state for taxes (1).
2. Those lands received from the United States by the State and known as swamp lands (2).

In a large number of cases, certain titles from the Levee boards were found defective for want of sufficient signatures, only one officer of the board signing where the statute required two. However such defects were cured by act of the legislature (3).

Eminent Domain.

As an agency of the State levee boards possess the power of eminent domain and until 1928 (4), could exercise that power without compensation to the owner of the land taken, except those situated in the City of New Orleans, on the principle of damnum absque injuria (5). In 1928 the constitution was amended so as to require compensation to all owners (6).

In all respects expropriation proceedings by levee boards should conform to formalities required in such proceedings in other cases.

Schools.

Schools, or rather School Districts acquire by Grants from the United States and from the State.

Purchase.

Donations inter vivos and mortis causa.

Eminent Domain.

Grants From the United States and the State.

Grants from the United States for the use of the schools were not made directly to the schools but to

1—Act 280 1910
2—Act 97 1890; 74 1892; 125 1902
3—Act 316 1926
4—Sect. 6 Art. 16 Const. 1921 as amended by Act 165 1928
5—Eagan v Hart 45 A.1858
6—Act 165 1928

the State. The principal grant was that of the sixteenth section in every township.

This subject has been discussed at length in the chapter entitled Patents so need not be repeated here.

Purchases.

In these cases the school boards stand in the same position as any other vendee and the formalities to be observed are the same.

Eminent Domain.

As a branch of the State, school boards exercise the right of eminent domain and that right is limited to necessity and use of the land expropriated and otherwise subject to the same rules as in other such proceedings.

Donations Inter Vivos and Mortis Causa.

These transactions come under the same rules and laws as donations of that character to individuals and require no further discussion.

The rules and laws governing acquisitions by the State, its subdivisions and agencies having been set forth in the foregoing, it now remains to discuss the alienations which may be made by them and the laws governing same.

ALIENATIONS BY STATE.

The State may alieniate by :
Grants and Patents.
Sales.
Donations.

GRANTS AND PATENTS

Grants are confined solely to the State's subdivisions and agencies and to the United States Government for governmental purposes.

Grants are made through the legislature to the sub-divisions and agencies for public purposes and uses and seldom, or never come into the public market and therefore the examiner is not particularly interested in these grants.

Patents issued by the State have been fully discussed in another chapter.

Sales.

Sales may be made by the State, but they are mainly made through a particular agency, generally by legislative enactments.

Donations.

Donations of land are confined to donations to the United States Government.

The rules governing such transfers are to be found in the special acts by which they are made; and in the constitutional provisions authorizing them.

Transfers Made By Political Sub-Divisions and Agencies

Alienations by the sub-divisions and agencies of the State are subject to all of the provisions contained in the acts creating them and must conform strictly thereto. In most cases such alienations can only be of property found to be of no further use for the purpose for which it was purchased, or to further the purpose of its purchase.

In some cases special consent of the legislature is required; in others such alienations are permitted by general statutes, which gives parishes general authority to dispose of surplus property.

Levee and school boards form an exception to this rule in the sale of lands which have been granted to them by the State and the United States as a source of funds to be used in accomplishing the purposes for which these boards were created.

Sales By Levee Boards.

These sales must conform to the rules established by the acts granting them and the essentials of sales by corporations. A number of titles issued by the levee boards were found defective by reason of the fact that only one officer of the board signed whereas the statute required two signatures (1). However, these titles were quieted by an act of the Legislature (2), although the courts have since held that the signature of either the Auditor or Register was sufficient for a valid title (3).

Sales By School Boards.

These sales in general follow the rules which prevail in alienations by a state agency, but in the proceedings necessary to effect the sale, the formalities to be obesrved are laid down by various statutes.

The Revised Statutes (4) provide for a vote by the people of the parish where the land is situated, and a majority vote in favor of the sale is necessary.

If the sale is authorized by the vote, the land must be surveyed, if not already surveyed; and an appraisement made by two appraisers appointed by the treasurer and recorder of the parish. The proposed sale must be advertised for thirty days in accordance with law.

Swamp lands are sold in the same manner as above, except there is no vote (5).

In 1906 an act was passed authorizing school boards to sell and lease timber and mineral rights

1—Lovell v Dulac, 31 Fed. Sup. 919
2—Act 316 of 1926
3—Barnett v State Mineral Board, 193 L.1055
4—Rev. Stat. 2958 to 2966, both inclusive
5—Act 151 of 1912

without obtaining a vote of the people (1) and in 1912 another act authorized the school boards to rent lands and lease mineral rights, but required an election to authorize sale of land and timber (2). An act of 1916, amended by an act of 1918, authorized the superintendent and the treasurer of a school board to execute leases of lands and sales of timber and authorized the treasurer to execute leases of mineral rights and make sales of land (3).

The question was raised at one time as to the right of the State to sell school lands, but it was settled in the affirmative by decisions of both the state and federal courts (4).

School lands reserved to State consisting of seminary lands, sixteenth sections and lands formerly the bed of bodies of water, were opened to entry and sale by an act of 1902 (5).

1—Act 120, 1906
2—Actt 100, 1912
3—Acts 120, 1916 and 142, 1918
4—Cooper v Howard 18 How. 173; State v Joyce 261, Federal 128
5—Act 124, 1902; Board Levee Com. v Capdeville 128, L.283

CHAPTER XVIII

Involuntary Alienations.

The term involuntary refers to those class of change of owner ship in which the change takes place without the consent of the owner which consent is not an element affecting the validity of title, as the transfer takes place by operation of law.

For convenience in discussing them, these alienations have been divided into different classes and they will be discussed and analyzed in order.

1   Public Sales, i. e. by sheriffs·

2   Judicial Sales, i. e. partitions and other sales made under order of court.

3   Sales of minors and interdicts' property.

4   Tax Sales

5   Eminent domain

6   Sales by Trustees under established trusts

7   Petitory actions and act of revendication, that is by reason of judgments of courts in suits involving those claims.

8   Bankruptcy sales.

There is a third class of change of ownership, involuntary in character, brought about by death, but the discussion of that class will be in a separate division as the laws controlling such a change are so numerous and important that it has been thought best treat them separately.

CHAPTER XIX

Public Sales.

The classification herein made between public sales and judicial sales is somewhat arbitrary, but is principally based upon the difference in procedure and the technical rules governing each class.

Public sales under the classification made, are those sales made by a sheriff or other officer of justice under a fieri facias or other writ issued for the enforcement of money judgments or its own orders by a court of competent authority.

A necessary part of the examiner's work is an examination of the proceedings leading up to these sales, and although in the main, third parties are protected by the judgment, decree or order under which such sales are made, certain essentials must be checked for assurance that such judgments, decrees or orders are valid.

These essentials are:
1. Jurisdiction of the court or other authority..
2. Petitions, parties and cause of actions.
3. Citation.
4. Answer, or
5. Default.
6. Judgment.
7. Appeal.

Jurisdiction.

The jurisdiction of a court depends upon two factors. The jurisdiction "ratione materia" and "ratione personam."

The jurisdiction ratione materia embraces the territory, the subject matter and the amount, involved in the suit. The jurisdiction of each court in the state of Louisiana has been fixed in the Constitution of the State, commencing with the constitution of 1812 up to and including the constitution of 1921 as amended.

No discussion of the provisions of the constitutions on the subject can be attempted here because of the necessary limitations as to the length of this work, but proper reference to the articles of the 1921 Constitution as amended, will be found in the foot notes at the bottom of the page (1).

The jurisdiction ratione personam embodies the principle that a defendant has the right to be sued at his own domicile and at one time he was forbidden to waive that right (2), but the rule as to waiver has been abrogated and it is now settled that he may so waive (3), and a voluntary appearance in court has been held to be such a waiver (4).

Even a citizen of another State may consent to be sued in this State (5), but not in matters of divorce or separation from bed and board (6), although such a suit is against the defendant personally marriage is a status and a court in Louisiana has no jurisdiction ratione materla where the matrimonial domicile is not in the state (7).

There are a number of exceptions to the rule that a defendant must be sued at his domicile, as for instance, in cases of trespass, personal damages, partnerships etc, found in the Code of Practice (8).

1—Section 31 Art 7 Const. 1921 as to district courts; Sec. 80 as to Civil Listrict Court New Orleans; Sections 35 and 81 as to amount and subject matter
2—Art 162 C. P.
3—Stackhouse v Zuntz, 36 A.529; Kelly v Lyons 40 A.498
4—Bernstein v Clarke Stave Co. 122 L.412; Phipps v Snodgrass 31 A.88
5—Franek v Turner, 164 L.532
6—Mann v Mann 170 L.958
7—Ibid
8—Arts. 163, 164 and 165 C. P.

A judgment rendered by a court without jurisdiction is invalid and cannot form a basis for any subsequent proceedings, hence a sale founded on such a proceeding is equally invalid.

Petitions, Parties and Cause of Action: The examiner is little concerned in the petition or the defects, except that it should conform to certain rules and that it is addressed to the proper court.

Parties: The names of both the plaintiff and defendant should be given; their ages and capacities and domiciles. This to establish clearly that the proper parties were before the court and that they could legally stand in judgment.

Where the suit is brought in behalf of an absentee, minor or interdict or a coporation, allegations sufficient to show authority should be in the petition, although this is of little consequence where the suit has gone to a definite judgment after appearance and trial. On the other hand, where a judgment is obtained by default, such a judgment is open to attack until prescription bars such a possibility.

As to the defendant of like character, the validity of the proceeding turns on citation rather than on formal allegations. Cause of Action: Generally speaking the cause of action in a suit that has reached judgment can have no bearing on its validity, insofar as an examination is concerned, but there are instances in which a judgment based on facts which can never give rise to a cause of action, is null and void ab initio, such as a contract which is contrary to public morals, or which furnish no grounds for relief as a divorce suit brought on grounds which did not constitute a cause of action.

All of the foregoing is of especial emphasis in those judgments obtained by default.

The Prayer: The prayer should be analagous to the allegations and the relief sought, as a judgment based on facts not alleged or which granted relief not prayed for, would be null and void (1).

Citation: The laws covering citation are to be found in the Code of Practice (2) and while it would be impossible to cite them in full, there are a number of essentials which should be touched upon as they are vital if any reliance is to be placed upon a judgment resulting in execution.

The citation must be addressed to the defendant; it must give the name of the court (3), title of the cause (4) and be served upon the defendant either personally or at his domicile (5). It should state the time for answering (6); where the answer should be filed (7); and finally it should be signed by the clerk (8) and sealed with the seal of the court (9).

A domiciliary service must be at defendant's usual place of residence and if he be absent, by delivering it to a person apparently above the age of sixteen and living in the house (10).

A citation on a person not sui juris must be made on his duly authorized representative personally or at the latter's residence (11).

All these essentials must be noted in the Sheriff's return.

Service upon corporations must be made in accordance with the statutes providing for such cita-

1—Litchenstein v Lyons 115 L.1051
    2-3-4-5-6-7-8-9-10-11 all the foregoing covered by Art. 176
    to 207 Code of Practice and by Act 179 of 1918 as amended
    by Act 48, 1932

tions and the provisions of the charter of each corporation (1).

For service upon an absent defendant through a curator or attorney at law, see the chapter on substituted service in this volume.

Answer Or Default: As it is the default rather than the answer which has significance here, it alone will be discussed.

A default cannot be entered until the time for answer has expired (2), not counting the day on which citation was made, nor the last day, if it falls on a dies non (3). A default must be entered. Unless it is entered the case is not put at issue and without it no judgment is valid (4). A judgment must be confirmed but not until the third day after default, excluding dies non (5). The claim must be proved (6).

Judgment: A judgment must be rendered in open court and dated (7). It must be signed by the judge. His signature on the minutes is not sufficient (8).

Where a defendant has been personally served or has answered no notice of judgment is required before execution of judgment, but where there has been domiciliary service and a default judgment rendered, notice thereof must be served upon defendant (9).

Execution: Execution may issue ten days after

1—C. P. 606; State ex rel Judge Civil District Court, 35 A.213,
    Dart Gen Statutes, Sec. 1117; Act 250 1928
2—C. P. 180; Font v Gulf State Land Co., 47 A.272; Helmer v United Gas Co. 175 L.285; State v Judge Civil District Court 128 L.918
3—Tessier v Jacobs 164 L.239; Catherwood v Shepard 30 A.677
4—Cavanaugh v Youngblood 10 La. App. 117
5—C. P. 312; as amended by Act 90 1904
6—   Ditto
7—C. P. 543; Laurent v Beelman 30 A.363
8—State v McLonald, 17 L.485
9—C. P. 575 and 624; State ex rel Mitchell v Kohn Flour & Feed Co., 135 Sou. 385

judgment is signed where no notice is required (1). but where such notice is required, the delay runs from the date of signing of the judgment (2). However, no appeal can be taken after one year from the signing of the judgment (3).

Appeal: The examiner should satisfy himself by checking the docket that no appeal has been taken from the judgment rendered and the character thereof as a suspensive appeal prevents execution whereas a devolutive appeal does not and the purchaser at a public sale is protected where there has been only a devolutive appeal (4).

The subject of appeals is covered in another chapter.

City Courts and Justices of the Peace.

All of the rules and statutes set out in the foregoing aply to these courts insofar as applicable. The jurisdiction of city courts and justices of the peace is established by the Constitution (5).

1—C. P. 575 as amended by Act 45, 1890 and 289, 1926
2—State ex rel Mitchell v Kohn Flour & Feed Co. 135 Sou. 385
3—C. P. Art 593
4—State ex rel v Judge 7th District Ct., 22 A.35; Bommarito v Br-
    nett Furn. Co. 171 L. 1027
5—Art. 7 Section 45, 51, 90 and 91 Const. 1921

CHAPTER XX.
Executory Process.

In addition to the suits and judgments discussed in the preceeding chapter, there are two suits or forms of action involving money demands which form a class in themselves as the enforcement of these demands follow a different procedure and in accordance with different rules. These suits are known as the "Executory Process" and "Hypothecary Action" and are essentially the same with one exception. Unless the act of mortgage contains the pact non de alienando the plaintiff must resort to the hypothecary action in the event that the property hypothecated has passed into the hands of third persons. If on the contrary the act does contain that pact, he may ignore the third possessor and without notice or demand, enforce the payment of the debt by the executory process.

The rules under which the executory process is authorized and enforced are found in a separate chapter of the Code of Practice (1).

The first article (2) in that chapter authorizes the executory process in the following cases: When the creditor's right arises from an act importing a confession of judgment and which contains a privilege or mortgage in his favor. When the creditor demands the execution of a judgment which has been rendered by a tribunal of this state different from that within whose jurisdiction the execution is sought.

The law authorizing executory proceedings being an extraordinary remedy must be strictly construed (3).

1—Chapter 7 C. P.
2—Art. 732 C. P.
3—Calhoun v Mechanics Bank 30 A.772

An act is said to import a confession of judgment in matters of privilege and mortgage, when it is passed before a notary, or other officer fulfilling the same functions, in the presence of two witnesses, and the debtor has declared or acknowledged the debt for which he gives the mortgage or privilege (1); when the creditor is in possession of such an act he may proceed against the debtor or his heirs by causing the property subject to the mortgage to be seized and sold on a simple petition and without a previous citation of the debtor, in the manner laid down in the third paragraph, second section, third chapter of the first part of this code (C. P.) (2). The Code further provides that the proceedings may be conducted against an executor, administrator, syn dic or other fiduciary officer (3), and also against the surviving spouse where community property is the subject of the mortgage, without making the heirs parties to the suit (4).

A holder of a note secured by special mortgage imparting confession of judgment, containing the pact de non alienando and a waiver of appraisement may enforce the mortgage by executory process notwithstanding the fact that the debtor has died and his succession was under administration in another parish (5). The holder of a note secured by mortgage containing the pact de non alienando may proceed directly against the original mortgagor and ignore subsequent transferees of the property (6). The existence of subsequent mortgages does not alter the right of seizure and sale under a prior mortgage

1—Art. 733 C. P. Dejean v Hebert 31 A.729
2—Art. 734 C. P. as amended by Act 148 1928
3—Act 148 1920
4—Act 57 1926 Dixon v Federal Land Bank 196 L.937
5—Freeman v Carmouche's Succ. 174 L.808
6—Lortz v Iberville B. & T. Co. 176 L.579

where subsequent mortgagees are not made parties to the proceedings (1).

As has been stated the executory process and the hypothecary action are in essence the same and both are proceedings in rem, a real action which follows the property subject to the claim in whatever hands it may be found, but are subject to different rules according as the property may be found in the possession of the debtor or his heirs, or of third persons (2). Where the property is in the hands of the debtor the creditor, in both cases, has a right to have the property seized immediately and sold for the payment of his debt, in accordance with the rules provided for executory process provided that he has, in addition to his hypothecary debt, a title importing a confession of judgment (3).

Both of these actions are proceedings in rem (4), hence there can be no personal judgment against the debtor rendered in these proceedings (5); and a cumulation of another cause with the hypothecary action is fatal (6).

The executory process based on an act of mortgage only is here discussed (though the executory process may issue in certain other cases). As a basis for the suit the mortgage must be by authentic act and must contain two clauses which are vital to the validity of the suit, viz: a confession of judgment (7) and a pact de non alienando (8).

The act itself must also conform with all the

1—Carite v Trotot, 105 U. S. 751, 26 L.1223
2—C. P. Art. 61 and 62
3—C. P. Art. 63; Art. 734 C. P.; Act 57, 1926
4—Wisdom v Parker 31 A.52
5—   ditto
6—Marchand v Sobral, 24 Fed. 316
7—Taylor v Pipes, 24 A.551
8—Waddill v Payne, 22 A.184

essentials of an authentic act, which essentials have been enumerated elsewhere.

Foreclosures Under Executory Process.

In foreclosure suits the essentials in a proper suit are similar to the essentials in other suits, such as to jurisdiction, parties, petition, cause of action, etc., but differ somewhat in each respect.

Jurisdiction: The defendant may be sued either in the parish where the property is situated or in the parish wherein the debtor has his domicile (1).

Parties: The holder of the mortgage note, whether he be the original mortgagee or a transferee may, sue, but in the case of a latter, he must establish his right to the note by authentic evidence as will be more fully explained hereafter.

The defendant need only be the original maker, although the property may have been transferred to others. A holder of a first mortgage with the pact de non alienando, may proceed by executory process without giving special notice to anyone except the debtor. Even though others are given second mortgages by virtue of the same instrument they are not entitled to notice (2). As it has already been stated if the debtor be dead, the action may be brought against his executor or administrator, or against the surviving spouse, without bringing the heirs in.

The petition, in addition to the regular averments in a suit on a note, should also aver that the plaintiff is the owner and holder of the note either as mortgagee or by transfer, that it was acquired for a valuable consideration before maturity, name

1—Arts. 163, 736 C. P. Reugger v DeBrueys, 146 L.283
2—N. O. Natl. Bank v LeBreton 120 U. S. 765; 30 L. ed 821. Jefferson v Stringfellow, 148 L.223

of and paraph of notary, amount interest and rate thereof, maturity of note or notes and or installments, if payable in that form, failure to pay notes when due, or installments as the case may be, the fact of demand or waiver of demand, acknowledgment of debt and confession of judgment, consent to the seizure and sale, pact de non alienando, accelaration of maturity by reason of non payment or non fullment of conditions, waiver and other security clauses in act, and such other allegation as will show right of enforcement by executory process.

If there have been partial payments, balance due must be shown supported either by the notes themselves, or in the case of installments by a sworn statement detailing amounts paid and what are due, and in cases where the plaintiff is a corporation such statements should be attested under seal by the secretary or other fiscal officer (1).

Two important elements in a foreclosure suit are to be carefully noted. 1. What may be claimed under the provisions of the act of mortgage? 2. What proof and in what form must such proof be in order to justify the issuance of the writ.

In addition to the amount of the note and interest there is usually other amounts representing attorneys fees, insurance premiums, and costs, the exact amount of which cannot be fixed in the act and are therefore not certain at the time of the execution are not barred for that reason from the benefit of the mortgage and of the executory process and may be included in the order for the writ (2).

It has been repeatedly held that practically the petition and all documents attached must prove

1—Act 179 1918 Art 191 Code Practice
2—Germainia Savings Bank v Waguespack 50 A.1289

themselves, and must be in authentic form (1), but the courts have been compelled by the nature of the suit to deviate from these rules to some extent. To illustrate: Where the purchaser and mortgagor has signed both the act and the note, indorsed in blank, a power of attorney to transfer the note forms no part of the evidence necessary to authorize the order of seizure and sale. When a promissory note is made payable to the order of the maker and endorsed by him (in blank) and this fact is recited in the authentic act of mortgage, possession thereof is sufficient authority for instituting executory proceedings (2). To the contrary, where a note is made payable to the order of a certain party, a mere endorsement by that party will not suffice. There must be a formal transfer made in authentic form (3).

Where a trustee in a bond issue sues out executory process to enforce payment of serial bonds due and to become due and alleges in his petition that the unmatured bonds have become due under the accellarating clause of the authentic act, such a declaration is sufficiently proved by the recitals of a written instrument, issued under the corporate seal and signed by the proper officials of the plaintiff corporation, and attached to the petition, authentic evidence being impossible from the nature of the case (4).

The evidence of non-payment of the note or notes is evidenced by the filing (5).

A copy of the resolution of the board of directors of the mortgaging corporation authorizing

1—Woods v Woods, 32 A.801
2—Franek v Brewster, 141 L.1031; Holiday v Logan, 134 L.427
3—Brock State Bank Com. v Messina, 200 Sou. Rep. 511
4—Colonial Trust Co. v St. John Lbr. Co., 138 L.1033
5—Franek v Brewster, 141 L.1031

the execution of the mortgage, taken from the copy certified by the secretary and attached to the original act of mortgage and certified by the notary before whom the act was passed, or from the conveyance or mortgage records, when the records show that the copy filed for record was certified by the secretary and certified by the recorder, shall be sufficient evidence of the authority of the officer or agent to execute same and no authentic evidence or further proof of the existence of the corporation or board of directors or of the personel or authority of the board to grant such, to execute the mortgage (1), is necessary. The holder or bearer of mortgage notes may maintain executory process foreclosure of mortgaged property without producing authentic proof of transfer of such notes from the original holder to present plaintiff (2).

An act of the legislature authorizes the secretaries of building and homestead assocations to certify statements of balances due on a note by a mortgagor, and gives to such a certification the character of authentic evidence (3).

The allegations of facts and figures in the petition should conform to and agree with those in the act of mortgage a certified copy of which should be annexed to the petition, which should be sworn to.

The prayer should be for the issuance of a notice of demand for payment or as it is sometimes termed, notice of judgment and notice of seizure, which is the term used in the Code of Practice (4); for recognition of the privilege and mortgage; and for the issuance of an order of seizure and sale.

1—Act 148 1910; American Trust Co. v Crescent Ice Co. 133 L.247
2—Nolen v Davidson's Succ. 190 Southern Report .826
3—Act 140 1932
4—Art. 735 C. P.

The Order: Should conform with the prayer and should be issued by the clerk and served by the Sheriff (1).

There is no citation in the technical sense of the word, but in all respects the service must meet the essentials of a citation and the service is in all essentials the same as in ordinary suits.

The creditor has the choice, in those cases where the debtor is domiciled in one parish and the property is situated in another parish, to sue either in the parish of the domicile or seize the property in the parish where situated (2). In the former case service is made on the debtor personally or at his domicile, and in the latter case, the service issues out of the court of the parish where the property is situated and the notice is served by the sheriff of the parish of domicile. It has been held that the proper course to be pursued in those cases where the creditor wishes to sue the debtor in his own domicile, is to proceed via ordinaria and then send the judgment for execution to the parish where the property is situated, for the reason that the sheriff of the debtor's domicile cannot either seize or deliver property situated in another parish (3).

The notice of demand for payment, or notice of seizure: It suffices that three days notice be given to the debtor if he resides in the parish in which the proceedings are had, or five days notice if he resides in another parish (4). The order is granted exparte; no previous notice is required and is not required before the order but before the seizure (5).

1—Hart v Pike, 29 A.262; Billgery v Ferguson, 30 A.84
2—Art. 163 C. P.; Reugger v DeBrueys, 146 L.283
3—Miles Planting Co. v Ware, 142 L.1026
4—Art. 735 C. P. as amended by Act 41, 1898 and 97 of 1928
5—McDonogh v Fost, I Rob. 295; Andrews v City Bank, 5 A.737

Prior to 1904 when the article was amended the debtor had three days delay after notice and for every twenty miles his residence was distant from the court, he was entitled to one additional day, not one day for every twenty miles or fraction thereof. Where the distance was thirty-five miles, he was entitled to only one additional day (1).

In the event that the mortgagor was served personally by sheriff of the parish where the property was situated, while he was within that parish temporarily, this was sufficient notice (2).

Absence of Debtor: If the mortgage debtor is absent and not represented in the State, or if he cannot be found and served after diligent effort though he may still reside within the state, the judge at the request of the plaintiff shall appoint an attorney to represent the debtor, to whom notice shall be given in the manner directed and contradictorily with whom the seizure and sale shall be prosecuted (3).

The absent mortgagor must be represented by a curator ad hoc (4).

The terms "curator ad hoc" and "attorney at hoc" have been declared to be synonymous. In 1924 an act was passed by the legislature requiring that attorneys for absentees must be duly qualified attorneys at law (5). Prior to that time they need not be. Second conditions which gives rise to the right of executory process: When a creditor has obtained against his debtor a judgment having the force of res judicata, in a tribunal of this state different from that in which he seeks the execution

1—Nagel v Clement, 113 L.192
2—Rhea v Taylor, 8 A.23
3—Art. 737 C. P. As amended by Act 130 of 1920
4—C. P. 963
5—Acts 190, 1904; 167, 1924

thereof, he may ,on this ground, proceed by executory process and cause the property belonging to his debtor to be seized and sold, without previous citation in the same manner as in privileged or mortgage debts contained in acts importing confessions of judgment (1).

It will be noted that it is only a judgment having the force of adjudicata which may be enforced in this manner, hence an appealable judgment cannot be enforced under the article, but such a judgment need not be one that has been rendered with an appearance of the debtor and a trial had thereon in due course, as a judgment by default or on attachment, may be the basis of the executory process (2). This provision has been strictly construed, it having been held that a judgment in another state, after defendant withdrew a plea, is not one by default within the meaning of this article. A default, under our laws, is where the defendant neither appears nor answers (3) In effect the judgment concerned was found not to come within the scope of the act.

All judgments from other states of the United States must be certified according to the act of Congress.

The Hypothecary Action.

If the hypothecated property be neither in the possession of the debtor, nor of his heirs, but is in that of a third person, the creditor has his action against that person, in order to compel him either to give up the property or pay the amount for which

1—C. P. Art. 746
2—C. P. Art. 747
3—Stone v Minor, 6 Rob. 29

it stands hypothecated.   This is the hypothecary
action properly speaking (1).

Both the executory process and the action referred to above are alike in that they seek to enforce rights against the mortgaged property, but
they differ principally in the methods to be employed in that enforcement.   In both cases the act of
mortgage must contain a confession of judgment and
must have ben executed in authentic form.

It is chiefly in the procedure by which the right
must be enforced that the two actions differ.   In
the executory process the suit may be brought
against the original debtor without notice to subsequent purchasers, whereas in the hypothecary action
there must have been an attempt made to collect the
debt from the mortgagor before action may be taken
against third possessors.

The pleadings: The jurisdiction is the same in both
cases and calls for no further comment.

Parties: The necessary parties are those who are in
actual possession of the hypothecated property and
these 'possessors include the debtor's heirs under
certain conditions which will be discussed hereafter.
In other respects the parties must be those who may
stand in judgment in the suit, and be brought in,
either as sui juris or through proper representatives.

Petition: As in all cases the petition must set forth
facts sufficient in law to constitute a cause of action
but must also contain allegations which show full
compliance with the requirements of the Code of
Practice which are: a demand made on the debtor,
his heirs and or widow for the payment of the debt
within thirty days after such demand; notification
to the third possessor of such a demand having been

1—Art. 68 C. P.

made, coupled with a demand that he pay same or surrender the property, and finally failure of all parties to comply with such demands (1).

As in the executory process authentic proof of the evidece must be furnished, which fact makes pertinent an inquiry as to how the proof of the demands above referred can be made so as to constitute authentic evidence, in view of the fact that these demands must precede the suit and hence are not made by the sheriff. It would seem that written notice sent through the registered mail and the receipt of the recipients should meet the requirements. The prayer: Should be in accordance with the allegations of the petition for recognition of the privlege and mortgage, notice of demand and order for seizure and sale.

The petition must be properly sworn to by the plaintiff or his authorized agent, or his attorney and should conform in facts and figures with the act of mortgage a certified copy of which must accompany it.

A question which is very pertinent to any discussion of these proceedings is: Who are third possessors? The original mortgagor is not a third person and is not entitled to the notice prescribed by Article 69 of the Code of Practice; nor is his vendee who is personally liable for the debt (2); nor is the purchaser of a mortgaged property who assumes payment of the mortgage (3); and if the debtor has died leaving a single heir who has accepted the succession, the hypothecary creditor may proceed against that

1—Art. 69 C. P.; R. C. C. Art. 340; Art. 70 C. P,
2—Duncan v Elam, 1 Rob. 135; Federal Land Bank v Cook, 179 L.361
3—Shlater v Greaud, 19 A.125; Woodward v Dishell. 15 L.184; Hebert
      v Doussan 8 A.267 Moriarity v Weiss 196 L.38

heir, as he could against the debtor himself (1);
where there are more than one heir and such heirs
have accepted the succession, and if the act imports
a confession of judgment and there has been no partition, such heirs are not third possessors, but if
there has been a partition among the heirs and the
property has fallen to the share of one of the heirs,
the proceedings must be directed against him (2).
If the act of mortgage contains no confession of
judgment the heir or heirs must be proceeded against
ordinarily and judgment obtained against each one
(3).

The rules governing the appointment of attorneys or curators to represent absentees are to be
found at length in the chapter entitled "Substitute
Service".

Injunctions and Appeals: The examiner is not concerned with these proceedings for the reason, the
actual sale of the property precludes issuance of the
injunction and an appeal in such a case could only be
devolutive and hence have no effect on the title (4).

1—Art. 65 C. P.; Arts 734, 735 C. P.; Soye v Price, 30 A. 93; R.
        C. C. Art, 1417, 1821—38
2—Art. 66 C. P., Saloy v Chexnaidre, 14 A.567
3—Art. 67 C. P.
4—Jefferson v Gamm, 150 L.372; Geoux v Lockport Central Lbr.
        Co., 156 L.889; 1st Natl. Bank v Hebert, 161 L.378;
        Bommarito v Barnett Fur. Co., 171 L.1027

CHAPTER XXI.

Sheriff's Deed.

The Code of Practice provides that the sheriff shall pass an act of sale to the purchaser within three days, but this is inoperative for the reason that the purchaser has the right to have an examination made of the title. It also provides the selling sheriff's successor, if he should resign, or die or be removed from office, shall have authority to execute and record the sale.

The act of sale must be made by and in the name of the sheriff in his official capacity with the place, the day month and year in which it was passed (1), and must also make mention of the writ under which the property was sold; of the title of the cause in which the writ was issued; of the names and surnames of the plaintiff, defendant and purchaser; of the nature of the object sold, with a description of it, as well as the price and conditions; of the manner in which the purchaser has paid the price or bound himself to discharge it; of the amount of the privileges or mortgages with which the property is encumbered, and which was made known at the time of adjudication; and finally of the special mortgage given for the purchase price, if any (2).

The sheriff shall conclude the act by selling and transferring to the purchaser all of the rights which the former owner had, pursuing the same forms as in ordinary sales (3). This act of sale adds nothing to the force and effect of the adjudication, but is only intended to afford proof of it; consequently the omission of any of the above formalities from the

1—C. P. Art 692
2—C. P. Art. 693
3—C. P. Art. 694

act, the adjudication is not void on that account if it otherwise appears that it was made by virtue of a legal authority and with all the forms requisite for its validity (1).

The sheriff shall deliver to the clerk of court a certified copy of the act of sale; and it is the duty of the said clerk to record same literally in a record to be kept by him; provided that in the City of New Orleans, the sheriff shall record the act in the Conveyance Office (2). The sheriff's deed is an authentic act (3) and its recitals prevail over those of his return and is full proof of the adjudication (4).

It will be noted that the Code of Practice does not require the sheriffs in the country to register the deed in the conveyance records but whether or not it is registered by the sheriff, it should be so registered to have effect against third persons (5).

Tax researches should be annexed to a sheriff's deed (6) and since 1938, a paving certificate must be obtained by the sherff, where the property is situated within a paving area (7).

Deputy sheriffs may act in place of the sheriff in all duties and may execute orders, though addressed to the sheriff himself (8).

The process verbal of the sheriff, if it fulfills all of the requirements of the Code of Practice has been declared as being in itself a deed (9).

1—C. P. 695
2—C. P. Art. 697
3—Perron v Maillon, 10 L.520; Lee v Darranson, 3 Rob. 160
4—McCall v Iron, 41 A.1126; Hughes v Edson, 129 L.866
5—Huntington v Bordeaux, 42 A.346; Harrison v Ittman, 111 L.730
6—Act 116, 1938, 235, 1940
7—Act 116, 1938
8—State v Wilson, 12 A.189
9—Strauss v Soye, 29 A.270

CHAPTER XXII.

Judicial Sales And Other Changes In Ownership Affected By Judgment And Decrees Of Court.

Sales made by sheriffs under writs of fieri facias and seizure and sale, are of course, judicial sales since they are made under order or judgment of court, but the term "Judicial Sales" is applied here to those sales made by order of court in settlement of successions, receiverships, bankruptcies and partitions, at public sales by auctioneers, administrators, executors, syndics and other fiduciary officers.

This term also includes changes in ownership effected by order of court and executed before notaries public, such as dation en paiements in liquidation of debts in successions, receiverships, bankruptcies and of minors and interdicts. It also includes changes in ownership effected by the judgment of the court itself, without further formalities or executions, such as rescissions, specific performances and petitory actions.

Though a rule of property is that judgments of competent courts, and the appointment of tutors, curators, receivers, syndics and trustees, cannot be attacked collaterally and therefore third parties need not look beyond such judgments or appointments, there are exceptions to this rule which will be noted hereafter.

The first exception is that a judgment rendered by a court without proper jurisdiction is absolutely null and void, hence the examiner must satisfy himself, insofar as he can, that the court rendering the judgment or making the appointment had full jurisdiction in the matter.

The jurisdiction of a court is based upon the subject matter, the amount involved (Ratione Materiae) and the domicile of the defendant. (Ratione Personam).

Under the present constitution (1921) with its amendments, district courts have exclusive jurisdiction in successions and probate matters including partitions, adoption of children, annulment of marriages, divorces and separations, in all civil matters and in all suits involving civil rights, where the amount involved is over one hundred dollars.

In the country the district courts have concurrent jurisdiction with justice of the peace courts (and with municipal courts where existing in suits up to three hundred dollars and in Orleans parish the Civil District Court has concurrent jurisdiction with the First and Second City Courts in suits involving amounts over one hundred dollars and not over three hundred dollars).

Neither city nor municipal courts have any jurisdiction other than suits in money demands and by landlords for possession of leased premises when the monthly rent does not exceed one hundred dollars. A judgment of the City Court of New Orleans cancelling tax sales has been held void (1). Nor may it cancel taxes (2).

In successions, receiverships and petitory actions the district courts have jurisdiction but not exclusive jurisdiction as to the last two proceedings as the Federal Courts may under certain circumstances take jurisdiction in such cases.

In bankruptcy matters the Federal District Courts have exclusive jurisdiction.

1—Quaker Realty Co. v Purcell, 131 L.496, 499; same, 134 L.1022
2—Ibid

Ratione Personam: The jurisdiction ratione personam of a court is to be determined by the nature
of the proceedings: In successions the court of the
deceased domicile has jurisdiction, but should he
have no fixed domicile, the court of the parish where
he had property would have jurisdiction (1); in a
petition suit, if it is a suit brought before the heirs
are sent into possession, the court of the place where
the succession was opened will have jurisdiction (2),
but if the co-heirs have been sent into possession or
if it is a suit among co-owners who have acquired
otherwise than by inheritance, the suit must be
brought in the place where the property is situated
(3).

In tutorship, curatorship, and receivership proceedings, they should be brought at the domicile of
the minor, interdict, or corporation as the case may
be. In all other cases the rules governing jurisdiction ratione personam have been discussed at length
elsewhere in this volume.

The next exception to the rule of property heretofore mentioned is to be found in the appointment
of a tutor, curator, administrator, executor, receiver,
syndic or trustee. In general, where such an officer
has been regularly appointed by an order of court,
duly signed, has taken the oath, has caused an inventory to be taken, has given bond, and letters
have been issued to him, his appointment may not
be attacked and his acts are valid acts (4).

However, the appointment of a dative tutor in
place of a natural tutor who is not barred by any
of the reasons set forth in the Civil Code, but who

1—C. P. 929
2—Art. 924, C. P. R. C. C. Arts. 1289, 1327
3—Medicis v Medicis, 165 L.171; C. P. 165; R. C. C. 1290, Succ.
   Kelly, 154 L. 585
4—Stackhouse v Zuntz, 36 A.528; McCoy v Derbonne, 109 L.310

for reasons of his own, refuses and declines to qualify as such, is null and void (1).

For other instances of the nullity of the appointment of such officers, the reader is referred to the chapter on "Defects and their cures" in this volume.

There are four kinds of tutors: natural tutor (2), tutor by will (3); tutor by effect of law; and dative tutor (4).

Hence there must be an order either confirming or appointing the tutor. A dative tutor could not have been appointed, under the provisions of Act 319 of 1926 because such proceedings could only be initiated by a tutor already qualified, but an act of 1934 (5) amended the act of 1926 so as to allow or permit the court to appoint a dative tutor without the convoking of a family meeting on the petition of any party at interest, that is, any such party may petition the court where there is a vacancy in the tutorship.

A tutor of whatever character must qualify by having an inventory and appraisment made (6); and he must, except the natural tutor and the tutor who is dispensed with giving a bond, furnish sufficient security for the fidelity of his administration the amount of which is to be fixed by the judge (7); and it must be recorded (8); but he may give a special mortgage (9); or a surety bond (10); and where the tutor is not required to give bond, the inventory

1—Succ Watt, 111 L.237; James v Meyer, 41 A.1103
2—R. C. C. 246
3—R. C. C. 257
4—R. C. C. 263
5—Act 47, 1934
6—R. C. C. 316
7—R. C. C. 317, 318
8—R. C. C. 319
9—R. C. C. 320
10—Act 88, 1926

must be recorded in the mortgage office of the tutor's parish and a certificate to that effect from the recorder of mortgages must be presented to the judge before he can make the appointment or authorize issuance of letters of tutorship. In those cases where a special mortgage or a surety bond has been given, the clerk's certificate must show this fact, together with the amount of the inventory or the amount of the bond as fixed by the judge.

Curators.

There are two kinds of curators: the curator of an interdict who is likened in all respect to a tutor and all the rules concerning the oath, the inventory, the security, the recording of the legal mortgage, the certificate of the clerk and the letters apply to such curatorships (1).

The curator of a vacant estate (or of an absentee) is in reality an administrator (2) and all the rules prescribed by law for administrators apply to the curator of a vacant estate.

He who claims the curatorship of a vacant succession, or one of which the heirs or part of them are absent and not represented, must present his petition to that effect to the judge of the place where the succession is opened (3); the judge on receiving this request must order public notice thereof to be given, with notice to all those who wish to make opposition thereof, to do it in ten days from date of such notice (4); the public notice to be given in this case, as in all other cases in which the law

1—R. C. C. 415
2—R. C. C. 1097
3—R. C. C. 1114
4—R. C. C. 1115; Art. 967 C. P.

requires it to be given, must be in the mode required by law for other judicial advertisements (1).

Such notice may and should be posted at the court house and at two other public places where no newspaper is published in the parish (2).

In effect the advertisement is a citation and is as essential as is a citation in ordinary cases (3).

A petition is a requisite whether the appointment is of a curator, administrator, or dative executor; and there should be an order signed by the judge requiring publication thereof (4).

Curator of Absentee.

When a person possessing property within this state, shall be absent and without representation, the judge of the place where that estate is situated, shall appoint a curator to administer the same (5).

All the rules applicable to a petition, appointment, advertisement, oath, inventory, bond or security and letters apply to the curator for an absentee.

In all these cases proper proof should be made as to the absence of the party whose estate is being administered.

Curators and Tutors ad hoc, Special Curators and Tutors and Attorneys for absentees.

As these officers are appointed in all sorts of proceedings and their appointment and qualifications are governed by different rules, a separate chapter has been devoted to the subject under the heading "Substituted Service."

Under Tutors And Under Curators

In all regular tutorships and curatorships of interdicts there must be an under tutor or under cura-

1—R. C. C. 1116, Art. 969 C. P.
2—Harriman v Janney, 31 A.276
3—Elkins v Canfield, 5 Mart. (N. S.) 505
4—Succ. Gusman, 35 A.404
5—Elkins v Canfield, 5 Martin (N. S.) 505

tor appointed. In cases of curators and tutors ad hoc, no under tutor or under curator is appointed, specially, but such tutors or curators are sometimes appointed where the regular tutor or curator cannot act, and in those cases the regular under tutor or under curator officiates.

In every tutorship there shall be an under tutor, whom it shall be the duty of the judge to appoint at the time the letters of tutorship are certified for the tutor (1); the under tutor shall, prior to his entering upon his duties, take an oath that he will well and faithfully fulfill his trust (2).

The appointment of an under tutor shortly before that of a tutor is valid (3).

It is the duty of the under tutor to act for the minor whenever the interest of the minor is in opposition to the interest of the tutor (4).

But it must be emphasized that an under tutor cannot act in place of the tutor where that tutor is disqualified, or may not act for the minor. He may only approve or disapprove, as in the partition of property owned in indivision by the minor, of any proposed action by the tutor; and also in seeing that the tutor renders the proper accounts (5).

All of the foregoing applies to the under curator. Inventories:

As an inventory is an absolute essential in administrations, executorships, receiverships, bankruptcies, tutorships and curatorships, one must be made in every case and generally should be prayed for in the petition applying for the appointment, unless one has already been made in the proceedings.

The inventory must be made by a notary and

1—R. C. C. 373; 2—R. C. C. 274; 3—Succ. Freid. 106 276; 4—R. R. C. 275; 5—C. P. 410

assisted by two appraisers appointed to value the property inventoried (1).

Oaths: The oath is equally essential to the validity of acts of all fiduciary officers (2).

Bond: A proper bond, based on the amount of the inventory, and in accordance with law, is required in every case, or the proper recording of the legal mortgage where other security is dispensed with by law (3).

Letters: The letters of tutorship shall not be delivered to the tutor until he shall have complied with the law as herein required. Until they have been delivered to him he shall not administer the property of the minor, and he shall not be recognized, confirmed or appointed nor permitted to act as tutor, until the judge renders and signs a decree authorizing letters of tutorship to be issued (4).

Administrators.

Administrators are appointed in all cases where there are no heirs, or where the heirs have renounced or accept under benefit of inventory and are qualified in accordance with the rules under which other fiduciary officers are qualified (5).

Administrators are appointed according to certain priorities laid down by the Civil Code, but the examiner is not concerned as to these, because purchasers at succession or other similar sales are protected by the order of court and the letters, provided that these are properly issued (6).

Where a succession is so small or in so much debt that no one will accept the curatorship or ad-

1—R. C. C. 49, 67, .316, 1101, 1112
2—R C.. C. 313, 334, 1126
3—R. C. C. 49, 318, 322, 323, 415, 1127, 1128
3—R. C. C. 335
5—Vide Chapter on Tutors and Curators; R. C. C. 1071, 1072
6—Vide. same

ministration, the judge, after having ordered an inventory, shall appoint the clerk of court curator of such a succession, provided that this does not apply to successions amounting to more than five hundred dollars (1).

The clerk does not have to give bond but sales made in such a succession must be made under the same conditions as are required in all successions sales.

In the parish of Orleans ,the estates of an absentee and vacant successions are administered by the Public Administrator (2).

Executors.

There are two kinds of executors, testamentary and dative testamentary. The rules applicable to all fiduciary officers apply to them. with the exceptions noted hereafter.

A minor cannot be a testamentary executor, but of course this is true of all fiduciary offices (3). A married woman, prior to 1928 could not accept a testamentary executorship without the consent of her husband, but since that time she may (4).

The testamentary executor does not have to give bond, unless required to do so by the testators, or upon the demand of a creditor or a claimant of a specific piece of property in the succession (5), but not on the demand of an heir (6).

The dative executor has to give bond (7).

There may be more than one executor named in a testament and should some of them fail to qualify for any reason, or resign or die after accepting,

1—R. C. C. 1190
2—Act 14, 1926
3—R. C. 1465
4—R. C. 1668
5—R. C. C. 1677Chretien v Benvenu, 41 A.671; Succ. Krantz, 115 L.546
6—Vide Citations, above.
7—R. C. C. 1679

the other executor or executors continue to function with the same power and authority as if no other executors had been appointed, and one executor may act for all (1).

Dative Executor.

The dative testamentary executor is or may be appointed in all testate successions, where the testator has failed to name an executor in his will (2), or the named executor refuses or fails to qualify or has died, or has been removed.

In all respects he has the same power and authority of a testamentary executor.

Executors shall continue in office until the estate shall be wound up finally (3); and even after the expiration of his administration he is bound to continue suits brought either by or against him on account of the succesion, until the heirs appear or cause themselves to be put into possession (4).

Receivers.

Receiverships are to be tested by the special acts of the legislature and the Acts of Congress regulating receivership, but they are too voluminous to be copied in this chapter and have been relegated to special exposition in another chapter. However, the examiner is only interested in certain requirements as the rules of property as to sales under order of court apply here as in other cases.

These requirements are:

Jurisdiction of the court.

Authority of the Receiver.

Issuance of proper judgment or order of court for sale.

1—R. C. C. 1658, 1681
2—R. C. C. 1672
3—R. C. C. 1672
4—R. C. C. 1676

Jurisdiction: Jurisdiction over receiverships is vested in the district courts of the State and of the United States (1); and the jurisdiction of a particular court is tested by the domicile of the corporation, if a domestic one, and of a foreign corporation by its designated domicile, if it has any, or if it has not designated any by the location of the property (2).

The court with proper jurisdiction may appoint a receiver under the provisions of the various state acts and of Congress; and in case of a defunct corporation under a special act of the Legislature (3).

The receiver must take an oath and give bond as fixed by the court and letters of receivership must issue as in all cases of fiduciary officers (4).

The examiner need look only to the jurisdiction of the court and the issuance of proper citation, for the purpose of deciding as to the legality of the proceedings in which the appointment of a receiver is made as third parties as in other cases are protected by the rule of property heretofore mentioned.

The essentials of a proper qualification of the receiver has been set out above, essentials which hold in all such cases.

Judicial Liquidators.

There are two classes of judicial liquidators. The first class of liquidators are those appointed by the court in receiverships (5) and the other class are those appointed by the Governor (6) in the execution of annullments of the charter of a corporation.

All liquidators must take an inventory, give a

1—Act 250, 1928; F. C. A. Title 11
2—Act 159, 1898; 117, 1916
3—Act 159, 1898; 224, 1902; 250, 1923
4—Vide previous pages
5—Act 250, 1928
6—Act 224, 1902

bond (except the Attorney General or District Attorney appointed under the provisions of Act 224 of 1902) and their authority attested by letters or by a commission from the Governor, as the case may be.

Syndics.

Sections 1781 to 1818 of the Revised Statutes cover the appointment, qualifying and duties of the Syndic in insolvency proceedings. These sections were in effect bankruptcy proceedings. As Congress has assumed jurisdiction over insolvencies, the state provisions have become practically obsolete.

These syndics were appointed under about the same conditions and with the same foramlities as in the case of Trustees in bankruptcy proceedings and as in the case of similar judicial officers the legality of their appointment may not be attacked collaterally (1).

In General.

In the case of a vacant estate which is insolvent, the creditors should be summoned in meeting for the purpose of deliberating upon the manner of selling the effects of the estate (2). These provisions are seldom followed at present and the failure to observe them can be ignored by the examiner for the reason that unless the creditors object before the date of sale, they are barred from any attack.

Curators of a vacant estate or of absent heirs who wishes to absent himself from the State for a time exceeding one year, must render an account and cause his place to be filled by some other (3).

In effect this provision amounts to a forfeiture of the office; and would apply to all fiduciary officers.

1—Cloutier v Lemee, 35 A.305
2—R. C. C. 1172, 1173, 1174, 1176, 1177, 1178
3—R. C. C. 1153

The temporary absence of such an officer would not work a forfeiture, provided he leave with some person resident of the parish or an adjoining one, his general and special power of attorney to represent him in all the acts of the administration and deposit an authentic copy of this power, before his departure, in the recorder's office in the parish where the succession has been opened (1).

Where parties appear in a succession proceedings through an agent, the procuration should be in authentic form.

1—R. C. C. 1154; Succ. Burbank, 129; Succ. Drysdale, 124 L.256

CHAPTER XXIII.

Public Sales By Auctioneers or Other Officers.

These are sales to pay debts of a succession or a corporation in liquidation; to pay legacies; to settle successions or the affairs of a corporation in liquidation; and to effect partition by licitation.

The essentials of the proceedings leading up to a sale in all of the above cases, that is the power and authority of the court and the authority of the officer seeking to bring about such a sale has been discussed in the preceeding pages; and it now remains to determine what are the requirements of a valid order of sale and under what conditions a sale may be invoked.

Sales By Tutors, or Curators of Interdicts to Pay Debts or For Their Advantage.

Owing to the peculiar nature of these sales, a separate chapter under the heading "Alienation of Minors and Interdicts property" has been devoted to these sales, hence nothing will be said here on the matter.

Sales By A Curator Of A Vacant Succession to Pay Debts.

The curator of a vacant succession, like the administrator, executor, receiver, liquidator, or syndic, should file a sworn list of debts, which amounts to an acknowledgment of them, but unliquidated debts should not be listed as he is without power to recognize them (1).

He then should file a petition citing the list and request that he be permitted to sell the property to pay them but he is bound to wait thirty days before filing his petition in order that he may know what

1—R. C. C. 1164, 1165

part of the property should be sold in order to pay
the debts.

Where in order to pay debts, it is necessary
to sell property engaged in argiculture, that is being cultivated, it must not be sold for one year after
the curator's appointment (1).

An order of sale to pay debts, valid on its face,
issued by a court having jurisdiction of the succession, protects the innocent purchaser (2); but that
order must comply strictly with the requirements
and formalities hereinabove set out.

In all cases, the sale must be at public auction,
to the last and highest bidder, after the advertisements and publications required by law, to-wit: ten
days for movables, thirty days for immovables.

Prior to a sale the property to be sold must be
appraised by two experts appointed and sworn by
the judge, and at the sale it must bring the appraised
value, if it has been sold upon the application of
creditors (3); if it does not it must be again read-
vertised and offered for sale and it may be sold for
anything it will bring on twelve month's credit (4).
No additional order of court is required to authorize
readvertisement, but the court in his discretion may
order the property re-examined and re-appraised (5).

The Legislature of 1938 authorizes executors and
administrators to sell property belonging to a succession at private sale to pay debts or any other purpose, but it must be strictly construed as the act
specifically designates those two officers and none

1—R. C. C. 1168
2—Kelerec v N. O. Land Co., 130 L.111: Succ. Balovich, 130 L.1043;
        Succ. Leman, 41 A.987
3—Arts. 990, 991 C. P.
4—Campbell v Owens, 32 A.265; Succ. Hood, 33 A.466.
5—Succ. Hood, 33 A.446

other and although the curator of a vacant estate
or the curator of an absentee are in fact administrators (1).

Curator of an Absentee.

Neither the Revised Civil nor the Code of
Practice specifically provide for the sale of the property of an absentee administered by a curator, except for the purpose of settling the estate and paying
in the proceeds to the State Treasury in lieu of known
heirs (2), and then only after a period of ten years
from the date the administration begins. As there
is rarely a case in which the absentee would not
leave debts of some kind, even though it be only taxes where there is immovable property, besides the
debts incurred in conducting the administration, such
as attorney's fees, court costs etc., the provisions of
the Code of Practice and the Revised Civil Code (3)
authorizes such sales to pay these debts.

Administrators.

With regard to the immovables belonging to the
estate, the administrator may not sell them until
the term given to the heir in which to deliberate
whether or not he will accept or reject the succession has expired, which term is thirty days counting from the date of the inventory, or the last one
if more than one has been taken (4).

All that has been said in preceeding pages, in
reference to the essentials leading up to the sale of
property to pay debts by a curator of an absentee
estate applies equally to the administrator that is
listing of debts, petition, etc., insofar as they are
applicable.

1—Act 290,1938
2—Art. 53 C. P. R. C. C.
3—C. P. Arts. 990, 991; 1164, 1187 R. C. C.
4—R. C. C. 1050, 1051

By Executors to Pay Debts And Legacies.

There are two kinds of Executors, testamentary and dative testamentary and all the rules governing administrators, curators of vacant estates etc., apply insofar as sales to pay debts are concerned, with the exceptions herein noted.

As regards the debts both executors possess the same powers and exercise the same rights.

The testamentary executor shall proceed to the payment of the debts of the succession in the same manner as is prescribed for curators of vacant successions (1). This necessarily applies to the dative testamentary executor. In default of funds sufficient to discharge the debts and legacies, the testamentary executor shall cause himself to be authorized to sell the movables, and if they are not sufficient, the immovables, to a sufficient amount to satisfy those debts and legacies (2).

A sale of property directed by the will of the deceased is valid (3); and although a testamentary executor who has not been granted seizin of the estate, is without power to do more than to see to the execution of the legacies and to cause an inventory etc., he may sell sufficient property to pay debts (4), and presumably the legacies of sums of money, under the provisions of the Code.

Neither sort of executor may sell any of the immovables except he is authorized by the will of the deceased to do so (5).

By Receivers to Pay Debts.

Where a receiver has been appointed by the

1—R. C. C. 1670
2—R. C. C. 1668
3—Succ. Massey. 46 A.126
4—Porter's Heir v Hornsby. 32 A.337: R. C. C. 1668
5—R. C. C. 1669

court and it appears that there is no reasonable ground for believing that the corporation can be so administered as to pay its debts and the possession of the property restored to the corporation, the court on application of any party at interest, after ten days notice on the order book, if there be no opposition, or after hearing on same, may order the sale of the property (1).

All orders for the sale of the property of a corporation must be entered in the Receivership order book in the clerk's office (2).

The above applies to receiverships in the state courts.

Sales by Judicial Liquidators to Pay Debts.

The law is silent as to the specific manner in which property belonging to corporations under liquidation may be sold, but the procedure usually followed in sales at public auction, would apply to such sales and render them valid sales.

Sales by Syndics to Pay Debts

The Civil Code provides for two sorts of syndics, which are in reality administrators, in the one case of an insolvent succession and in the other case of an insolvent debtor.

The first class of syndics are appointed in those successions where no one will accept the administration of a succession and the creditors are authorized to appoint a syndic, at a meeting held for that purpose. The articles of the Code are two in number (3).

Other articles of the Code (4) provide for the appointment of the clerk of court in such situations,

1—Act 159, 1898
2—Act 159, 1898
3—Arts. R. C. C. 1224, 1225
4—Arts. R. C. C., 1190

but these appointments are limited to those successions possessing property of less than five hundred dollars value.

The articles of the Code regulating the appointment and powers of a syndic in case of an insolvent debtor are to be found in paragraph 5 Section 1 Chapter 5 under the heading of Cessions (1).

The interest of the examiner in both of these cases is some what academic for the reason that for a long number of years, there had been no appointments made in either case because the practice of appointing syndics in insolvent successions has ceased; and in the insolvency of debtors the codal provisions have been repealed by the enactment of bankruptcy laws by Congress.

In the event that a link is found in the chain of title being examined, which consists of a sale by either kind of syndic, prescription will have obviated the necessity of passing upon the validity of the proceedings

In General.

The rules given heretofore in succession matters have special application to sales to pay debts but they also apply as far as they fit to sales of succession property for the purpose of a settlement of the succession itself. There are three provisions of the Civil Code covering these latter sales, namely where an absentee has not been heard from for the space of ten years his curator shall apply to the court setting out these facts and the further fact that he has no known heirs in the state, upon due

1—R. C. C. Arts. 2170 to 2184

and satisfactory proof the judge shall order the sale of the property (1). Whenever an heir shall declare that he is not willing to accept the succession other than under the benefit of inventory, the administrator shall proceed to the sale of all of the property and to the settlement of the succession (2). If, at the expiration of one year from the appointment of a curator of a vacant succession, there be immovable property belonging to the succession which has not been sold, the judge is bound, at the request of the curator, to order the sale of them to be made at public auction (3).

Before proceeding to this sale, the judge is bound to cause the property to be sold to be estimated by experts appointed by him and sworn, and if at the sale two-thirds of the estimated value be not offered for it, the sale shall be suspended and the curator is bound to have it again exposed, after the same advertisements and formalities prescribed by law at one, two and three years credit (4), but then the property must be sold at the price offered.

This provision applies to all sales to pay debts or to effect the settlement of an estate made on the application of a representative of a succession, whether it is an executor, administrator, curator or any other, in any succession, legal, testamentary, or irregular, vacant or not, accepted with the benefit of inventory, or unconditionally, whether the heirs

1—R. C. C. 53
2—R. C. C. 1058
3—R. C. C. 1169, 1170
4—R. C. C. 1170; Huckaby v Huckaby; 134 L.107; Thibodaux v Thibodaux, 138 L.227

be all of age, or minors or both, present or absent (1).

Representatives of successions shall have the right to cause sales of the property administered by them to be made by the sheriff, or an auctioneer, or to make it themselves (2).

Sales may be made for less than the appraised value in order to pay debts (3). At one time it was the opinion of the bar that minors' property could not be sold for less than the appraised value, even to pay debts but this was decided squarely to the contrary by the Supreme Court (4).

Sales to pay debts are not dependent upon the filing of an account of administration or tableau of distribution (5). The order may issue merely upon filing of a list of debts.

All orders or judgments affecting sales of property should be signed in open court   (6).

1—Huckaby v Huckaby, 184 L. 107; Lacroix v Crane, 133 L.227
        Thibodaux v Thibodaux, 112 L.906; Succ. of Hood,83 A.466
2—R. C. C. 1171
3—Succ. of Stolz, 23 A.175
4—Ibid
5—Succ. of Tabor, 33 A. 343
6—C. P. 546

CHAPTER XXIV.

Partitions By Licitation.

The general law and jurisprudence governing partitions will not be discussed here as they are treated under the heading "Partitions" in this volume, but although the alienation of minors' and interdicts' properly is specially treated under a separate title, it is included in this chapter for the reason that, practically speaking, minors and interdicts stand in the same position in these suits as persons sui juris, with one exception which will be noted hereafter.

The essentials of a valid partition by licitation are:

1. Jurisdiction of the court
2. Petition
3. Parties
4. Appointment, oath and report of experts to advise as to the divisibility or nondivisibility of the property; and to appraise the property.
5. Prayer
6. Citation
7. Judgment

District courts as probate courts have exclusive jurisdiction of partitions (1); The particular district court in which the suit must be brought is determined by the place where a succession is opened or where the property is situated when a succession is not involved (2). Where heirs have been recognized and sent into possession a suit for a partition is not for a partition among heirs but between co-owners and suit must be brought where the real estate is situated (3).

Between co-owners who are not heirs the gener-

1—Sec. 35, Art. 7, Const. 1921; Constitutions, 1913, 1898, 1879
2—Art. 924, C. P.; R. C. C. 1289, 1327
3—Medicis v Medicis, 155 L.171

al rules governing partitions will govern but such rules as are inapplicable are not sacramental (1).

Petition: The petition should set forth the names of all the co-owners, ages and domiciles; a description of the property; the acquisition thereof; and where inherited proper reference to the proceedings if the heirs have been placed in possession, by judgment of court, and to the registration of said judgment. However, if the parties or any of them, are heirs, they may ask for recognition as such and to be placed and sent into possession, in the petition in the partition suit, as the ownership of the property sought to be partitioned must be established (2).

There should be an allegation covering the divisibility or non-divisibility of the property (3); and appropriate clauses asking for the appointment of experts to determine this (4); and for an appraisement (5), if none has been made within the year (6).

Parties: All co-owners should be made parties to the suit, either as plaintiffs or as defendants (7).

If there are several minors with the same tutor a special tutor ad hoc must be appointed for each minor in the partition suit (8).

A partition may be sued for by any heirs testamentary or ab intestado (9); and the action of partition will not only lie between co-heirs and legatees, but between all persons who hold property in common,

1—Paul v Lamothe, 36 A.318
2—Aucoin v Engeron. 165 L.319
3—R. C. C. 1339
4—Cameron v Lane, 36 A.722; Rayner v Rayner, 171 L.1050
5—R. C. C. 1324
6—Supra
7—R. C. C. 1329
8—Buddecke v Buddecke, 31 A.572; Metcrlf v Alter, 31 A.394;
         Metcalf v Green, 140 L.957
9—R. C. C. 1307

from whatever cause they may hold it (1) ; any heir or
co-owner, tutor of minors, curator of interdicts, when
duly authorized by the judge (on the advice of a family meeting prior to 1926, or by the judge alone since
then (2) ; curator of absentees, and of vacant successions (3); may sue for partition. Married women pri-
or to 1921 could not sue without the consent of their
husbands, or of the judge (4) but since then they
may (5).

Tutors of minors and curators of interdicts do
not need the authorization of a family meeting or of
the judge to defend a partition suit (6). Co-owners
who are sui juris may be represented by an attorney
in fact but the act of procuration must be special and
in authentic form but the attorney or agent may not
represent several co-owners (7) ; nor can a tutor of
a minor or curator of an interdict represent such minor or interdict in such cases where the tutor or curator is an interested party (8); nor where there are
several minors, or interdicts. Each minor or intedict
must be represented by a tutor or curator ad
hoc (9). In an action for the partition of the effects
of an ordinary parternership, where the deceased left
minor heirs, they cannot be properly represented by
an attorney for absent heirs; and it is not competent
for such administrator and attorney without other
parties to obtain a valid judgment for a partition and

1—R. C. C. 1308
2—Act 319, 1926
3—R. C. C. 1315, 1186
4—R. C. C. 1316
5—Act 34, 1921
6—R. C. C. 1314
7—Metcalfe v Alter, 81 A.389; Metcalfe v Green, 140 L. 957
8—Metcalfe v Alter, 81 A. 389 ; Gassan v Palfreyy, 9 A.560
9—Crawford v Binion, 46 A. 1261

they are not proper parties to represent the succession in a sale to effect partition (1).

The subject of curators, attorneys, attorneys to represent absentees and absent heirs, tutors and curators ad hoc, is fully discuss in a chapter under that heading.

Appointment, oaths and reports of experts: Two experts should be appointed and sworn by the judge (not a notary) to report upon the divisibility or non-divisibility of the property; and to make an appraisement of the property (2). It is necessary to have an inventory and appraisement made, if none has been made within the year (3). An inventory is unnecessary when there is only one piece of property (4).

The reports of the experts must be made in writing.

The inventory need not be homologated (5).

All above mentioned orders should be dated and signed by the judge.

Prayer: The prayer should in every respect correspond to the allegations of the petition.

The judgment: The court should decide as to whether or not the partition should be made and whether it should be made in kind or licitation; it should appoint an auctioneer to conduct the sale if by licitation; and a notary public to continue the partition.

Execution of The Sale By The Auctioneer: It is unnecessary to discuss here the esentials of a public sale, as to appraisements, advertisements, etc., as a sale to effect a partition must follow the requirements of all public sales.

1—Savage v Williams, 15 A.250; Bank v Choppin, 46 A.633
2—R. C. C. 1339
3—R. C. C. 1324, 1325, 1326
4—Blandid v Blandid, 126 L.319
5—Giglio v Giglio, 159 L.46

There is one important fact to be noted and that is, the property even where a minor is interested, may be sold for less than the appraisement, but not less than two thirds thereof, at the first bid (1).

In the execution of the formal deed, if possible all co-owners or their representatives should join.

Proceedings before the notary public, after completion of sale: The examiner should follow up the proceedings to the extent that he should check to see that the proceeds of the sale belonging to a tutor or curator have been deposited in the registry of the court, where there are minors or interdicts interested in the partition. Formerly, under the jurisprudence, the purchaser was not protected until not only the purchase price had been deposited in the registry of the court, but the share of the minor had been ascertained and reinvested (2), but under later decisions, it is only required that the share of the tutor or curator be deposited in the registry of the court (3). The title of the purchaser can then be cleared of the minor's mortgage by a simple rule.

It is absolutely vital that all of the formalities and requisites of the law be observed in such a partition (where the interests of a minor or interdict are attempted to be divested) as a failure to comply with them strikes down the partition which becomes merely provisional (4). Purchasers at partition sales must not only look to the jurisdiction of the court which ordered the sale, but also the power of the court to render the order (5); in effect such sales are the

1—Buddecke v Buddecke, 31 A.574; Schaffet v Jackson, 14 A.154; R. C., C. 345, Arcenaux v Cormier, 175 L.948; Succ. of Hocd, 33 A.466
2—Succ. of Aron, 48 A.817; Koehl v Solari, 47 A.890
3—Schmidt v Schmidt, 155 L.155 L.103; Wilson v O'Quin, 131 L. 126
4—R. C. C. 1372; Rhodes v Cooper, 118 L.299
5—Mackins v Willes, 106 L.1

exception to the general rule, that third parties are not forced to do more than satisfy themselves that the court had jurisdiction.

On the other hand, when the formalities required with regard to minors or persons under interdiction, either for the alienation of immovable property, or in a partition of a succession, have been complied with, they are considered as to these acts, as though they had executed them, as being of full age or before interdiction (1).

1—R. C. C. 2231

CHAPTER XXV

Alienations and Changes of Ownership Effected by Acts before Notaries Public, Under Order of Court

These alienations or changes of ownership made by order of court, occur in the following instances:

1. Sales at private sale to pay debts.
2. Dation en paiements.
3. Partitions in kind.

Sales of minors' and interdicts' interests to effect partition or otherwise, are not included here as they are the subject of a separate chapter.

Until 1924 all sales of succession property, corporations, etc., had to be sold at public auction, but the legislature of that year passed an act (1) which authorized receivers or judicial liquidators whenever they found it advantageous to the corporation that its property either in part or in whole, be sold at private sale, to sell in that manner, by petitioning the court for an order to that effect. The petition in such case to set forth either a special proposition previously made for the purchase at private sale of the property, or outlining a proposition which should be invited and accepted for a private sale. Upon receipt of such a petition a rule issued directed to the corporation, and any co-receiver or co-liquidator, if such there be, and the creditors, to show cause within the delay fixed by the court, why the sale as prayed for, should not be made.

This rule was to be served upon the corporation and the co-receivers or co-liquidators, as in citation and must be published for ten days in the usual manner for judicial notices, to-wit, three times in ten days.

1—Act 43, 1924

Upon the trial of the rule, whether or not there was opposition, due proof of the necessity of the sale and the advisability thereof, must be made and if the prayer was granted, the court must fix the terms and conditions as it deems proper.

This act applies solely to receivers and liquidators, but this authority was extended by the legislature in 1938 (1). Owing to the fact that this act contains a number of special requirements which have been strictly construed, it is deemed best to give the act verbatim, instead of a summary thereof: Whenever it shall appear to the executors or administrators of any succession or estate of a deceased person to be to the manifest advantage of the succession or estate, its creditors or heirs, to sell any movable or immovable property at private sale, in whole or in part or in indivision, for cash, in order to pay debts, legacies or both, or for any other purpose, the executor or administrator may, although not obliged so to do, file a petition in the district court having jurisdiction of the succession proceedings setting forth a full description of the property to be sold, the price and conditions of the proposed private sale, and the reasons which make it advantageous to the succession, heirs or creditors to dispose of the property.

In any sale of succession assets under the provision of this act there shall be no priority as between movables and immovable property, provided, however, that the administrator or executor shall set forth his reason if he recommends the private sale of immovable property before the movable property has been exhausted.

Whenever such petition shall be received by the court, the judge thereof shall order that due notice

1—Act 290, 1938

be given by publication, in the manner prescribed for judicial advertisements, of said application to sell movable property, or immovable property, or both, at private sale, and said notice shall require all those whom it may concern, including the heirs, to make opposition, if any they have, to such course, within ten days, including Sundays and holidays, from the day whereon the last publication appears. If no opposition be made to the granting of the authorization prayed for ,the judge shall, if he deems it expedient, so order and shall fix the minimum price to be accepted. If the opposition be made, the judge shall hear the matter and determine thereon in a summary manner.

The attention of the examiner is directed to several points of importance in the act. First: The expression "for any other purpose" in the act seems all embracing and some members of the bar have been inclined to consider it as authorizing sales for any and all purposes, including even partitions, but such an act, constituting as it does, a radical departure from long established practices and legislation, must be strictly construed, until at least the courts have established a line of jurisprudence thereon.

The period of advertising referred in the act is three times in ten days and five times in thirty days for movables and immovables respectively.

Prior to 1938 an act (1) had been enacted by the legislature authorizing any executor or administrator of a succession to make a dation en paiement of any property belonging to such succession which is encumbered by mortgages of an amount in excess of the value of such property and the requirements as to petition, reasons, advertisement, delay etc., are the same as the above mentioned act.

1—Act 121, 1934

In accordance with the law in general there must be a valuation of the property for the purpose of establishing that the mortgage or mortgages exceed in amount the value of the property.

While other fiduciary officers, such as the curator of a vacant estate, are in fact, administrators the explicit and exclusive use of the terms "executor" and "administrator" preclude any extension of the authority conferred by both acts on the latter officers, to the former.

The requirements of the authentic act by which the above transfers are carried out, must be complied with to the same extent as in ordinary sales.

While it is said that the requirements of the Act 1934 are the same as Act 290 of 1938, as to advertisements etc., there is a discrepancy in the wording of the act in regard to the time in which opposition may be made. In the Act 1938 opposition must be made within ten days after the last publication appears, but the act of 1934 reads ten days from the date of the first publication, though in both cases the period of advertising is the same, three times in ten days for movables and five times in thirty days for immovables. There must be an error in the printed statute, but it would seem to be the safer practice for the days to be computed from the last day of advertisement.

CHAPTER XXVI.
Partitions In Kind.

Partitions in which minors or interdicts are interested are not included in this chapter for the reason that they are the subject of another chapter entitled "Alienation of Minors' and Interdicts' property," hence there is little to be said here as if the co-owners are all present or represented and sign the process verbal of the partition in kind ordered by the court, they are bound thereby, and if they do not so sign and file opposition, the judgment of court thereon is conclusive (1).

However, lots should be formed and the parties should draw for the same, as provided by the Codal provision on this kind of partition (2), as lesion beyond moiety may give ground for attack.

If any of the co-owners are represented by an agent or attorney in fact, such agency must be in authentic form and annexed to the act; and if more than one owner is represented, each must be represented by different agents or attorneys in fact (3).

The process verbal of the partition must be homologated in accordance with the codal provisions (4), and the notice of ten days provided therein served, in accordance with law, on the parties, for the reason that if one of the parties was not present or represented, he would not be bound unless served with such notice (5).

The notarial act by which the partition was made should be seasonably registered in the conveyance office.

1—Blanchard v Blanchard, 7 A.529; R. C. C. 1374; Hollinsworth v
      Caldwell, 195 L. 33
2—R. C. C. 1367
3—Metcalfe v Alter, 31 A.389
4—R. C. C. 1374
5—Reynolds v Reynolds, 43 A.1118

CHAPTER XXVII.

Alienations And Changes Of Ownership of Property Belonging To Minors And Interdicts by Order of Court.

All the rules governing minors and tutors apply with equal force to curators of interdicts, and to interdicts themselves, so in discussing the alienation of the property of either minors or interdicts, it will not be necessary to specifically mention the latter. The person interdicted, is, in every respect, like the minor, who is under a tutor, both as respects his person and estate, concerning the oath, the inventory and the security, the recording of the legal mortgage, the mode of administering, the sale of the estate, the commission on the revenues, the excuses, the exclusion or deprivations of the tutorship, the mode of rendering the accounts, and the other obligations, apply with respect to the curatorship of the person interdicted (1).

The rule of property being that the acts of a duly qualified tutor (or curator) cannot be attacked collaterally and the innocent third party is protected by the order of court (2), the examiner is only obliged to inquire into those proceedings which go to the taking of the oath, security and letters, with one exception; the father cannot either refuse a tutorship (3), resign (4), or be removed from the tutorship of his children, except for the causes provided in the code (5); so the appointment of anyone else, even a trust company is invalid (6).

The examiner must also inquire into the power of the court, that is, its jurisdiction.

1—R. C. C. 415
2—Succ. Hawkins, 35 A.591; Robinson v. Scharfenstein, 148 L.364
3—James v Meyer, 41 A.1103; Succ. Watt, 111 L.937
4—Ibid
5—R. C. C. 302, 305
6—James v Meyer, 41 A.1103; Succ. Watt, 111 L.937

The appointment, recognition or confirmation must be made by the judge of the parish where the minor has his domicile, if he has a domicile in the state, or if he has no domicile in the state by the judge of the parish where the principal estate of the minor is situated (1).

The domicile of the tutor is the domicile of the minor, hence if the tutor removes his domicile, the judge of the parish to which the tutor removes has jurisdiction over the minor (2).

Courts outside the State cannot appoint guardians or tutors to minors domiciled in Louisiana (3). Appointments of tutors or guardians to minors outside of the State of Louisiana are valid in Louisiana; proceedings to alienate the minor's real property in Louisiana must be brought in the court of the parish wherein the property is situated, such as a sale to effect a partition, to pay debts etc. (4).

Petition: Application should be made by the party seeking the appointment and show facts which would serve to establish jurisdiction of the court and relationship to minor.

Order: There should be an order signed by judge appointing or confirming the tutor upon compliance with the law as to oath, inventory, recordation, security, etc. (5).

Inventory: An inventory must be made in accordance with the formalities required (6).

Recordation: The inventory (or bond) must be recorded (7), unless a surety bond is given.

1—R. C. C. 307
2—Fraser v Zylick, 29 A.533; State v Pettit, 14 A.565
3—Succ. Vennard, 44 A.1076
4—R. C. C. 363
5—R. C. C. 284, 334, 335
6—R. C. C. 316, 317, 318
7—R. C. C. 321, 323, 325, 326, 328. et seq.

Oath: His oath must be taken and filed (1). The tutor can perform no acts binding the minor he represents unless he has taken his oath (2). Every tutor must take an oath (3).

Letters: The letters of tutorship shall not be delivered to the tutor until he shall have complied with the law as herein required. Until they are delivered to him he may not administer the affairs of the minor. The tutor is not recognized, confirmed or appointed, until the judge signs an order authorizing letters of tutorship be issued (4).

The letters are the basis of the tutor's authority to act and hence should be issued only after all the formalities have been complied with.

Under-tutor: An under tutor must be appointed and sworn. Any alienation of a minor's property without his presence at family meeting is void (5).

The foregoing sets out the law governing tutors (and interdicts) in general and is discussed in detail in the chapter entitled "Minors and Their Tutors".

A minor's property may be alienated or its ownership changed in the following cases.

1. To effect a partition (6).
2. To pay debts (7), or when it is found advantageous to him that his property be sold (8).
3. To adjudicate to a parent (9).

It may also be mortgaged for his benefit (10).

The immovables of the minor cannot be alienated, or mortgaged unless on the representation of the

1—R. C. C. 334
2—Verret v Aubert, 6 L.350; Boyer v Tassin, 9 A.491
3—R. C. C. 335
4—R. C. C. 335
5—R. C. C. 273; Doucet v Fenelon, 120 L.18
6—R. C. C. 345
7—R. C. C. 345; Act 149, 1924
8—R. C. C. 345; Act 209, 1932
9—R. C. C. 343
10—R. C. C. 339-40

tutor that it is for the interest of the minor (1).

The sale of a minor's property, except it is to be made to effect a partition, must be at public auction, after having been duly advertised in the manner required for other judicial advertisements, during ten days for movables and thirty days for immovables (2).

Such are the codal provisions on the subject of the alienation of minor's property. They have not been repealed and any alienation made in accordance therewith would be perfectly valid.

The legislature, however, has seen fit to pass certain statutes which provide a different procedure in connection, not only with the sale of a minor's property, but with other matters concerning minors and which legislation is a radical departure from the articles of the Civil Code on the same subject, but which is merely permissive and not mandatory.

Prior to 1870 a minor's property could, under no circumstances, be sold without a strict compliance with the following requirements:

1. The convoking of a family meeting to advise upon the subject.

2. A sale at public auction.

The Revised Statue of 1870 (3) first permitted, without a repeal of the codal articles, a sale of a minor's property with the advice of a family meeting, to be effected at private sale to effect a partition. The section of the Revised Statutes embodying this provision was amended specifically in 1878 (4), 1912 (5), 1918 (6), 1920 (7) and finally in 1924 (8).

1—R. C. C. 339
2—R. C. C. 340
3—Sect. 2667, R. S. 1870
4—Act 25, 1878
5—Act 50, 1912
6—Act 245, 1918
7—Act 248, 1920
8—Act 221, 1924

The Revised Statues and each of the aforesaid acts dealt exclusively with the one object, to-wit: The alienation of a minor's (or interdict's) property at private sale to effect a partition. It is significant that the act of 1924 (1) stipulated that its provisions were not to change or effect, in any way, Act 110 of 1920 which authorized the waiving of a family meeting in every instance where the law required the convoking of a family meeting, thus emphasizing the fact that the act of 1920 was general in its nature and each act was to be considered as separate and distinct legislation.

Each of the titles of the aforementioned acts (except Act 110 of 1920), recited the fact that it was an amendment and re-enactment of the Revised Statutes, Section 2667 as amended by the previous acts.

Act 110 of 1920 was the first of a series of enactments which permitted family meetings to be dispensed with in matters concerning a minor or interdict. The act was amended in specific terms by an Act of 1926 (2). The latter act was followed in 1934 (3) by an act which was apparently new legislation on the subject, as it contained no other reference to previous enactments, except the general repealing clause· The 1934 act was amended in 1935, 2 E.S. (4). The title of each of these acts, however, read exactly the same, viz: "An act authorizing (or to authorize) the Judge of. a Court of competent jurisdiction (or authority) to render decrees or orders with reference to minors and interdicts in all matters without convocation of family meetings."

The body of these acts differ very little from

1—Act 149, 1924
2—Act 319, 1926
3—Act 47, 1934
4—Act 18, 1935, 2 E. S.

each other, except that the act of 1926 includes in specific words, "including any and all proceedings to effect a partition of the property of a minor or interdict," a clause which was omitted from Act of 1934 and the amendment of 1935 and in this, that in the act of 1920 and of 1926 the proceedings were to be taken contradictorily with the under tutor or under curator, but in the amendment of 1935 this provision is omitted, unless the under tutor or under curator fails or refuses to concur in the recommendations of the tutor or curator.

Both from the titles and from the body of the acts it is evident that these acts contained but one object, that is, the dispensing or waiving of the convocation of family meetings.

Nor do any of these acts provide for any procedure or requirements other than the presentation of the recommendations of the tutor or curator in regard to the subject matter, so that it hardly can be argued that this general provision justifies the ignoring of other requirements of the Code in reference to minors, especially the sale of their property, etc., such as appraiser's report as to the divisibility or non-divisibility of the property in matters of partition, etc.

The first legislation authorizing the sale of a minor's or interdict's property at private sale when it is found to be to the advantage of the minor or interdict that it be sold (this refers to property owned entirely by the minor or interdict) was passed in 1924 (1). The language was somewhat ambiguous, but it was evident that it had no reference to a partition. It provided for a rule to be taken on

1—Act 149, 1924

on behalf of any such minor or interdict, the delib-
erations of any such meeting to be approved and homologated by the district court of the parish in which
such minor or interdict resides. The tutor of any
minor, or the curator of any co-owner may initiate
such proceedings in his discretion without the necessity of its being authorized by a family meeting
so to do.

"Section 7—Whenever to effect a partition it is
desired to sell an entire property in which an undivided interest belongs to a minor or to an interdict who is absent from the State and not represented by a tutor or curator, the Court having jurisdiction of the property, may appoint, upon the petition
of any party interested a tutor or curator and an
under tutor or under curator, as the need may be, to
represent the said absentee in the proceedings, without the necessity of convoking a family meeting to
advise and consent to such appointment. Such tutor or curator, under tutor or under curator to serve
under oath, but without bond.

"Section 8—Any property sold under this act
may be purchased by any co-owner or co-owners
thereof.

"Section 9—None of the provisions of this act
are in any way to change or affect Act 319, 1926.

The provisions of Section 7 of the foregoing act
is decidedly confusing insofar as the interdict is
concerned, because it provides for the appointment
of a curator and an under curator, officials never appointed until and unless there has been a judgment
of interdiction. If such a person has been interdicted in the State and the curatorship is vacant and
the interdict absent, the court having jurisdiction

over such a person should properly make the appointments mentioned. If on the other hand the absentee interdict was interdicted in another state, the fact that he was interdicted would have to be established legally and to do this his guardian would have to be contacted and would have a right to appear in the proceedings in his capacity as guardian.

The repealing clause repeals specifically Section 2667 of the Revised Statutes 1870, Act 25 of 1878, 50 of 1912, 245 of 1918, 248 of 1920 and sections 1, 2, 3, 4 and 6 of Act 77 of 1928. Section 5 of that act was not repealed as it is the prescription clause but otherwise the entire act was repealed.

It will thus be seen that the above act (209 1932) covers the entire subject of the alienation of a minor's property, and provides two forms of procedure, one to be followed where a sale of property owned by the minor either in its entirety or in indivision with others is desired in all cases other than to effect a partition; and the other procedure to be followed in the case of a partition.

There seems to be a difference of opinion among the members of the Bar as to the procedure to be followed in those cases where a minor owns property in indivision with others. Some hold that a sale under such condition is in reality a sale to effect a partition and that therefore Section 6 of the Act of 1932 should be followed. That section requires a family meeting which has the duty of deciding as to the advisibility of the sale, to appraise the property and to fix the price and terms upon which the interest of the minor is to be sold.

They further hold that the Act of 1934 as amended by the Act of 1935 2 E.S., permits the family meeting to be dispensed with and hence it is only necessary to go into court with a petition by the tutor, concurred in by the under tutor, setting forth the facts, including the indivisibility of the property, the appraised value thereof, the price and terms offered and recommending the sale for the price and on the terms set forth in the petition. If the court approves, the tutor's recommendations are to be homologated. The order of court homologating the recommendatons and ordering the sale, is deemed sufficient to constitute a valid sale of the minor's interest.

Others hold that, unless an actual partition is necessary because co-owners demand it, section 1, 2, 3, and 4 of the Act should be followed in accordance with the procedure laid down therein. It is a matter of frequent occurrence that a bona fide offer of purchase for a stipulated price is received by the owners of the property and they desire to accept it and it becomes necessary that the sale of the minor's interest be authorized. To use the procedure provided by Section 6 on the ground that such a sale is in reality a partition, is but a subterfuge. It is held that to proceed under Section 6 and then dispense with the family meeting and thus prevent the performance of the duty of appraising the property and fixing the price and terms imposed upon it, is to nullify the provisions of that section and to give the tutor and the under tutor almost unlimited authority to dispose of a minor's property for such price and for any reason they may see fit.

Due to the fact that the courts have not as yet had occasion to interpret any of the foregoing acts, it would seem that a word of caution is in order.

There can be no question that the compilers of
the Civil Code and the Code of Practice, consented
with reluctance to the alienation of minor's property
and endeavored to establish safe guards of all kinds
to prevent the defrauding of such minors. The courts
up to the present time have looked askance at every
such alienation and have closely and keenly scrutiniz-
ed every alienation which has been brought to their
attention and have insisted that all the formalities
prescribed by law be strictly observed; and it is sure-
ly within every lawyer's knowledge that even where
the letter of the law itself leads to an absurdity,
they have insisted that the letter be followed (1).

In view of the lack of jurisprudence which
would serve as a guide at this time, and in view of
further fact that no error would be made in following the provisions of Act 209 of 1932 in all alienations of a minor's property, it is suggested that such
a course should be followed as a matter of precaution.

1—Massey v Steeg, 12 A.78; Lyons v Women's League, 124 L.722

CHAPTER XXVIII.

Adjudication of a Minor's Interest to Parent.

The procedure required in an adjudication of a minor's interest in property owned in common by the parent and minor, is specifically and clearly set out in the Civil Code. The article which authorized the adjudication read prior to 1916 as follows:

Whenever the father or mother of a minor has property in common with him, they each can cause it to be adjudicated to them, either in whole or in part, at the price of an estimation made by experts appointed by the judge and duly sworn, after a family meeting duly assembled, shall have declared that the adjudication is for the interest of the minor, and the under-tutor shall have given his consent thereto and in this case the property so adjudicated shall remain mortgaged for the security of the payment of the price of the adjudication and the interest thereof (1).

Partly, it is to be supposed, because the idea of adjudicating the parent's as well as the minor's interest to that parent seemed an absurdity, and partly because there were cases in which, not only were the minor and parent co-owners in the property but others as well, it seemed a further absurdity and a legal impossibility to adjudicate the interest of those other co-owners, the profession fell into the error of only adjudicating the minor's interest to the parent instead of the whole property. However logical this view point was, the error was in the face of a decision of the Supreme Court which had emphatically declared that the adjudication should be of all of the property and not merely the interest of the minor. (2)

1—R. C. C. 843
2—Massey v Steeg, 12 A.78

This procedure was accepted and followed by the profession generally with the consequences that title after title containing a link of this character, was rendered fatally defective.

Finally the issue again came before the court in a case involving an adjudication made in the manner referred to, that is, the interest of the minor and not the whole property, had been adjudicated to the parent, and met the condemnation of the court, which said that where a parent held property in common with a minor, and desired to purchase the minor's interest, the whole of the property must be adjudicated. (1)

So many titles were thrown into doubt that the Legislature had to come to the rescue by passing acts quieting these titles (2), and as a further means of clarifying the situation amended the article so as to make it possible to adjudicate the minor's interest and not the whole property. (3)

As the illegality of these adjudications affected other titles in which majors had been co-owners, another act (4) was passed quieting such titles, by a six months' prescription.

As it was found that in certain cases, the minor whose interest had been alienated erroneously, had been interdicted since the attempted alienation, another act was passed authorizing the ratification of the attempted sale by a family meeting held for that purpose in accordance with the act. (5)

The procedure to be followed at the present time may be summarized:

1—Lyons v Women's League, 124 L.222
2—Acts 53, 1912, 78 of 1914
3—Act 23, 1916; 17, 1928
4—Act 17, 1928
5—Act 131, 1924

1. A petition by the surviving parent filed in a court of proper jurisdiction.
2. An adjudication in accordance with Article 343 R. C. C.
3. An appraisement by duly appointed and sworn appraisers.
4. A decree of adjudication (1)
5. A recordation of the decree of adjudication in the mortgage office (2).
6. A registration of the alienation in the Conveyance Office.

A legal mortgage results from the recording of the decree in the mortgage office, but this mortgage may be eliminated before or after recordation by a special mortgage (3); or a bond (4).

The right of adjudication granted by the article of the Civil Code is not restricted to community property. It makes no distinction as to the source of the acquisition of the parent and minor (5).

Community property being partly owned by two major heirs of deceased wife, could not be adjudicated to husband (6).

Sale to Pay The Debts of A Minor

Until 1932 these sales had to be at public auction therefore the rules heretofore discussed in preceding chapters apply thereto.

The legislature that year passed an act (7) which by its all embracing language has authorized the sale of a minor's property at private sale whenever it is

1—Succ. Burguieres, 104 L.52
2—R. C. C. 343-44
3—R. C. C. 344; Act 223, 1900; 68, 1924; 283, 1926
4—Act 283, 1926
5—Berteau v O'Brien, 2 A.162
6—Brewer v Brewer, 145 L.835
7—Act 209, 1932

deemed to the advantage of the minor that the property be sold. This statute both in the title and in the body thereof recites that it is an act passed for the purpose of authorizing the sale of a minor's property, whenever it appears to the tutor of a minor or the curator of an interdict, who owns property either in its entirety, or in indivision that it is to the advantage of the minor or interdict to sell such property at private sale.

Clearly the act authorizes a sale to pay debts of the minor because the payment of a debt is to the advantage of the minor.

The same governs any other sale of a minor's property where the tutor may show that the minor will advantage from a sale.

CHAPTER XXIX

Tax Sales.

In Roussel v. Railways Realty Company, reported in the 132 La. 379, the Court said: It is historically well known and abundantly appears in our jurisprudence, that before the Constitution of 1898 the status of tax titles was such as can only be described as chaotic. As a consequence . . . an immense amount of valuable property had to be taken over for taxes by the State . . .

This confusion did not arise from any defect in the laws under which the collection of taxes were enforced, as those laws are and always have been clear enough and free from ambiguity, but it arose from other factors inherent in the fundamental principles upon which the enforcement of the payment of taxes were based.

Though the lawmakers recognized that the State fisc must be served and taxes collected, they realized that the means by which they were collected were harsh and that the taxpayer lacked the protection given by the courts and the orderly rules of judicial process, to other classes of debtors. So realizing, statutes were enacted which carefully provided the formalities and conditions by which and under which collection of taxes were to be made by the collecting officers. The courts, in turn, have never favored the enforced alienation of the tax payer's property, and they have uniformily required the strictest compliance with the formalities prescribed by the tax laws and have thrown the burden of full proof of the observance of such laws upon the tax purchaser. Necessarily under such a condition tax titles were practically of no value.

And even today, unless a tax title has behind it the constitutional prescription of three (now five) years, or has been quieted by the proceedings prescribed for that purpose (1), it is almost the poorest link in a title known to examiners.

Because of this fact no attempt will be made here to analyse or discuss or set out the laws governing tax sales· It would require too much space to little avail, hence the validity of a tax title which has been strengthened by prescription or by the proceedings to quiet tax titles as aforesaid, will be the subject of this chapter.

Prior to the Constitution of 1879 none of the previous constitutions contained any provisions for the collection of taxes, leaving the entire matter subject to legislative will. The constitutions of 1898, 1913 and 1921 are alike in the main essentials except the constitution of 1879 did not contain the prescription and the quieting of titles clauses. These clauses are to be found in various articles of the Constitutions of 1898 (2), 1913 (3), and 1921 (4).

The lawmakers, still mindful of the lack of judicial sanction in tax sales, skillfully and ingenuously encouraged judicial tests of such titles, first, by inviting tax purchasers to confirm their titles in court, with the reward that, if the tax debtor made no defense, or if having made such defense, a judgment quieting their titles would be valid against the world; and second, by affording the tax debtor an opportunity during a certain period of time, of proving the invalidity of the alienation, in a direct action, or by a defense in an action by the tax purchaser, with the

1—Act 101, 1898, Act 134, 1928
2—Art. 238, Const. 1898
3—Art. 233, Const. 1928
4—Sec. 11, Art. 10, Const., 1921

penalty of being forever barred from contesting such a title, if he failed to take advantage of the opportunity.

The courts, though they reluctantly bowed to the constitutional mandate, did not do so until 1907 when they decided that the constitutional prescription applied (1), except for the causes enumerated in the constitutions, although they held as late as 1901 (2), that want of notice was not cured by the prescription. Almost, immediately thereafter, however, the courts gave full recognition to the constitutional prescription as cutting off all defenses except prior payment of taxes, as set forth in the three constitutions referred to, even want of notice, but as early as 1901 they indirectly indicated that there were possible exceptions, such as want of possession by tax purchaser, non assessment, or assessments so vague as to preclude identification of the property, etc., saying in one instance (3): Irregularities and all errors of form not of such a character as to render a tax deed absolutely null and void, are cured by the prescription of three years. In a later case (4) the court discussing possession at length, inferred at least, that if the tax purchaser did not have possession corporeal or constructive, the prescription did not apply.

Gradually through the years the courts have formulated principles which constitute rules of prop erty and which form exceptions to the constitutional prescription.

These rules are:

1. No actual possession.
2. No assessment.

1—Canter v Williams, 107 L.77
2—Foreman v Hinchville, 106 L.295
3—Boyle v West, 107 L.347
4—Ashley Co. v Bradford, 109 L.641

3. Insufficient assessment or a description which fails to identify the property.
4. Property not subject to taxation.
5. No recordation of tax sale.

No Possession: There are three kinds of possession (1).

1. Corporeal Possession.
2. Constructive possession (i. e. Civil Possession).
3. No possession on part of tax purchaser and corporeal possession on part of tax debtor.

Corporeal Possession: In the 107 (2) La. case, the court found corporeal possession in the tax purchaser and none in the debtor and found on that ground in favor of the former, as have the court since in similar cases.

Constructive Possession: Constructive possession in the tax purchaser is in effect civil possession, as evidenced by his title, though it may be augumented by other facts, such as payment of subsequent taxes, etc. Where the property is susceptible of corporeal possession and the tax debtor does not have such possession, the civil possession of the tax purchaser prevails over that of the tax debtor (3). It is not necessary for the tax purchaser to take possession; it suffices that the original tax debtor be not in possession (4). Possession by any one other than the owner will not suspend prescription (5). The prescription accrues where the possession is merely flowing from a tax title, or constructive possession following the termination of corporeal possession of the tax debtor.

1—Ashley Co. v Bradford, 109 L.641
2—Canter v Williams, 107 La.77
3—Pickens v Dillinger, 163 L.529; Levenberg v Shanks, 165 L.419, Progressive Realty Co. v Levy, 177 L.749
4—Byrns v C. M. Sec. Co., 7 A.667
5—Ibid

Where the property is "wild" or swamp lands not susceptible of corporeal possession, it is sometimes difficult to decide the question pro or con. However, the corporeal possession which is required in property where actual corporeal possession is possible, is not required where such corporeal possession is difficult or impossible.

Facts which would evidence an intention to possess as owner; payment of taxes; posting of property, hunting thereon and other acts would constitute possession sufficient to defeat the claim of a tax purchaser whose only possession arises from his tax deed (1).

A mere survey does not prove possession (2), but where such a survey is made a part of the public records it would be corroborative.

. It would be impossible to lay down any set rule in these cases. Each case would have to be decided on the facts then existing.

No Possession on Part of Tax Purchaser and Corporeal Posesssion on Part of Tax Debtor: The entire jurisprudence is based upon the theory that the actual possession of the tax debtor is in continuous conflict and a continuous protest against the tax sale (3). This possession may be through a debtor's tenant (4).

This prescription applies to minors (5).

No Assessment: The essential factors in reference to assessments are that the property is actually as-

1—Blanchard v Garland, 6 La. App. 508
2—Zahn v Ferraro, 17 La. App. 167
3—Baronet v Houssiere, 143 L.72; Adsit v Park, 144 L.934; Bradley v New Orleans, 153 L.281; Byrne v Commercial Sec. Co., 7 LA. App. 667; Mire v LaSalle Realty Co., 176 L.663; Bonvilain v Richaud. 153 L.431; Charbonnet v State Realty Co. 155 L.1044; Williams v Raymond. 163 L.764; Kivlen v Horvath. 163 La. 901; Wils.n v Joseph, 158 So.661
4—Flanagan v Land Dev. Co., 145 L.843
5—Doyle v Negrotto, 124 L.100; McNamara v Nider, 136 L.159

sessed and that the assessment was substantially of the same property as was sold for taxes.

The fact that the assessment is in the name of one person or another or in no name, or that the owner in possession was not notified, or that the sale was not advertised, is of no consequences. If the property was assessed that is sufficient (1).

On the contrary where there has been no assessment, a tax sale of the property not assessed, is an absolute nullity (2).

Insufficient Description: The question of sufficiency or insufficiency of description is determined by identification. In other words, if the description is sufficient to reasonably identify the property, a tax sale under such a description is valid, but if the description fails to establish identity, or if the identity of the property cannot be reasonably established, the sale is null (3). In numerous cases the rule that an insufficient description is not cured by the constitutional prescription is upheld.

Property not Subject to Taxation: The sale of property belonging to the State or a political subdivision or of any property specifically exempted by the constitution from the payment of taxes is not protected by the constitutional prescription (4).

No Recordation of Sale: Where there has been no recordation of the tax sale, it forms no exception to the rule, but it does suspend the three years pre-

1—Griffin v Taft, 151 L.442; Byrne v Commercial Sec. Co., 7 L. App.667; Quaker Realty Co. v Purcell, 134 L.1024; Slattery v Heolperin, 110 L.86; Cordill v Quaker Realty Co., 130 L.933.
2—Hollingsworth v Schanland, 155 L 925; Close v Rowen, 171 L.263
3—Bd. Comrs. v Concordia Land & Timber Co., 141 L.247; Close v Rowen, 171 L.263; 3rd District Land Co. v Villavaso, 172 L.917; Claiborne v Lezine, 175 L.635; Thomas v Stricker Land Co., 181 L.784
4—The Puritan Co. v Clarkson, 146 L.1099; Stockbridge v Martin, 4 La. App., 410; Neal v Pitre, 142 L.737

scription and hence the title is still open to attack, although more than the three years (or five) have elapsed since the tax sale (1).

The constitution of 1921 omits dual assessment as one of the exceptions to the three years prescription. This omission was made clearly on the ground that it was surplusage, as a plea of dual assessment would be of little avail, where there had been no payment under either assessment, whereas a prior payment of taxes under either assessment would be sufficient to bar the prescription.

The Constitution of 1898 (2) ordered the legislature to provide for the manner and form of preceeding to quiet tax titles after a lapse of twelve months from the date of recording the deed and in compliance with the mandate the legislature of that year passed an act which is set out in full here for the reason that its provisions must be strictly followed:

The manner of notice and form of proceeding to quiet tax titles in accordance with Article 233 of the Constitution shall be as follows:

After the lapse of twelve months from the date of recording the tax deed in the conveyance records of the parish where such property is situated, the purchaser, his heirs or assigns may institute by petition and citation, as in ordinary actions against the former proprietor or proprietors of the property, in which petition must appear a description of the property, mention of the time and place of the sale and name of officer who made same, reference to page of record book and date of record tax deed, notice that petitioner is owner of said property by virtue of said tax sale and notice that the title will be confirmed unless

1—Edmiston v Tulane Inv. Co., 9 La. App. 112
2—Art. 233, Const. 1898; Act 101, 1898, 144, 1928

a proceeding to annul is instituted within six months from date of service of the petition and citation. This suit shall be brought in the parish where the property is situated, unless it lies in two or more parishes, in which case this suit may be brought in either of such parishes. The petition and citation shall be served as in ordinary suits; provided that if the former proprietor be a non-resident of the State or unknown, or his residence is unknown, the court shall appoint a curator ad hoc to represent him and receive service, and said curator shall receive not more than ten dollars. After the lapse of six months from service of petition and citation, if no proceeding to annul the sale has been instituted, judgment shall be rendered quieting and confirming the title.

Section 3 of the same act as amended in 1928 (1) reads:

In all cases where tax titles have been quieted by the prescription of three years, under the provisions of the constitution of this state, the purchaser, his heirs or assignees, may, if he or they so desire, either obtain a judgment of the court, confirming said title, same to be done by suit in the manner and form as above set out, except the delay for answer shall be ten days, instead of six months, provided that the failure to bring suit shall in no manner effect said prescription title; or the said purchaser, his heirs or assignees, may at his or their option, quiet said title by monition proceedings, as provided by law, relative to sheriff's sale and tax sales.

Section 2 provides that two or more former owners of separate property, though they have no privity or community of interest, may be joined in the suit.

1—Act 144, 1928

The following is essential:

1 Strict compliance with the act as regards the allegations which the act requires.

2 Citation on all the owners, if there are more than one, who appear of record as last owner or owners.

3 In the case of absent or unknown owners, an allegation as to these facts and the proper appointment of a curator ad hoc.

4, An answer by the curator ad hoc, who may not waive any proof or admit the truth of any allegation, but must require strict proof thereof.

Suit must be brought against all the former owners, that is all owners who have become such since the owner in whose name the property was assessed and sold (1).

A judgment which is rendered in accordance with the provisions of the act is valid against the world, the courts holding: but we held and we still hold, that the correctness as distinguished from the validity of a judgment of confirmation obtained contradictorily with the true owner of the property is not open to investigation by any third person whomsoever . . . from all of which it follows, as a matter of course and a fortiori, that a valid judgment against the true owner passes the title absolutely to the successful litigant, and is res judicata against all the world, regardless of the grounds or lack of grounds on which it is based. And this is particularly true of a judgment confirming a tax title (2). And it was further held: Act 101 of 1898 and Constitution 1921, Art. 10, Sect. 11, governing proceedings to quiet tax titles, not requiring joining of every person having color of title,

1—Lemoine v Dupis, 2 La. App. 726; McIlhenny v Lemoine, 2 La. App. 733; Lemoine v Dupis, 2 La. 734
2—Rousel v Railways Realty Co., 132, La. 379

plaintiff in tax sale annulment suit held affected by proceedings to quiet tax title though not made a party therein, there being assessment and sale thereunder in name of party appearing as land owner with deed from same author from whom plaintiff claimed title, antedating his claim, and former proprietor being cited through curator ad hoc . . . (1).

In the case referred to above, Stockbridge purchased the property from one O'Neal in 1909, but it was assessed to O'Neal for the years 1918 and 1919 and sold to the City of South Highland for municipal taxes of 1918. It was again assessed in the name of O'Neal for the year 1919 and sold to Martin defendant.

There is another form of procedure for the curing of defects in titles (2) and which may be used in quieting tax titles.

However, as the proceedings referred to affect other forms of titles they have been made the subject of a chapter under the title "Monition Proceedings".

There are four kinds of tax titles:

Those based on the three or five years constitutional prescription which have not been quieted by either of the afore mentioned proceedings.

2 Those which have been so quieted.

3 Those based upon ten years prescription.

4 Those based on thirty years prescription.

The first mentioned class of titles are valid prima facie titles provided that the exceptions to the constitutional prescription as discussed previously, do not exist. Of these exceptions, possession or lack of possession require the proper proof de hors the record. The record should dispose of the other excep-

1—Stockbridge v Martin et al, 4 La. App. 410
2—Sec. 2370, Rev. Stat.

tions as the assessment rolls will disclose whether or not there has been an assessment, sufficiency of description for indentification, and whether or not the property is exempt from taxation. The conveyance records will show lack of recordation, or if recorded date thereof.

In the second class of titles, the proceedings and judgment should satisfy the examiner as to the validity or invalidity of the title, as quieted.

The third class of tax titles depend for their validity upon the prescription of ten years based upon a title translative of property, which the courts have declared a tax title to be, and are subject to all the rules governing titles of that character.

The fourth class of tax titles, thirty years prescription are valid, provided there has been actual corporeal possession or at least constructive possession in the case of wild or swamp lands; and that there are no minors as thirty years prescription does not run against them, or interdicts.

CHAPTER XXX

Eminent Domain.

The examiner is so rarely called upon to pass on a title which involves eminent domain, or expropriations, because property acquired by the exercise of that power is seldom passed back into commerce, and for the further reason that there are so many acts of the legislature conferring this power on corporations organized for public purposes that it would require far too much space to list them here, no attempt will be made to do so or to dissect them.

The State itself exercises this power by reason of its sovereignty, but it has granted the same power to public utilities, school boards, levee boards, corporations for educational or charitable purposes, railroads, navigation, gas, telegraph and telephone companies, etc.

Procedure in expropriation cases is to be found in the Civil Code (1), and the Revised Statutes (2).

1—R. C. C. 2626, 2639
2—Rev. Stat. 1479, 1489, 1481, 1482; Acts 117, 1886; 96, 1896; 227, 1902; 208, 1906 ;123, 1910; 176, 1928; Rev. Stat. 696 Acts 124, 1880; 268, 1916; 16, 1917 E. S.; 18, 1871; 39, 1917 E. S. 39, 1906; 80, 1908; 12, 1892; 82, 1890; 181, 1916

CHAPTER XXXI

Alienations By a Trustee Under a Trust.

Trusts have never been favored by Louisiana and it was not until 1918 (1) that they were authorized. The act of that year was followed in 1920 by two others, one of which authorized charitable and educational trusts (2); and the other certain individual trusts, with limited scope (3)· In 1935 individual trusts were abolished and the statutes on the subject repealed (4), but in 1938 (5) an act was passed in which minute restrictions and definition are set out.

Neither of the acts of 1918 or 1920 grant any specific authority to a trustee to alienate or mortgage property entrusted to his care, and although there has been no jurisprudence in this State on the subject, it would seem, that under certain conditions, such property could be sold under authority of court, that is to say act 167 of 1920 authorizing trusts for charitable and educational purposes, does not so authorize, but Act 107 of the same year, contains the following provision on the subject:

Said trustee or trustees shall administer the property entrusted to them in conformity with the directions contained in the act of donation, and shall have the powers needed for such administration, and can mortgage, pledge, alienate or encumber the designated property whenever necessary in the opinion of the trustee, unless prohibited by the donor . . .

It was provided in said act that vacancies in the trusteeship should be filed by the judge, if the method has not been provided for by the donor.

1—Act 72, 1918
2—Act 167, 1920
3—Act 107, 1920
4—7, 1935—3 E. S.
5—Act 81, 1938

The Act of 1935 (3) E. S. repealed the acts establishing private trusts, and attempted to terminate the then existing trusts established under the previous acts, but this was declared unconstitutional (1).

The specific provisions of the 1938 act as to the powers and limitations of the trustee of a trust estate are as follows:

The nature and extent of the duties and powers of the trustee shall be determined, 1 by the terms of the trust; and 2, in the absence of any provision in the terms of the trust, by the rules stated in this title and by law.

The proper court may direct or permit the trustee to deviate from the terms of the trust, if, owing to circumstances not known to the settler and not anticipated by him, compliance would defeat or substantially impair the accomplishment of the trust; and in such case, if necessary to carry out the purposes of the trust, the proper court may direct or permit the trustee to do acts which are not authorized or are forbidden by the terms of the trust.

No trustee shall directly or indirectly buy or sell any property for the trust from or to itself or an affiliate, where the trustee is a corporate trustee; or from or, to a director, officer or employee of such trustee, or of an affiliate, or from or to a relative, employer, partner or other business associate, where the trustee is a non corporate trustee.

Except as above provided, the trustee shall exercise such powers personally as: 1 conferred upon him by specific words by the terms of the trust, or,

1—Succ. Manning, 185 L.894

2 are necessary or appropriate to carry out the purposes of the trust and not forbidden by the terms of the trust.

If there are two trustees, the powers conferred upon them shall properly be exercised only by both of them, unless it is otherwise provided by the terms of the trust, or otherwise directed by the court.

The trustee shall have power to sell trust property if, 1; a power of sale is conferred in specific words, or 2; such sale is necessary or appropriate to enable the trustee to carry out the purpose of the trust, unless such sale is forbidden in specific words by the terms of the trust, or unless it appears from the terms of the trust that the property was to be retained in kind in the trust.

In passing upon a title derived from a trust estate, the examiner should examine into: 1: The instrument creating the trust: 2; that the trustee has qualified by formally accepting the trust and making bond, if required: 3; that the trustee was especially authorized by the terms of the trust to sell, or was not specifically forbidden to sell: 4; that where a sale was necessary to carry out the purpose of the trust, or under conditions and circumstances not known to the settler and not anticipated by him, or where a non sale would impair the accomplishments of the trust, that this necessity was made to appear by proper presentation to the court and a judgment ordering the sale, was rendered.

5. The instrument by which the alienation was accomplished.

The power to sell as outlined above is discretionary with the trustee, unless forbidden by the instrument establishing the trust, and the courts cannot control the exercise of this power, unless to prevent abuse.

In connection with the sale of property which is part of Trust Estate, a question was recently raised which was res novo and which has not been answered authoritatively through the courts. Under such circumstances it does not properly belong to this work, but as it involves title it is included here merely for the purpose of bringing the matter to the attention of the bar in general.

A creates a Trust Estate by will executed in 1934, for the use and benefit of a minor grandchild. The trustee is authorized by the testator to sell any of the property of the Trust Estate in specific terms. The question presented is: May property belonging to a minor, though held in Trust, be alienated without a compliance with the law governing the alienation of minor's property?

The Trust Act makes no provision for such a contingency.

Under a trust a beneficiary's ownership is deferred and title to the property is suspended and may never vest in the beneficiary insofar as any particular property may be concerned, hence, it may be said that a sale by a trustee, when authorized by the terms of the trust, is not a sale of a minor's property, but a change in the character of the asset belonging to the trust.

Again, it may be considered that a Trust is a form of mandate, which under authority of the Trust Act, may be executed after the death of the principal. Hence, the authority to sell is a mandate to sell or not to sell property belonging to the principal. The only right the minor could have would be, and is a right to the property as it existed at the time the trust ceased.

There can be no objection, however, to a proceeding taken in accordance with the laws covering the alienation of a minor's property in conjunction with a sale by the Trustee.

CHAPTER XXXII

Change of Ownership By Judgment of Court.

All suits involving title to real estate, such as petitory action, specific performances, revendications, etc, result in one of three decisions; one in favor of the plaintiff, in which there is a change of ownership; one in favor of the defendant, in which event there is a confirmation of title in him as against the claim of the plaintiff; or one dismissing the suit as in nonsuit; in which case the title remains in doubt. These remarks apply of course to other than specific performance suits. In these latter cases, it very often occurs that they are brought about by some alleged defect in the title and the judgment rendered in the case puts at rest the doubt thrown on the title, so that the examiner is not at a loss as to whether the title is good or bad anent the defect.

The judgment itself decides the issue, hence the examiner is not concerned as to the merits of the case, he is only concerned as to the jurisdiction, citation and other formalities such as signing, delay for appeal, etc·, especially in case of default.

In all such suits, the purchaser is protected by the rules which have been established by the courts and which are discussed in the chapter on Third Parties in this volume.

CHAPTER XXXIII

Bankrupt Sales.

In effect an adjudication in bankruptcy divests the bankrupt of title in the property surrendered in bankruptcy, so that neither, he, his heirs nor his creditors may be heard to attack any sale by the bankruptcy court.

Of course that court cannot create a new title, consequently such a title is open to attack by third parties other than the class mentioned above. In other words, the court cannot sell any more than the bankrupt has, but insofar as his rights are concerned, he is without the right or power to complain of any divestiture of his title made by the court. The examiner therefore is concerned only with the proceedings by which the property in bankruptcy is sold; that the formalities and requirements of the bankrupt laws governing such sales have been complied with, constitutes the only concern the examiner need have in his examination of such a link.

Title to a bankrupt's property vests in the Trustee at the time of filing of petition (1). The sale is made by the Trustee (2); The sale may be ordered by the judge or during his absence by the Referee (3). There must be ten days notice to creditors, but the court may shorten the time or order the sale without notice (4). The sale may be either at public sale or by private sale (5). The sale when made must be approved by the judge and must bring at least a price which is seventy-five per cent of the appraisal (6); which

1—Sec. 70 (a) U. S. C. A.; FCA
2—Sec. 110 (g) Ibid
3—Sec. 110 (f), Title 11 U. S. C. A.; Fed. C. A.
4—Sec.110 (94) Ibid
5—General Orders, 18 Ibid
6—110, F. Title 11 U. S. C. A.; F. D. C.

must be made by duly appointed appraisers (1).

When sale is made at auction, all the formalities required in a judicial sale, as to advertisement, etc., must be complied with· No officer of the court, and this includes Receivers, Referees and Trustees, may purchase any property of a bankrupt (2), but bankrupt may (3).

The Trustee is required to record in the conveyance office of each parish where the real estate of the bankrupt is located within ten days after he has qualified, a certified copy of the approval of his bond (4). Unless this has been done, a purchaser without knowledge of the bankruptcy proceedings is protected (5).

It has been held that the discretionery power of the referee to direct a private sale of a bankrupt estate ought not to be disturbed unless it clearly appears to have been improvidently exercised (6); but a sale of a bankrupt's property at private sale without the order of court and without appraisal and which has not been approved by the court, vests no title in the buyer (7).

As in all public sales a defective and inadequate description is fatal to the validity of title and so it has been held in bankruptcy sale (8).

A notice of sale of real estate which was merely a notice of meeting of creditors to consider the advisability of a sale of bankrupt's property, and directed such creditors to attend the sale to be held later on

1—Sec. 110 (f) Title 11, U. S. C. A.
2—Sec. 67 (b) Ibid
3—Clark v Clark, 17 Howard (U. S.) 15
4—Sec. 75 (c) U. S. C. A.; FCA
5—Vombrack v Warra, 331, Ill., 508, 17 AMB 122
6—In re Hawkins, (D. C. N. Y.) 11 AM. BR 49; 125 Fed. 633
7—In re Monsarrat (D. C. Hawaii); 25 AM. B. R., 815, 819
8—Ibid

the same day, if a sale was decided upon at the meeting, is no notice at all.

There are no specific sections in the bankruptcy act governing the administering of what has been styled "burdensome" property of a bankrupt, such property being that burdened with liens and mortgages amounting to more than the true value of the property, or in other words where there is no equity existing over and above the privileged debts owed on the property, but the jurisprudence holds that a Trustee should not administer such a property (1).

On the petition of the lien or mortgage holder, the Trustee will release such property and waive all claims against it. This release should be made only with the consent of the creditors given at a meeting called after ten days notice, or by unanimous written consent, and with the approval of the court.

1—United Realty and Home Corp. (DCMD.) 27 Fed. (2) 138; 12 AMB (N.S.) 452. In re Am. Magneston Co. (DC. Ill.) 34 Fed. (2) 681; 14 AMB (NS.) 218

CHAPTER XXXIV
Inheritance·

A succession has been defined by the Civil Code as the transmission of the rights and obligations of the deceased to the heirs (1); and also as signifying the estates, rights and charges which a person leaves after his death, whether the property exceeds the charges or the charges exceed the property, or whether he has left only charges without any property (2).

It also includes subsequently accrued rights and charges since opening of the succession as well as new charges (3). Finally it includes that right by which the heirs take possession of the estate of the deceased (4).

There are three sorts of successions.

1. Testamentary successions
2. Legal successions; and
3. Irregular successions. (5)·

Testamentary succession is that defined as that which results from the institution of an heir by last will and testament (6).

Legal succession is defined by the Civil Code as that which the law has established in favor of the nearest relations of the deceased (7); and irregular succesion is that established in favor of certain persons, or the state, in default of other heirs legal or testamentary (8).

Consequently in accordance with the above, there are three kinds of heirs. Testamentary, or instituted heirs; legal heirs or heirs of the blood; and iregular heirs (9).

1—R. C. C. 871
2—R. C. C. 872
3—R. C. C. 873
4—R. C. C. 874
5—R. C. C. 875
6—R. C. C. 876
7—R. C. C. 877
8—R. C. C. 878
9—R. C. C. 879

Prior to 1938, the husband or wife, called to the succession of the deceased spouse whether the property inherited was separate or the community property of the deceased, was obliged to have seals affixed, and to have an inventory made in the presence of a person representing the interest of the absent heir, if any (sic) and give sufficient security (1). Finally the surviving spouse could not take possession of the effects of the deceased unless authorized to do so by the judge.

These provisions still apply to the inheriting of the separate property of the deceased by the surviving spouse (2), but such spouse inherits the share of the deceased spouse in the community as a legal heir and as such takes with no more formality than would any other heir. Article 915 of the Code as amended (3), reads in part as follows: . . . shall go to the surviving spouse, who shall inherit as a legal heir by operation of law, and without the necessity of compliance with the forms of law provided in this chapter for the placing of irregular heirs in possession of the succession to which they are called.

As the essentials of a proceeding to put heirs in possession are, in the main, the same in all successions, with such exceptions as will hereafter be pointed out, the requirements of a proceeding to put legal heirs (ab intestato) will first be set forth.

These requirements are:

1. Jurisdiction of the court
2. Proof of death and heirship
3. Acceptance of the succession
4. Proof that deceased died intestate

1—R. C. C. 930
2—R. C. C. 917 and 927
3—Act 408, 1938

5. Proof that he never adopted anyone, or was adopted by anyone
6. Marital status
7. Proof as to whether or not there were any debts left by deceased
8. Location of property and inventory or listing thereof
9. Payment of inheritance tax, if any are due
10. Prayer and judgment
11. Registration of judgment.

Jurisdiction of the Court

The district courts, of course, have exclusive jurisdiction in probate matters, and the jurisdiction of the particular court is determined by the articles of the Code of Practice (1) and the Civil Code (2) on the subject.

The various articles (3) of the two codes established the jurisdiction of the courts substantially as follows:

1. In the parish where the deceased resided, if he had a domicile or fixed place of residence in the state.
2. In the parish where he left immovable property, if he had neither domicile nor place of residence in the State; or in the parish in which it appears by the inventory that his principal property was situated, if he had property in different parishes.
3. In the parish where he died, if he had no fixed residence in the State ,nor any immovable property in this State.

The courts have decided that Article 929 of the

1—929 C. P.; 935 R. C. C.
2—935 R. C. C.
3—929 C. P.; 935 R. C. C.

Code of Practice establishes the rules as to the jurisdiction of a probate court (1), although the articles of the Revised Civil Code do not diffor essentially from those of the Code of Practice. However, after a comparison of the articles of the two codes on the subject, the Supreme Court has decided finally that the ownership of real estate is the certain test of jurisdiction and that the situs of the landed or fixed property of a non-resident determines the place of the opening of the succession (2).

While the domicile of the husband is that of the wife, yet if he abandons her, she retains her former domicile for the purpose of probate proceedings, upon her death at that place (3)·

Proof of Death and Heirship: The succession, either testamentary or legal, becomes open by death or presumption of death caused by long absence, in the cases established by law (4).

Absence, though not of sufficient length to create a legal presumption of death, if coupled with other strong circumstances will be sufficient to establish death (5).

Where a succession has been opened in a parish where decedent had his domicile and that portion of the parish where he had his domicile, is made part of a new parish, the court of the old parish doesnot lose jurisdiction, unless the record of the succession has been removed by law to the new parish (6).

Where a succession has been administered for years in one parish where the deceased owned real estate, that court will not lose jurisdiction merely

1—Armstrong v Bakewell, 18 A.39
2—Randolph v Kraft, 128 L.743
3—Succ. Lasseigne, 124 L.1095
4—R. C. C. 934
5—Boyd v New England Mut. Life Ins. Co., 34 A.848
6—Beadle v Walden, 11 Rob. 67

because proof is made that deceased died in another parish (1). This merely means that whatever may have been the error made as to domicile in the opening of the succession, discovery of that error would not vitiate the proceedings nor render a change of courts necessary, where the real estate was within the jurisdiction of the original court.

Proof of Death and Heirship: The proof of death should be in the form of an official death certificate, but the affidavit of two witnesses who were well acquainted with the deceased and were in a position to certify to his actual death, would be sufficient, provided that the place and date of death were positive.

The proof of heirship should be in the form of a family tree establishing the names, ages and domiciles of each living heir and their relationship to the deceased, and the dates of death of deceased persons who might have taken, if alive.

This evidence should also show in what capacity each heir takes whether in own right and in what degree.

Proof that deceased died intestate: A search for a will is often made and the proces verbal of the notary, is sufficient. A proper affidavit by disinterested witnesses, if of a positive nature, is also sufficient.

Proof that deceased never adopted anyone or that he was not adopted by anyone: The law governing adoptions makes an adopted child or an adopted parent a forced heir and renders such proof imperative. An affidavit is about the only proof possible in most cases. This proof should also include the same information as to a predeceased heir who might have taken if

1—Gary v Sandoz, 16 L.11

alive, in such cases where representation occurs, or could have occurred.

Marital Status: This proof should be full and precise, even to the extent of an averment that the deceased, if married, was never judically separated from his spouse, this because such a separation would have put an end to the community, even though the parties had become reconciled, or a divorce had not followed, and hence affected his rights. It should also include the marital status at time of death of any heir who through predeceased might have taken, if alive.

Proof as to whether or not there were any debts left by the deceased: Affidavits are sufficient to cover this requirement, which is not of much importance, in view of the fact that it would not preclude creditors from suing.

Location of property and inventory or listing thereof: A recent act of the legislature (1), requires either an inventory or a sworn list and valuation of the property left by the deceased with the valuation thereof, should be filed in the succession (2). A full description should be given and the acquisition thereof, as a convenience to future purchasers.

Payment of Inheritance Tax, if any: This payment, or the exemption thereof, should be established with the approval of the Inheritance Tax Collector, as heirs may not take unless this is done (3). As part of this requirement, it must be alleged and proved that the deceased made no donation or other conveyance of property without due consideration prior to his death (4).

1—Act 127, 1921; 44, 1922
2—Ibid
3—Ibid
4—Ibid

Prayer and judgment: The prayer should be for recognition as heirs and for the putting and placing them in possession; and the judgment which contains a full description of all immovable property should conform thereto, be dated and signed by the judge in open court.

The acceptance of the succession by the heirs should be specially pleaded and if any of the heirs are domiciled elsewhere and represented by an agent, the authorization to accept should be in authentic form and filed in the proceedings.

Tutors and Curators may accept for their wards, (1) but it has been held that such acceptance must be by authority of the judge, on the advice of the family meeting and with the benefit of an inventory (2). Family meetings having been dispensed with, the authorization of the judge only is now necessary. In any event the minor is not liable beyond the amount of the property inherited (3), so the question is somewhat academic, unless the creditors intervene within the prescribed period.

The judgment should be properly registered.

A judgment putting the heirs in posssession is prima facie evidence of the right of the parties to have possession of the estate (4).

A summary of the codal provisions and jurisprudence thereon follows:

If the deceased has left no will, or if the will is null and void the succession is then open in favor of the legitimate heirs by the mere operation of law (5).

The opening of a succession is not necessary in

1—R. C. C. 354
2—Pargoud v Pace, 10 A.613
3—Fonelieu v Fonelieu. 116 L.866; Stephenson v Hebert, 27 A.302
4—Succ. Lisso, 194 L.828
5—R. C. C. 886

view of the principle that a legitimate and regular heir succeeds the deceased at the moment of death without any action being required on the heirs' part (1), but in practice, especially since the tax on inheritances has been imposed, the proper probate proceedings are necessary in all cases.

There are three classes of legal heirs, to-wit: The children and other lawful descendants: The fathers and mothers and other lawful ascendants; and the collateral kindred (2).

The nearest relation in the descending, ascending or collateral line, in accordance with the rules laid down by the code, is called to the legal succession (3). A child of former marriage may inherit share of mother in community acquired during second marriage (4).

The propinquity of consanguinity is established by the number of generations and each generation is called a degree (5); and the series of degrees form the line: the series of degrees between persons who descend from one and another is called the direct or lineal consanquinity, and the series of degrees between persons who do not descend from one and another, but spring from a common ancestor is called the collateral line of collateral consanquinity. The direct line is divided into a direct descending or ascending line. The first is that which connects the ancestor with those who descend from him; the second is that which connects a person with those from whom he descends (6).

In the direct line there are as many degrees as there are generations. Thus, the son in regard to the

1—Succ. Sarthon, 6 La. App. 33
2—R. C. C. 887
3—R. C. C. 888
4—Succ. Pavelka, 161 L.728
5—R. C. C. 889
6—R. C. C. 890

father is in the first degree, the grandson in the second and vice versa with regard to the father and grandfather towards the sons and grandsons (1). Children are descendants in the first degree; grandchildren in the second degree (2).

In the collateral line the degrees are counted by the generations from one of the relations up to the common ancestor exclusively and from the common ancestor to the other relations .Thus brothers are related in the second degree; uncle and nephew in the third degree, cousins german in the fourth degree and so on (3).

In matters of legal succession no difference of sex and no primogeniture are known; but they are regulated by the most perfect equality (4).

Of Representation.

Representation is a fiction of law, the effect of which is to put the representative in the place, degree and rights of the person represented (5). Representation take place ad infinitum in the direct descending line. It is admitted in all cases whether the children of the deceased concur with the descendants of a predeceased child, or whether all the children having died before him, the descendants of the children be in equal or unequal degrees of relationship to the deceased (6). In the collateral line representation is admitted in favor of the children and descendants of the brothers and sisters of the deceased, whether they come to the succession in concurrence with the uncles and aunts, or whether the brothers and sisters of the

1—R. C. C. 891
2—Walker v Vicksburg R. R., 110 L.719, 718
3—R. C. C. 892
4—R. C. C. 893
5—R. C. C. 894
6—R. C. C. 894

deceased having died, the succession devolves on their descendants in equal or unequal degrees (1).

Children of a predeceased brother take in the succession of an uncle by right of law. Though their father might not have taken by reason of certain acts or omissions, they are not estopped on that account (2).

In all cases in which the representation is admitted the partition is made by root; if one root has produced several branches, the subdivision is also made by roots in each branch and the members of the branch take between them by heads (3). Person deceased only can be represented; persons living cannot (4).

One who has renounced the succession of another may still enjoy the right of representation with respect to that other. Thus it is not necessary that the children who succeed by representation should have been heirs of their father or mother. Although they should have renounced their succession, they are nevertheless competent to represent them in the succession of their grandfather or other ascendants (5).

If a person has been disinherited by his father or mother, or excluded from the succession for unworthiness, his children cannot represent him in the succession of their grandfather or grandmother, or other ascendants if he be alive at the time of the opening of the succession, but they can represent him if he died before (6). Legitimate children, or their descendants inherit from their father and mother, grandfathers or grandmothers without distinction of

1—R. C. C. 897; Succ. Jacobs, 129, 432; Succ. Morgan, 23 A.290
2—McKenzie v Breen, 40 A.157
3—R. C. C. 898
4—R. C. C. 899
5—R. C. C. 900
6—R. C. C. 901

sex or primegeniture and though they be born of different marriages. They inherit in equal portions and by heads, when they are in the same degree and inherit in their own right; they inherit by roots when all or part of them inherit by representation (1).

Ascendants.

If any one dies leaving no descendants, but a father and mother, and brothers and sisters or descendants of these last, the succession is divided into two equal parts, one of which goes to the father and mother, who divide it equally between them, the other to the brothers and sisters of the deceased, or their descendants, as is prescribed in the following section (2). This Article and Article 911 of the Civil Code refer to intestate successions; Article 1493 and 1494 refer to testate successions. There is this distinction between the distribution of an estate under Articles 903, 904 and 911 of the Code; if the deceased leaves no will his property is distributed and controlled by the latter articles; if on the contrary he disposes of his estate by last will and testament, he is bound to leave his parent, or parents, one-third of his estate; he may leave them more, but he cannot leave them less (3).

If the father or mother of the person who has died without issue, has died before him, the portion which would have been inherited by such deceased parent, acording to the terms of the preceding article will go to the brothers and sisters of the deceased or descendants in the manner directed by the following article (4).

1—R. C. C. 902
2—R. C. C. 903
3—Succ. Messina. 123 L.469; Succ. Jacobs. L.456
4—R C. C. 904

Where only one parent survives, that parent inherits one-fourth of the estate, the brothers and-or sisters inherit three fourths (1).

If the deceased has left neither descendants nor brothers nor sisters nor descendants from them, nor father nor mother, but only other ascendants these ascendants inherit to the succession to the exclusion of all collaterals in conformity with the articles which follow (2).

If there are ascendants in the paternal and the maternal lines in the same degree the estate is divided into two equal shares, one of which goes to the ascendants in the paternal line and the other to the ascendants in the maternal line, whether the number of ascendants on each side be equal or not. In this case the ascendants in each line inherit by heads (3).

But if there is in the nearest degree but one ascendant in the two lines, such ascendant excludes all other ascendants of a more remote degree and alone takes the succession (4). In other words representation does not take place in the ascending line.

Ascendants to the exclusion of all others inherit the immovables given by them to their children or their descendants in a more remote degree who die without posterity, when these objects are found in the succession. In the event that these objects have been alienated by the donees, such objects revert to the donor because of the happening of a condition which is part of the alienation (5).

If a person dies, leaving no descendants and his father and mother survive, his brothers and sisters or

1—Grover v Clark. 7 A.794; Monroe v Pitre, 149 L.910
2—R. C. C. 905
3—R. C. C. 906
4—R. C. C. 907
5—R C. C. 908

their descendants only inherit one-half of his succession. If the father or mother only survive the brothers and sisters or their descendants inherit three-fourths of his succession (1).

The property so inherited by the father or mother under the above provision, reverts to the brothers and/or sisters of the deceased, in the event of the remarriage of either parent, under Article 1753 of the Code, but this article has been repealed (2).

If a person dies leaving no descendants, nor father or mother, his brothers and sisters or their descendants inherit the whole succession to the exclusion of the ascendants and other collaterals (3). The partition of the three-fourths or the whole of the succession falling to brothers and sisters as mentioned in the two preceding articles, is made in equal portions, if they are all of the same marriage; if they are of different marriages, the succession is divided equally between the paternal and maternal lines of the deceased; the german brothers and sisters take a part in the two lines, the paternal and the maternal brothers and sisters, each in their respective lines only; if there are brothers and sisters in one line only they inherit the whole succession to the exclusion of all other relatives of the other line (4). When the deceased has died without descendants, brothers or sisters, or descendants from the latter, or father or mother, ascendants in the paternal or maternal lines, his succession passes to his collateral relations. Among the collateral relations he who is the nearest in degree excludes all the others, and if there are several in the same degree they partake equally and by heads, ac-

1—R. C. C. 911
2—Act 238, 1918
3—R. C. C. 912
4—R. C. C. 913

cording to their number (1). No distinction is made between whole and half blood among collaterals, but where brothers and sisters are of the whole and half blood (2), that is, some are of the whole blood and some of the half blood, the former take three-fourths and the latter one-fourth of the succession (3). A half brother or sister takes one-sixth, while children of a predeceased sister or brother of the whole blood will take five-sixths (4).

It has been said a collateral heir need only aver that there are no heirs in a descending line, and he need not prove it, nor need he prove that his kindred died intestate, unmarried and without issue, unless evidence is offered to the contrary (5), but as in the event that the contrary was true, his right would be affected, proof at least in the form of sworn affidavits, should be filed in the proceedings, especially, where brothers and sisters take, as in such cases representation takes place ad infinitum. This is particularly true where a brother or sister has died since the death of the person whose succession is involved.

There are two factors which may be interjected in succession proceedings, whether they be testate or intestate, and so do not belong particularly to legal succession but may as well be discussed here as in any other kind of succession.

Those factors are the renunciation by the widow or wife and the renunciation by the heir.

These renunciations present several questions which should be answered. First: The form in which

1—R. C. C. 914
2—Pierson v Grice, 6 A.232
3—Sharp v Kleinpetor, 7 A.264
4—King v Neely, 14 A.165; R. C. C. 909
5—Hooter v Tippot, 12 Martin (O.S.) 390; Miller v McElwee, 12 A.476; DeGentile v White castle Lbr. Co., 130 L.705

such renunciation should be made: and Second: The effect of such renunciations.

In both cases the renunciation, if not made judically, as in the succession proceedings (in which event the pleadings should be signed by the renouncer), it should be made by a public act before a notary and two witnesses (1). The latter is the form prescribed by the Civil Code (2), but the renunciation may be made judicially (3).

The words wife or widow are used as the wife may renounce in divorce proceedings and the widow renounce in successions, but in either event the effect is the same.

Whether widow or wife, her renunciation places her in the position of an entire stranger to the community property (4) with the result that any residue which may remain after payment of all debts of the community may not be claimed by her (5), such residue reverting to the husband, or his heirs as the case may be. The wife's or widow's renunciation is generally made for the purpose of avoiding personal responsibility for the community debts, but occasionally the widow makes a renunciation for the benefit of the heirs. In the latter case, it would amount to a donation and would be subject to all the rules obtaining in that class of transfers.

The heir who renounces may do so to avoid personal responsibility for the debts of the community, or he may make it for the benefit of his co-heirs. The whole subject of renunciations has been fully discussed in another chapter, but there is one phase

1—R. C. C. 1017, 2415
2—R. C. C. 1017, 2415
3—Union Nat'l Bank v Chopin, 46 A.629
4—Smith v Reddich, 42 A.1055; R. C. C. 2411
5—R. C. C. 2411

which requires some inquiry in connection with the reversion which takes place where the renunciation has been in favor of the coheirs.

The portion of the heir renouncing the succession, goes to his coheirs of the same degree; if he has no co-heirs of the same degree it goes to those in the next degree. This right of accretion only takes place in legal or intestate successions. In testamentary successions, it is only exercised in relation to legacies and in certain cases (1).

This article has given rise to serious doubts in the minds of the members of the profession (2), as to who would take in certain cases. For instance: There are four brothers, A. B. C. and D. A dies leaving B and one child of C who predeceased A. Ordinarily B, D and the child of C would inherit equally, the latter by representation, but D renounces. The question arises, does the provisions above quoted, preclude the child from inheriting D's share? The article does provide that in the event of a renunciation, accretion takes place in favor of those who are in the same degree with the renouncer and a nephew is not in the same degree with an uncle, but as Article 894 R.C.C. provides that representation is a fiction of law, the effect of which is to put the representative in the place, DEGREE and rights of the person represented, it would seem that the child of C is by that fiction of law in the same degree as B.

In the case of the Union National Bank versus Choppin, reported in the 46 La. Ann, 629, it was decided that a mother's heirs having renounced her succession, which succession included the mother's interest in her brother's succession, that interest de-

1—R. C. C. 1022
2—4 T. L. Review 445

volved upon her brothers and sisters, but the decision seems to have turned on the point that the children themselves, in renouncing their mother's succession, in effect renounced her brother's succession.

Forced heirs of an heir who has renounced in a succession are not creditors who might have attacked the renunciation under Article 1021 of the Civil Code and have no interest in property held by one under the benefit of the renunciation (1).

Creditors may accept in the stead of an heir who has renounced but this right is barred by prescription.

The Civil Code requires a renunciation to be made before a notary and two witnesses, in authentic form, but it may be made by judicial proceedings (2). A renunciation to be a real renunciation and not a donation, must have as its intent to renounce the renouncer's interest in toto. One made, however, in favor of all the heirs without distinction is a renunciation, provided that it is made without consideration past or future (3).

One who renounces cannot revoke his renunciation, after the co-heirs have accepted the succession (4).

1—Aurienne v Olivet, 164 L.1071
2—Carter v Fowler, 33 A.100; Union Nat'l. Bank v Choppin, 46 A.629
3—Aurienne v Olivet, 164 L.1071
4—Succ. Hymel, 49 A.461

CHAPTER XXXV

Irregular Successions

The rules in irregular succession as to jurisdiction, parties etc., are the same as in other successions, but the family tree is not required. However, certain other essentials must be contained in the proceedings·

There are three classes of irregular heirs: The surviving wife or husband; natural children and parents; the State. Each class takes according to different rules.

The surviving spouse, as has been shown, insofar as the community property is concerned, is no longer an irregular heir, having been placed among the legal heirs taking according to the rules governing that class of heirs (1), but in reference to the separate property left by the deceased spouse, he or she can only take possession of the succession property in accordance with the provisions of the Civil Code as hereinafter set forth.

Natural children and their natural parents, the other class of irregular heirs, inherit from each other only under conditions which vary according to which parent they inherit from, and vice versa, which parent inherits from the child.

The allegations and proofs produced in the proceedings must conform to whatever condition exists.

These allegations and proofs in the case of a surviving spouse are:

If the wife survives the husband, she must prove;

1. That her husband left no lawful descendants, ascendants or collaterals.

2. That she has not been separated or divorced from her husband.

1—Act 408, 1938

Separated means judicially separated (1).

If it is the husband who has survived he must prove, in addition to the foregoing, that his wife left no natural children, duly acknowledged.

The wife living apart from her husband, but not separated from him if he dies intestate and leaving no ascendants, descendants, or collateral relatives, inherits from him (2).

This article is the sole rule governing a wife's right to inherit the separate property of her husband, who has died intestate (3).

The wife inherits from her husband, who has left no legitimate relations to the exclusion of his natural children, although they have been acknowledged by him (4). Also his natural collaterals (5).

The husband, whose wife dies intestate, must allege and prove.

1. That she died leaving no ascendants, descendants, or collateral relatives.

2. That she left no natural children, duly acknowledged by her.

3. That he has not been judicially separated or divorced from his wife.

As a matter of fact he inherits from his wife to the exclusion only of the State (6), her natural father, mother, brothers, sisters and other natural collaterals (7).

The allegations and proofs required in the case

1—R. C. C. 924, Gates v Walker, 8 A.277; Succ. Rogge, 50 A.122
2—Gates v Walker, 8 A.277
3—Dirmeyer v O'Hara, 39 A.961
4—Victor v Tagliasco, 6 L.646; Johnson v Sugar, 163 La. 785
5—Succ. Miller, 27 A.69
6—R. C. C. 924
7—Duplassis v Young, 11 A.120; Felix v Bruce, 14 Orleans La. App. 64; Penn v Jones, 5 La. App. 371

of a natural child inheriting from a natural mother are:

1. That he has been duly acknowledged by his mother
2. That she has left no lawful children or descendants

Under articles (1) of the Civil Code a duly acknowledged child of a wife, born before her marriage, inherits her share of the community to the exclusion of the husband, and this nothwithstanding the fact that a surviving wife inherits the community to the exclusion of her husband's natural children (2).

If he inherits from his natural father he must allege and prove:

1. That he has been duly acknowledged by his father
2. That his father left no descendants or ascendants or collaterals·

Bastard, adulterous or incestuous children shall not enjoy the right of inheriting the estates of their natural father or mother, in any of the cases mentioned above, the law allowing them nothing more than mere alimony (3); nor do natural children inherit from the legitimate relations of their father or mother, or vice versa (4).

The father and/or mother called to the inheritance of a natural child must allege and prove:

1. That he, she or they have duly acknowledged the natural child

2. That he left no children natural or legitimate

Brothers and sisters called to the succession of a deceased brother or sister must allege and prove:

1—R. C. C. 915, 918, as amended by Act 160, 1920
2—Brooks v House, 168 L.542
3—R. C. C. 920
4—R. C. C. 921

1. If any take by representation (1) they must show that their ancestor through whom they take ,is dead.

2. That the deceased never married or was not married at the time of his death.

Natural brothers and sisters do not inherit to the exclusion of natural children (2).

In all cases where natural children are called to the succession of their parents, they may take possession of the estate only upon order of the judge (3) and upon calling in the relations of the deceased who would have inherited in default of natural children, if they are present or represented in the State, or by appointing a person to represent them, if they are absent from the State, in the case of the mother (4); and upon taking an inventory in the presence of a curator or other representative of absent heirs, appointed by the judge, and upon giving sufficient security in an amount of two-thirds of the inventory in the case of the father (5).

The surviving husband or wife called to the succession of the other must cause the seals to be affixed, and be authorized to take possession of the estate by. the judge, after having caused a true and faithful inventory to be made, in the presence of a person appointed to defend the interest of absent heirs of the deceased, if any, and having given good and sufficient bond as prescribed in the following article (6).

The natural father, mother and children called to the succession of each other as hereinbefore set forth,

1—R. C. C. 923
2—Bourriaque v Charles, 107, 221
3—R. C. C. 925, 926
4—R. C. C. 926
5—R. C. C. 927, 928
6—R. C. C. 929

can not alienate the immovables belonging to the succession, unless it be under authority of the court at public auction and in cases in which their alienation is deemed necessary (1).

Natural persons who are related to other natural persons may inherit from each other, as an acknowledged natural child from her natural aunt (2), but they may not inherit from a legitimate relation (3). There is no law authorizing the aunt to inherit from her illegitimate nephew. Collaterals as used in Article 917 means lawful collateral relatives (4).

The State inherits, or rather the property escheats to the State only to the exclusion of unacknowledged children or bastards (5). Bastards are barred from inheriting under all circumstances (6).

The following articles of the Civil Code are of the utmost importance as the rights of those who claim under them are rigidly regulated and prescribed.

In all cases when either husband or wife shall die, leaving no descendants, nor ascendants and without having disposed by last will and testament of his or her share of the community property, such undisposed share shall be inherited by the survivor in full ownership (7). Prior to 1910, the share of the deceased spouse went to the nearest of the kin. The Act of that year put the surviving spouse ahead of all relations except the descendants or ascendants but the Supreme Court held that if the deceased did leave a father or a mother, the surviving spouse did not inherit and the share of the deceased in the commun-

1—R. C. C. 932
2—51 A.1584
3—R. C. C. 921; Montagut v Bacas, 42 A.169
4—Ibid
5—Succ. Vance, 110 L.764
6—R. C. C. 919
7—R. C. C. 915

ity property devolved upon the surviving ascendant and the brothers and sisters, if any (1).

Under further amendments enacted in 1916 and 1920, if either spouse dies intestate, the surviving spouse inherits one-half of the deceased's share of the community and the father and/or mother inherits the other half, provided they or either of them survive the deceased, otherwise the whole goes to the surviving spouse (2).

As has been shown, the surviving spouse, in regard to the community property has been placed among the legal heirs (3), so that Article 915 is no longer a part of irregular succession.

When the deceased left neither lawful descendants nor lawful ascendants, nor collateral relations, the law calls to the inheritance, either the surviving husband or wife, or his or her natural children, or the State in the manner and order hereafter directed (4).

Natural children are called to the succession of their natural mother, when they have been acknowledged by her, if she left no lawful children or descendants, to the exclusion of her father and mother and other ascendants or collaterals of lawful kindred. (5).

The brothers and sisters of a natural child acknowledged by the mother, succeed to that child's estate, if there is no other legal impediment. Acknowledgement is a prerequisite in such a case. Person, issue of an illegitimate union leave no heirs unless they are acknowledged. The property goes to the State by operation of law (6).

1—Lehman v Lehman, 130 L.960
2—Acts 80, 1916 and 160, 1920
3—Act 408, 1938
4—R. C. C. 917
5—R. C. C.918
6—Succ. Gravier, 125 L.733; Cordill v Quaker Realty Co., 130 L.933

Natural children are called to the inheritance of their natural father who has duly acknowledged them when he has no descendants nor ascendants, nor collateral relatives, nor surviving wife, to the exclusion of the State only (1).

Bastards, adulterous or incestuous children shall not enjoy the right of inheriting the estates of their natural father or mother, in any of the cases above mentioned, the law allowing them nothing more than a mere alimony (2)·

The law does not grant any right of inheritance to natural children to the estate of the legitimate relations of their father or mother (3).

The estate of a natural child deceased without posterity belongs to the father or mother who has acknowledged him, or to both when both have acknowledged him (4).

If the father or mother of the natural child died before him his natural brothers and sisters inherit his estate (5).

If a married man has left no lawful descendants, nor ascendants, nor any collateral relations, but a surviving wife, not separated from bed and board from him, the wife shall inherit from him to the exclusion of any natural child or children duly acknowledged (6).

If on the contrary it is the wife who died without leaving any lawful ascendants, nor descendants, or collateral relations, her surviving husband not separated from bed and board from her, shall not inherit

1—R. C. C. 919
2—R. C. C. 920; Marshall v Smedley, 166 L.364; Prieto v Succ. Prieto. 165 L.710
3—R. C. C. 921; Succ. Cloud, 7 A.407
4—R. C. C. 922; Perkins v Brownell-Drews Lbr. Co., 187 L.337
5—R. C. C. 923
6—R. C. C. 924

from her, except she should leave no natural child or children duly acknowledged by her (1).

The following seven articles (2), prescribe the manner in which irregular heirs shall be permitted to take possession of the estates of those from whom they inherit, all of which has been outlined in previous pages.

1—R. C. C. 924
2—R. C. C. 925, 926, 927, 928, 930, 931, 932

CHAPTER XXXVI

Testate Successions

In testate successions, the probate proceeding, that is the jurisdiction, parties, allegations and proofs, should conform as far as is practical to those rules prescribed for intestate successions.

The family tree is necessary in order to establish correctly either that the deceased left no forced heirs, or if he left any, just who they are, including ascendants and descendants, adopted children or adopted parents.

The next step in the proper order of proceeding in these kind of successions, is the probate of the will or testament of the deceased, under the provisions of which the estate is to be distributed·

The Civil Code provides minutely for the proof and execution of wills.

No testament can have effect unless it has been presented to the judge of the parish in which the succession is opened (1); the execution of a testament shall not be ordered until the death of the testator has been sufficiently proved to the judge to whom the testament is presented (2); when this has been done, the judge shall immediately proceed to open the will, if it be sealed and to the proof of it (3).

Nuncupative testaments received by public act do not require to be proved that their execution may be ordered; they are full proof of themselves, unless the are alleged to be forged (4).

Nuncupative testaments under private signature must be proved by the declaration of at least three of the witnesses who were present when they were

1—R. C. C. 1644, 928, 929, 935
2—R. C. C. 1645, 932
3—R. C. C. 1646
4—R. C. C. 1647

made (1) to the effect that they recognize the testament as being the same that was written in their presence or which the testator had declared had been written out of their presence, and which he had declared contained his last will and testament; and also that they recognize their signatures and that of the testator if they signed, or the signature of him who signed for them in case of their not having been able to sign for want of knowledge (2).

The execution of mystic wills can not be ordered until they have been in like manner proved by the declaration under oath of at least four witnesses who were present at the act of superscription (3), which declaration must be in substance that they recognize the sealed packet presented as being the same package delivered by the testator to the notary in their presence; and also that they recognize their signatures and that of the notary, if they have signed it, or the signature of him who signed it for them, if they knew not how to write (4).

In all of the above cases, when it is impossible to obtain the necessary number of witnesses to the will, because of death or absence from the State, it will be sufficient to prove the signature of the testator by two creditable witnesses who were well acquainted with his signature (5).

The olographic testament shall be opened, if it be sealed and proved by the testimony of two credible witnesses, who must attest that they recognize the instrument as being entirely written, dated and signed in testator's handwriting. The judge shall satisfy

1—R. C. C. 1648
2—R. C. C. 1649
3—R. C. C. 1650
4—R. C. C. 1651, 1652
5—R. C. C. Arts. 1653, 1654

himself that the witnesses are familiar with the testator's handwriting, and make mention of the whole proceeding in his proces verbal (1). He shall then order the execution of the instrument and direct the filing of such testaments as have not been passed by public act, after having paraphed the document ne varietur at the top and bottom of each page (2).

The judge must appoint counsel to represent heirs who are absent and not represented, from the State (3).

Testaments made in foreign countries and in other States of the Union, cannot be carried into execution as to property in this State, without being registered in the court having jurisdiction over the property (4). Where immovables are situated in different parishes it will be sufficient that the succession be opened and the testament registered in the parish where the principal property is situated (5).

The will may be ordered executed without any proof than that it has been proved before a competent judge of the place where it was received. If it has not been proved there it must be proved in the Louisiana Court (6), even though the foreign State does not require probate (7). In all cases the original will or a certified copy thereof must be produced before execution can be ordered (8).

The foregoing is but a prelude to any examination of a title based upon a testamentary disposition because before it is completed the examiner will have occasion to resort to more than a third of the articles

1—R. C. C. 1655 ; Grandchamps v Billis, 124 L.117
2—R. C. C. 1657
3—R. C. C. 1661
4—R. C. C. 1688
5—Act 176, 1912; C. P. 919
6—R. C. C. 1689, Succ. Drysdale, 121 L.816; Succ. Butler,30 A.890
7—Roberts v Allier's Heirs, 17 L.18
8—Succ. Henry, 113 L.790

contained in the Civil Code as embraced within the range of the examination, which are the principles of law governing donations, forced heirship, legal and irregular heirs, the capacity of the testator to donate, the capacity of the heirs and legatees to receive and the requisites for a valid will.

The subject of donations has been treated in part in connection with other links so the discussion here will be confined to the donation mortis causa and the principles of law governing same.

Property can neither be acquired nor disposed of gratuitously unless by donations inter vivos or mortis causa made in the forms hereinafter established (1); a donation mortis causa (in prospect of death) is an act to take effect when the donor shall no longer exist, by which he disposes of the whole or a part of his property (2); all persons may dispose or receive by a donation mortis causa, except such as the law expressly declares incapable (3); the incapacities are absolute or relative; absolute incapacities prevent the giving or receiving indefinitely with regard to all persons; relative incapacities prevent the giving to certain persons or receiving from them (4); it is sufficient if the capacity of giving exists at the moment the donation is made (5); with regard to the capacity of receiving it is sufficient if it exists at the moment of the opening of the succession of the testator (6). Status at the time of death determines capacity to inherit (7).

When the donation depends upon the fulfillment of a condition, it is sufficient if the donee is capable

1—R. C. C. 1467
2—R. C. C. 1469
3—R. C. C. 1470
4—R. C. C. 1471
5—R. C. C. 1472
6—R. C. C. 1473
7—Succ. Vance, 110 L.765

of receiving at the moment the condition is accomplished (1). One must be of sound mind in order to be able to make a donation mortis causa (2); the minor under sixteen years cannot dispose of any property by donation mortis causa (3); but the minor above the age of sixteen may, to the same extent as can a person of full age, even to the prejudice of the usufruct enjoyed by law to the father and mother during marriage on the property of the minor, and he does not need the authorization of his tutor (4); the wife may dispose of her property by a donation mortis causa without the authorization of her husband (5).

The minor above the age of sixteen may not make a donation mortis causa in favor of his tutor, nor his preceptors or instructors, whilst he is under their authority (6); nor can he even when he becomes of age, make such a donation in favor of his tutor, unless the final account of tutorship has been previously rendered and settled (7). The two cases above mentioned do not apply to the relations of the minor who have been his tutors or instructors.

Those living in open concubinage are respectively incapable of making a donation mortis causa to each other (9). If they afterwards marry this rule does not apply (10).

In order to be able to receive by donations mortis causa, it suffices to be conceived at the time of the death of the deceased, but the donations of the last

1—R. C. C. 1473
2—R. C. C. 1475
3—R. C. C. 1476
4—R. C. C. 1477; 373
5—R. C. C. 135
6—R. C. C. 1478
7—R. C. C. 1479
8—R. C. C. 1479
9—R. C. C. 1481; Succ. Filhiol, 119 L.998; Lazare v Jacques, 15 A.599
10—R. C. C. 1481

will can have effect only in case the child is born alive (1); natural or acknowledged illegitimate children cannot receive from their natural parents donations mortis causa, beyond what is strictly necessary to procure them sustenance or an occupation or profession, whenever the father or mother leave legitimate children. These donations shall be reducible in case of excess according to the rules laid down under the title "Father and Child" (2); when the natural mother has not left any legitimate children or descendants, natural children may acquire from her by donation mortis causa, to the whole amount of her succession (3); when the natural father has not left legitimate children, or descendants the natural child or children acknowledged by him may receive from him by donation mortis causa the amount of the following proportions; one-fourth if he leaves legitimate ascendants, or legitimate brothers or sisters of descendants from such brothers or sisters; and one-third if he leaves more remote collateral relations. If by sale or disguised donation a father attempted to give illegitimate children unacknowledged by him, more than one-fourth, the transaction is absolutely null (4). In all cases where the father gives his natural children the portion permitted by law, he is bound to dispose of the rest of his property in favor of his legitimate relations; every other disposition shall be null except those which he may make in favor of some public institution (5).

This article does not constitute his legitimate relations forced heirs; nor does it render void the dispo-

1—R. C. C. 1482
2—R. C. C. 1483; 213; 918
3—R. C. C. 1484
4—R. C. C. 1486; Bobinette's Heirs v Verdun's Vendees, 14 L.547
5—R. C. C. 1487

sitions in favor of his natural children, though he makes no disposition of the residue of his estate, or subsequently dispose of it in favor of persons not his legitimate relations. He could will his property to any of his legitimate relations he chose (1).

Natural fathers and mothers can in no case dispose of property in favor of their adulterous or incestuous children, except the mere amount necessary for their sustenance or to procure them an occupation or profession by which to support themselves; Doctors or surgeons who have professionally attended a person during the sickness of which he died, cannot receive any benefit from donations mortis causa made in their favor by the sick person during that sickness. To this however there are the following exceptions:

1. Remunerative dispositions

2. Universal dispositions in case of consanquinity.

The same rules are observed with regard to ministers of religious worship (2).

Donations mortis causa may be made in favor of the stranger when the laws of his country do not prohibit similar dispositions from being made in favor of citizens of this State (3); every disposition in favor of a person incapable of receiving shall be null, whether it be disguised under the form of an onerous contract, or be made under the names of persons interposed. The father and mother, the children and the husband and wife of the incapable person shall be reputed persons interposed. This article does not ap-

1—Compton v Prescott, 12 Rob. 56; Nelder v McCarty, 7 A.86;
Prevost v Martel, 10 Rob. 516
2—R. C. C. 1488
3—R. C. C. 1490

ply to duly acknowledged natural chidren of testator, though children of incapable persons (1).

Proof is not admitted of the disposition having been made through hatred, suggestion or captation (2). This article has been the means of cutting off in this State, a vast amount of litigation which, in common law states, arise in innumerable cases.

Forced Heirship: While the law covering this subject is clear and explicit, the examiner has the task of checking the probate proceedings to ascertain as far as possible, whether or not the dispositions made by the testator violate them. It is to be understood, of course, that such violations must appear in the record as he is not compelled to seek elsewhere. Equally so where all the known forced heirs have been made parties to the proceedings and they have accepted the succession in whatever proportions the testator may have fixed· Again prescription may have cured whatever defects exist. However, in the Chapter entitled "Defects and their Cures," wiil be found discussion covering all these points, this chapter being intended to give the law as it exists and as furnishing the basis of what should be found in these proceedings.

Donations either intervivos or mortis causa cannot exceed two-thirds of the property of the disposer if he leaves at his decease a legitimate child; onehalf if he leaves two children and one-third if he leaves three or a greater number. Under the name of children are descendants of whatever degree they may be, it being understood that they are only counted for the child they represent (3).

1—Compton v Prescott, 12 Rob. 62
2—R. C. C. 1492
3—R. C. C. 1493

Donations inter vivos or mortis causa cannot exceed two-thirds of the property, if the disposer having no children, leaves a father, mother or both (1). Legitime of father and mother is one-third if child makes a will and one-fourth if he does not (2). In the cases prescribed by the last two preceding articles the heirs are called forced heirs because the donor cannot deprive them of the portion of his estate reserved to them by law, except in cases where he has a just cause to disinherit them (3). To protect legitime forced heirs may contest recitals in ancestors deed (4). Where there are no legitimate descendants, and in case of previous decease of the father and mother, donations inter vivos or mortis causa may be made to the whole amount of the property of disposer saving the reservation made hereafter·

Forced heirs have the right to annul absolutely and by parol evidence the simulated contracts of those from whom they inherit and shall not be restricted to their legitime (5).

The disposable quantum maybe given in whole by an act inter vivos or mortis causa, to one or more of the disposer's children or successible descendants, to the prejudice of his other children or successible descendants, without it being liable to be brought into the succession by the donee or legatee, provided it be expressly declared by the donor that this disposition is intended to be over and above the legitime (6).

This declaration may be made, either by the act

1—R. C. C. 1494
2—R. C. C. 1495; Succ. Marks, 35 A.993; R. C. C,903
3—R. C. C. 1495
4—Boone v Carroll, 35 A.281
5—Act 5, 1884; Chachere v Superior Oil Co., 192 L.193;
    Succ. Black, 137 L.302
6—R. C. C. 1501

containing the disposition or subsequently by an instrument executed before a notary public and two witnesses (1). The declaration must be explicit and not left to inference (2).

Immovable property brought back into the succession through the effect of a reduction is brought free of all charges and mortgages created by the donee (3); the action of reduction or revendication may be brought by the heirs against third persons holding the immovable property which has been alienated by the donee, in the same manner as they may against the donee himself ,but only after discussion of the property of donee (4).

Last Will and Testament

In no other part of the Civil Code, are there more exact minute and strict regulations for the confecting of an instrument than in those articles and chapters devoted to last wills and testaments. In addition the courts have insisted upon the closest adherence to these requirements, so that unless a will meets those requirements, it is without the slightest validity.

No disposition mortis causa shall henceforth be made otherwise than by last will and testament. Every other form is abrogated. But the name given to an act of last will is of no importance and dispositions made by testament under this title, or under that of institution of heirs, of legacy, codicil, donation mortis causa, or under any other name indicating the last will, provided that the act be clothed with the forms required for the validity of a testament and that the clauses in it, or the manner in which it is made, clearly established that it is a disposition of

1—R. C. C. 1501
2—Succ. Ford, 130 L.442
3—R. C. C. 1516
4—R. C. C. 1517

last will. Thus an act of last will by which an individual disposes of his property, in any manner whatsoever, whether he has instituted an heir, or only named legatees, whether he has or has not charged anyone with the execution of his last will, is considered as a testament, if it be, in other respects, clothed with the formalities required by law (1). A testament is the act of last will clothed with certain solemnities by which the testator disposes of his property, either universally or by universal title, or any particular title (2). A simple direction to distribute the estate among the legal heirs according to law, is a will (3). A testament cannot be made by the same act by two or more persons. either for the benefit of a third person, or under the title of a reciprocal or mutual disposition (4). Two different acts on the same day not prohibited (5).

The custom of willing by testament by the intervention of a commissary or agent in fact, is abolished. Thus the institution of an heir and all other testamentary dispositions committed to the choice of a third party, are null, even should that choice be limited to a certain number of persons designated by the testator (6).

Testator cannot leave the selection of charitable institutions to receive bequests to his executors (7).

All testaments are divided into three principal classes, to-wit:

1. Nuncupative or open testaments

2. Mystic or sealed testaments

1—R. C. C. 1570
2—R. C. C. 1571
3—Succ. Schiller, 33 A.1
4—R. C. C. 1572
5—Wood v Roane, 35 A.865
6—R. C. C. 1573; Succ. Villa, 132 L.714
7—Succ. Burke, 51 A.538; Succ. Purkert, 184 L.803

3. Olographic testaments (1)

Testaments whether nuncupative or mystic must be drawn up in writing either by the testator himself, or by some person under his dictation (2).

Any will may be made, even by a notary, on a Sunday or other holiday (3).

The custom of making verbal testaments, that is to say resulting from the mere disposition of witnesses who were present when the testator made known to them his will without having reduced it to writing, is abrogated (4); the nuncupative testaments by public act must be received by a notary public in the presence of three witnesses residing in the place where the will is executed, or of five witnesses not residing in the place. This testament must be dictated by the testator and written by the notary as it is dictated. It must then be read to the testator in the presence of the witnesses. Express mention is made of the whole, observing that all those formalities must be fulfilled at one time, without interruption and without turning aside to other acts (5). It is not sufficient for testator to hand the notary slips of paper with his wishes thereon, saying "Like that" (6), but witness may read draft when testator repeats (7).

The nuncupative will by public act must mention every formality as having been observed, for the reason that the lack of such statements in the will cannot be supplied by oral testimony, or testimony of any kind (8).

Some latitude has been permitted in the observ-

1—R. C. C. 1574
2—R. C. C. 1575
3—Keller v McCallop, 12 Rob. 639
4—R. C. C. 1576
5—R. C. C. 1578
6—Succ. Theriot, 114 L.611
7—Golden v Executors of Burke, 35 A.160
8—LeBlanc v Borr's Heirs, 16 L.88; Succ. Davis, 37 A.834

ance of the formalities where the language of the Code is not explicit, as for instance while the testator must dictate his wishes, his counsel may assist in selecting words and shaping phrases which testator uses (1); and, it is not required that notary use the exact language of testator provided that he does not change its meaning (2).

In other respects the courts have insisted upon a precise and close following of the requisites of the law. Not only must the will be dictated by the testator and written down by the notary, but express mention of the fact that this was done must be made (3). The statement that the witnesses were competent has been held as not a sufficient compliance with the law. The will as confected must state that these witnesses resided in the parish, or that one or more of the five required if three witnesses residing in the parish cannot to be found, resided in another parish (4). On the other hand the turning aside to other acts, prohibited by the article, has been interpreted to mean acts which are not connected with the confecting of the will, a discussion of the phraseology and other matters connected with the making of the will, not constituting turning aside to other acts (5).

Express mention of the whole: The above and foregoing was written by me, notary, as dictated to me, by the said testator, the said Donald Monroe, in the presence of the said A. B. and C., and then read by me notary to the testator in the presence and hearing of said witnesses, all at one and the same time

1—Laundry v Tcmates, 32 A.113
2—Starrs v Mason, 32 A.8
3—Succ. Vidol, 44 A.41; Dalton v Wickliffe, 35 A.355;
    Renfrow v McCain, 185 L.135
4—Oglesby v Turner, 127 L.1097; Succ. Valnier, 40 A.593
5—Starrs v Mason, 32 A.8

without interruption and without turning aside to other acts, has been held to satisfy the requirements of the law (1).

This testament must be signed by the testator. If he declares that he knew not how to, or is not able to sign, express mention of his declaration, as also of the cause that hinders him from signing must be made in the act (2). The testatrix having declared that she could not write made her usual mark, held to be good (3), but to the contrary the recital that the testator being illiterate signs his mark has been held as not sufficient and the will to be null (4).

The article itself is very explicit and clear· Therefore the declaration in the will should not only show that testator cannot sign but show that he declared that he cannot sign and give the reason therefor, as never having learned how to write or sign his name, weakness, injury, etc.

The testament must be signed by the witnesses, or at least one of them for all, if the others cannot write (5); a nuncupative testament under private signature (6), must be written by the testator himself, or by any other person from his dictation; or even by one of the witnesses in the presence of five witnesses residing in the place where the will is received, or of seven witnesses residing out of the place; or it will suffice, if in the presence of the same number of witnesses, the testator present the paper on which he has written or caused it to be written out of their presence declaring to them that the paper

1—Monroe v Liebman, 47 A.155
2—R. C. C. 1579
3—Brand v Baumgarden, 24 A.628; Rostrup v Succ. Spicer, 183 L.1091
4—Succ. Carroll, 28 A.388; Succ. Whittington, 26 A.89;
       Succ. Nelson, 163 L.463
5—R. C. C. 1580
6—R. C. C. 1577

its being necessary in that case to increase the number of witnesses (1).

Those who do not know how or are not able to sign their names cannot make dispositions in the form of a mystic will (2); if any of the witnesses to the act of superscription know not how to sign express mention shall be made thereof· In all cases the act must be signed by at least two witnesses (3).

The Olographic Will and Testament

The olographic testament is that which is written by the testator himself. In order to be valid it must be entirely written, dated and signed by the hand of the testator himself (4).

It needs no witnesses; it may be written in pencil; clauses written after the will and not signed are good if followed by one which is signed, though not dated, if congruous and continuous (6); the date may be placed below the signature (7); the day is part of the date and the month and year without the day of the month is insufficient for a valid will (8).

Erasures not approved by the testator are considered not made; and words added by another as not written.   If the erasures are so made as to render it impossible to distinguish the words covered by them, it shall be left to the discretion of the judge to declare if he considers them important; in this case only to decree the nullity of the testament (9); it suffices for the validity of a testament that it be valid under any one of the forms prescribed by law,

1—R. C. C. 1585
2—R. C. C. 1586
3—R. C. C. 1587
4—R. C. C. 1588
5—Succ. VanHilla, 49 A.107; 13 Laurent, 173, Sec. 171
6—Lagrue v Merle, 5 A.280
7—Zerega v Percival, 46 A.605
8—Heffner v Heffner, 48 A.1088; Succ. Robertson, 49 A.368
9—R. C. C. 1589; Act 87, 1871

however defective it may be in the form which the testator may have intended to make it (1).

The following persons are absolutely incapable of being witnesses to testaments:

1. Children who have not attained the age of sixteen years complete
2. Persons insane, deaf, dumb or blind
3. Persons whom the criminal laws declare incapable of exercising civil functions
4. Married women to the wills of their husbands (2).

An executor may be a witness to the will in which he is named as executor (3). One who does not understand the language of the testator is incompetent as a witness (4). Actual residence is all that is necessary (5).

Neither can testaments be witnessed by those who are constituted heirs or named as legatees under whatsoever title it may be (6); mystic wills are excepted from the preceding article (7); by residence of the witnesses in the place where the testament is executed is understood their residence in the parish where the testament is made; that residence is necessary only when it is expressly required by law (8). The formalities to which testaments are subject by the provisions of the present section must be observed; otherwise the testaments are null and void (9); but the testaments made in foreign countries or the States or Territories of the Union, shall take ef-

1—R. C. C. 1890; Brontin v Vassant, 5 Mart. 182; 6 Mart (N.S. 262)
2—R. C. C. 1591; Act 30, 1908
3—Davenport v Davenport, 116 L.1009; Succ. Feitel, 187 L.626
4—Succ. Dauterive. 39 A.1094
5—Oglesby v Turner, 127 L.1097
6—R. C. C. 1592
7—R. C. C.1593
8—R. C. C. 1594
9—R. C. C. 1595

fect in this State, if they be clothed with all the formalities prescribed for the validity of wills in the place where they have been respectively made (1). An act of 1912 (2) provides that a last will and testament executed without this State in the mode prescribed by the law, either where executed or of the testator's domicile, shall be deemed legally executed and shall be of the same force and effect as if executed in the mode prescribed by the laws of this State; provided said last will and testament is in writing and subscribed by the testator. But it does not change the law as to the construction of the contents of the will (3).

Wills of people domiciled in Louisiana must be probated in Louisiana (4).

Testamentary Dispositions: Testamentary dispositions are either universal, under a universal title or under a particular title (5); a universal legacy is a testamentary disposition by which the testator gives to one or several persons the whole of the property which he leaves at his death (6); the legacy under a universal title is that which a testator bequeaths a certain portion of the effects of which the laws permit him to dispose, as half, a third, or all of his immovables or all of his movables (7).

The preceding articles are of interest to the examiner for the reason that they may affect title to real property, in view of the fact that particular legaies that fail, go to the universal legatee, but not to the legatee under a universal title. For example: If A

1—R. C. C. 1596
2—Act 176, 1912
3—Succ. Withers, 45 A.556
4—Succ. Drysdale, 121 L.834
5—R. C. C. 1605
6—R. C. C. 1606
7—R. C. C. 1612

leaves B a particular house ,that is a particular legacy; and to C all his remaining real estate, that is a legacy under a universal title. Should the legacy to B fail as by his death prior to the death of the testator, the particular house does not go to C but to the testator's heirs. If A leaves B, after making several particular legacies, all the remainder of his estate, failure of the legacies under a particular title benefits the legitimate heirs and not the legatee under a universal title (1)·

Rogrou (2) uses this illustration . "I bequeath to A and B all of my estate which I leave at my decease." This, he says, comes under the head of a universal legacy. "I bequeath to A and B each one half of my estate." This is a legacy under a universal title. In the first case, if A refuses to take, B takes the whole. In the second case, if A refuses to take, it does not increase B's share.

This distinction is based on the wording of the two articles. Article 1606 sets out that a universal legacy is a testamentary disposition by which the testator gives to one or several persons the whole of the property which he leaves at his death. It is the quantity bequeathed and not the number of persons which is to be considered. Article 1612 defines a universal title as that by which a testator bequeaths a certain portion of his property as a half, a third, or all of his immovables or all of his movables. In this instance it is the proportion that is to be considered as being bequeathed to each legatee.

In the first example it is the whole of the property which is disposed of to several persons. In the second example it is only one-half of the property

1—Compton v Prescott, 12 Rob. 56
2—Rogrou Art. 1003

which is bequeathed to each person. It is as if the testator had said: "I leave one-half of my property to A and I leave another half to B." Clearly a legacy under a universal title. Where a testator, having no forced heirs, wills his whole estate to his wife and his two sisters, stipulating that each is to have one-third each, they will be considered as universal legatees succeeding to the whole of the estate he died possessed of, to the exclusion of all others (1). But suppose one of the legatees had died before the testator. Would her share have gone to the other legatees instead of the heirs? Did not the use of the word "one-third" to each legatee constitute this a legacy under a universal title? A proper analysis of the case must decide the first question in the affirmative and the second in the negative. Reference to the language of the testator shows that he used the very language of article 1606. He gave the "whole of the property which he left" to several persons. The court so considered it as it decides that the parties were universal legatees.

A legacy of the whole estate to two people in Louisiana, to be divided equally between them is conjoint and survivor is entitled to the whole by accretion (2).

According to Rogrou the words "all of my estate" is equivalent to the "whole of my estate." A legacy of the residue (or balance) of any property of every description is a universal legacy (3)

In the above, the language used is equivalent to the whole and also refers and evidently means property of every description testator might leave at his

1—Shane v Withers Legatees, 8 L.489
2—Mackie v Story, 93 U.S. 589
3—Succ. Marks, 35 A.1055; Succ. Burnside, 5 A.708

death, and if a particular legacy fails it certainly reverts to his estate.

On the contrary, if a testator makes several particular legacies and then gives all the remainder of his estate to one and the particular legacies fail, the legatee of the remainder does not take, for the reason that by the use of the word "remainder" the testator evidently referred to the estate as it then existed and the bequest of the remainder of the estate as it then existed is under a universal title. The use of the words "I die possessed of" or words equivalent thereto would establish that the testator intended a universal legacy and not a legacy under a universal title.

Disinherision: The matter of disinherision can be of little interest to an examiner for the reason that if that question appears in the examination, it must have appeared in the will and in the proceedings and would have probably gone to judgment, in which event the judgment rendered will have settled all questions involved.

Particular Legacies

Particular legacies involve no question not already discussed under donations and testamentary dispositions, except that a mere judgment recognizing the legatee as such will not suffice as a title. He must be put into possession by an authentic act executed by the executor, unless the heirs have accepted the succession and have been put and sent into possession and have voluntarily made title to the particular legatee.

CHAPTER XXXVII

Putting Heirs of Absentee In Possession

Chapter Two of Title III of the Civil Code (1) covers the putting in possession the surviving spouse of community property and the heirs of their share of all property.

The title of the heir and spouse under such a possession is precarious unless there has been litigation and all proofs have been judicially supplied. There can be no certainty otherwise, as no presumption arises as to the death of the absentee, unless one hundred years have elapsed from the time of his birth (2).

There are circumstances, which coupled with the fact that his whereabouts are unknown, justify a presumption that he is dead (3). But these circumstances are facts which unless established judicially are of little value in determining the validity of the possession or of the death of the absentee. It has been held that collaterals must show the death of the absentee's relations in the ascending line, but not in the descending line, but it would seem that they must allege these facts (4). Unless, however, the title has the support of a judicial decision, it is open to attack at any time until the lapse of thirty years when prescription acquirendi causa occurs to quiet it.

Chapter Three of the same title, covers the case where an inheritance or other rights accrue to an absentee since his disappearance. Whoever shall claim a

1—R. C. C. 57 to 75
2—Hayes v Berwick. 2 Mart. (O.S.) 138: Succ. Vives, 32 A.305; Iberia Cypress Co. v Thoregson, 116 L.218; Succ. Herdman, 154 L.477
3—Morlene v Wall, 107 L.737; Tobin v U. S. Safe Deposit Bank, 115 L. 366; Succ. Butler v Lory, 166 L.227
4—Owen v Mitchel, 5 Mart. (N.S.) 667; Hooter v Tippet, 12 Mart. (O.S.) 390

right accruing to a person whose existence is unknown, shall be bound to prove such person existed at the time the right in question accrued, and until this be proved his demand shall not be admitted (1).

In case a succession shall be opened in favor of a person whose existence is not known, such inheritance shall devolve exclusively on those who would have had a concurrent right with him to the estate, or on those upon whom the inheritance should have devolved if such person had not existed (2).

These two articles pose several problems which must be solved. First: The death or non-existence of the absentee; second, who are his heirs, and third, if he left any heirs, where are they? As for instance, a man disappears, leaving a son. He is not heard from and his whereabouts are unknown. When he left he was a comparatively young man and may have married and left children, or he may have collateral relatives, but the existence of such children or relatives are unknown. His son dies intestate, unmarried and without issue. His father, the absentee would have inherited if alive. A brother is alive and does inherit. Under the article the brother inherits concurrently with the absentee but the interest of the absentee would not devolve upon the brother, if the former should have left children (3).

So it must be said that a title of this character, that is a possession based upon these articles of the code, is a dubious one, and only thirty years' prescription can remove the doubts which must arise under the circumstances, notwithstanding the fact that the courts have decided that a party who has disappeared

1—R. C. C. 76
2—R. C. C. 77
3—Succ. Williams, 149 L.197

or whose whereabouts is unknown has no right in a succession in which he might have taken as an heir (1) but this would be dependent upon facts which would have to establish by a preponderance of proof that he had never been heard of and did not leave children·

1—Succ. Derigny, 183 L.382; Pfister v Casso, 161 L.940; Martinez v Wall, 107 L.737

CHAPTER XXXVIII
Adoption

Adoption poses several questions to the examiner.

1. Validity of the act of adoption
2. The right of the adopted person to inherit from the adopting person.
3. The right of the adopting person to inherit from the adopted person.
4. Rights of blood relatives of both parties to act of adoption·

Validity of the Act of Adoption

Until 1924, the entire subject of adoption was contained in Article 214 of the Revised Civil Code, unamended and unchanged until that year, except by one amendment adopted in 1872 (1).

The original article of the Code read:

Any person may adopt another as his child, except those illegitimate children the law prohibits him from acknowledging, but such adoption shall not interfere with the rights of the forced heirs.

The person adopting must be at least forty years old and must be at least fifteen years older than the person adopted.

The person adopted shall have the rights of a legitimate child in the estate of the person adopting him, except as above stated. Married persons must concur in adopting a child. One of them cannot adopt without the consent of the other.

Beyond the clause prohibiting the adoption of illegitimate children, the clause covering the ages of the adopter and the adoptee, the clause in reference to the rights of the adopted person and those of the forced heirs, the act was decidedly vague, making

1—Act 31, 1872

no provision for the method of adoption, or the rights of the adopting person, or of anyone else.

By the provisions of subsequent acts, the age of the adopting person was reduced to twenty-one, and then to twenty years; required the written consent of the adopted person's parents or parent if only one was alive, or if one had abandoned the family, or by the tutor or by the representative of any charitable institution who had charge of the child; eliminated the prohibition against illegitimate children (bastards); required that the adoption be made by authentic act and the recordation thereof in the mortgage office, the approval of the courts (district) where the person adopted was under 17 years of age; forbade the adoption by a person of one race of a person of another race (omitted in the act of 1940 covering the adoption of persons over the age of seventeen (1)).

The jurisdiction of the adoption of minors under the age of seventeen years was vested in the Juvenile Courts by the Act of 1932 (2), but this jurisdiction was declared unconstitutional (3). Subsequently the Constitution was amended so as to give jurisdiction in adoption of persons under seventeen years of age (4), to the Juvenile courts.

Discussion as to the validity or invalidity of prior acts of adoption may be pretermitted for the reason that all such adoptions or attempted adoptions have been confirmed and validated by six months prescriptions by two acts of 1938 (5), as to the adoption of persons under the age of seventeen years, and by the

1—Acts 31, 1872; 48, 1924; 46, 1932; 44, 1934; 233, 1936; 428, 1938; 413, 1940
2—Act 46, 1932
3—Succ. Dyer, 184 L.251; Gorges v Embry, 181 L.1025
4—Act 324, 1936; 233, 1936
5—Act 233, 1936; 428 1938

same prescription in the case of adoptions of persons over seventeen years (1).

These prescriptions, however, apply only to matters of jurisdiction and procedure, so that defects arising from other causes, as for instance, the adoption of a person of one race by a person of another race, would not be cured by those acts.

Under the present legislation an act of adoption of a person over the age of seventeen must conform to the following requirements:

1. The person adopting must be over 20 and the adopted person must be over seventeen.
2. The adoption must be by authentic act.
3. The act must be registered in the office of the clerk of court in the parishes outside of Orleans parish and in the office of the register of conveyance in the latter parish.
4. The act must be signed by both the adopting parent or parents and by the adopted person, if a major, or an emancipated minor; or by the adopting parent or parents and the living parent or parents of the adopted person, or guardian or tutor, or a tutor ad hoc appointed for the purpose, where the adopted person is an unemancipated minor over seventeen years of age.

There is no prohibition contained in the act of 1940 (2) against the adoption of a person of one race by a person of another race and the act repeals all laws or parts of laws in conflict with the act, hence so far as the adoption of a person above the age of seventeen is concerned such an adoption would be legal.

1—Act 169, 1940
2—Ibid

Where the person adopted is under seventeen years of age, it must conform to the following:

1. The person adopting must be over twenty years of age and of the same race as the person adopted.

2. If the adopting person is married, both spouses must join in the adoption.

3. The adoption must be initiated by a petition to the Juvenile Court of the parish in which either the adopted child or the adoptive parent or parents live.

4. There must be a final decree of court, after due investigation and procedure prescribed by the act.

As an adoption is an artificial status created by special laws all of the requirements of those statutes must be strictly complied with and are strictly construed (1).

Right of adopted person to inherit from adopting person: It has been settled both by law and by the jurisprudence that an adopted person inherits from its adoptive parent (2) in the same manner as a forced heir, where there are no forced heirs surviving the parent, and where there are forced heirs he inherits only after the legitime of the legitimate or blood child has been provided for.

The jurisprudence is equally clear to this right (3). The principle as outlined above is recognized and emphasized.

1—Gros v Millers Indem. Underwriters, 153 L.357; Hardy v Mobley, 183 L.668

2—R. C. C. 214; Act 31, 1872; 38, 1924; 233, 1936; 428, 1928

3—Vidal v Commagere 13 A.516; Cunningham v Lawson, 11 L.1024; Succ. Hawkins, 139 L.228; Houghton v Hall, 177 L.237; Hardy v Mobley, 183 L.668

Right of the adopting person to inherit from the adopted person: Until 1936 the adoptive parent or parents were without right of inheriting from the adopted person. By act of that year (1), the right of the adoptive person is clearly defined. The act reads: Adoptive parents shall have all the rights of inheritance of parents in the estate of their adopted children as are enjoyed by parents in the estates of their legitimate children·

Rights of blood relatives of both parties to the adoption: The act of 1938 (2) cuts off the right of the parents of the adopted person to inherit a right they formerly possessed, but there has not been any judicial interpretation of that clause. The examiner, though must ask himself this question. Is not this provision of the act unconstitutional, in view of Section 16 of Article 4 of the Constitution of 1921, which prohibits the passage of any law which changes the laws of forced heirship? The act deprives a natural parent of his right of forced heirship, hence it is a decided change.

As to the rights of other relatives of the adopted person and the adoptive brothers and sisters, both the law and the jurisprudence is silent on the subject so that one can only speculate. It is certain though, to judge from the jurisprudence anent the right of an adoptive parent to inherit from an adopted child, established prior to 1938, such relatives could not inherit, nor would the adopted child inherit from the adoptive brothers or sisters.

1—Act 256, 1936
2—Act 428, 1938

CHAPTER XXXIX

Appeals

An examiner is not concerned with appeals beyond ascertaining that the delays for a suspensive appeal has elapsed, and if any appeal has been taken by either party, what the decision was and whether or not the delays for a rehearing in the Supreme Court have elapsed, and the delays for a rehearing and for a writ of certiorari have elapsed and that a notice of the decision in the Court of Appeal has been notified to the party cast, as pending such notice the delay for the writs do not run (1) .

An innocent third party is protected by the judgment rendered whether it be for a money judgment or for a thing, if there has been no suspensive appeal (2).

Another fact to be mentioned is that the interruption of prescription prescribed by Article 3519 of the Civil Code does not apply to appeals· It was once held to the contrary (3) but these decisions were over ruled (4).

1—Act .7, Const. 1921, Sec. 24; Morning Star, Bap. Ch. v Martina 150 L. 951
2—Continental Sec. Corp. v Wetherbee, 187 L.773; Harty v Flaty, La. 192 La. 782; Blappert v Paglieuhi, La. App. 192, Sou. 135
3—Hibernia Bank v J. A. Zimmerman & Sons, 167 L.814 Good v Picone, 18 La. App. 42
4—Verret v Savoie, 174 L.844; United Railwaymen Oil Co. v Dupuy, 171 L.177

CHAPTER XL

Boundaries, Descriptions and Surveys

These subjects are grouped together for the reason that they implement each other and an analysis of one requires an analysis of the others.

A proper and correct description, which would be binding on third parties and which would establish definitely the location of the property, as a first step in identifying it, should be the parish, or parishes, district, township, range and section in which it is located, together with such other descriptive language as will accurately fix the amount of land conveyed and its exact position as regards the section and adjacent and surrounding property (1).

Where the property is situated in municipalities and subdivisions which have been officially surveyed and divided into squares, with proper reference to the district, township and range and section in which it is located, and the surveys made have been recorded in the parish records according to law (2), it will be sufficient that reference be made to the parish, municipality and square in which it is located with the square boundaries and a proper reference to the particular recorded survey. The exact location of the property in the square and accurate measurements are necessarily a part of the description.

No description which does not tie in with a well established point, which in the case of a square is the corner thereof and in the case of rural property, is a monument, a section corner, or other well known and established point. This is also true in matters of survey in locating the property surveyed.

1—Castera v N. O. Land Co., 125 L.877; Brock v McIlhenny, 186
     L.903; Tircuit v Burton-Swartz Lbr. Co., 162 L.319
2—Act 182, 1912; 201, 1932

In the City of New Orleans, it is the custom to recite in the act, the parish, district (municipal district into which the city is divided), the number of the square, the boundaries thereof and the designation of the lot by number or letter and of course the measurements. The omission in such an act of all but the parish and boundaries of the square, the location of the lot and the measurements thereof would be sufficient, all other items being merely for convenience·

Difficulties often confront an examiner in reference to property located in squares, especially in the City of New Orleans, due to frequent re-divisions of the lots in the square, which results in the inclusion of parts of other lots and changes in the measurements and even in change of frontage on a street, making the identity of the property very difficult, especially where the change has been made without a survey. It will be frequently found that there is a duplication of the number or other designation.

Certainty of description as affecting the identity, location and amount of land conveyed is of prime importance (1), especially as the prescription of ten years is of no avail where a description fails to be sufficiently certain as to identify the property (2). It is also a decisive factor in boundary disputes and other actions involving title. However, any description which leaves no doubt on these points is sufficient, although the language used is more or less ambiguous. A description which omits the township or other legal subdivision but places the property on a particular stream in a designated parish, bounded

1—Wilfert v Duson, 131 L.21
2—Hargrove v Hodge, 9 La. App., 434; Continental Land & Fur. Co. v Lacoste, 192 L.561

by well known properties with the number of acres contained therein, or a sale of a plantation or residence by name and locality is sufficient (1). The proper reference to the vendor's acquisition such as the book and folio of the conveyance records wherein it was recorded, will serve to amplify, correct and supply ambiguous misdescriptions and omissions in purchaser's deed (2).

Errors which do not materially affect the identity or location of the property, such as an error in the range or the number of a square or of a section, provided that the rest of the description will serve to otherwise identify the property, is of no importance (3).

On the other hand an act describing a piece of land "situated in the corporate limits of the Town of "A" and being part of Section 7, S.R-E. of the eastern district of Louisiana and bounded on the south by Bayou Q" is too vague to convey title (4), or a conveyance of lands without description of boundaries or location merely as all other lands owned by vendor in the State of Louisiana, conveys nothing (5).

A general description which manifestly was intended to be summing up of the intention of the parties as to the property conveyed controls all prior words or phrases used, if that description is sufficient to identify with certainty the property as conveyed (6).

As to amount of land conveyed: A sale per aver-

1—Thornhill v Burthe, 29 A.639; Bryan v Wisner, 44 A.832;
       Robinson v Atkins, 105 L.790; Phelan v Wilson, 114
       L.813; Lee v Long, 166 L.1084
2—Render v Chew, 129 L.849; Lee v Long. 166 L.1084
3—Willis v Ruddock Cypress Co., 108 L.255
4—Miller v Brugier, 176 L.106
5—Kernan v Baham, 45 A.810; Kirk v Kansas City So. R. R.,
       51 A.673
6—Smith v Chappell, 177 L.311; 188 L.884

sionem determines the amount of land conveyed, whether it be more or less (1). Boundaries govern as to quantity of land conveyed as against measurements and quantities recited in the act (2) but not as against a survey unless such a survey is too vague and indefinite to be reliable (3), but the language used must clearly show that the sale was intended to be per aversionem.

A sale which recites "All that certain piece or portion of land bounded by the property of A on the north, by the property of B on the south, by the property of C on the east and by the property of D on the west, which contains forty-five acres" (or which measures 1050 feet on the north, 1050 feet on the south, 1450 feet on the east and 1450 feet on the west) would be considered a sale per aversionem and the measurements or acreage would not prevail, it being presumed that the vendor intended to sell the whole tract as bounded, and that the acreage or the measurements were merely estimates. On the other hand, a description which reads "A piece or portion of land measuring 250 feet on the highway, the same width in the rear by a depth of 1050 feet between equal and parallel lines and which is bounded on the north by the public highway, on the south by the property of A, on the east by the property of B, on the west by the property of C." the measurements would determine the amount of land sold.

Reference in an act by which the vendor acquired for a more perfect description, would aid in piecing out the description of the property sold, provided that

1—Passera v N. O., 167 L.199; Consol. Cos. Co. v Haas Land Co. 10 La. App. 608
2—Leonard v Forbing, 109 L.220; Ganauches v Monnot, 130 L.463 Beugnot v N. O. Land Co., 139 L.687; Johnson v Sylvester, 5 La. App. 720; Charnley v Edinborn, 163 L.945
3—Futrell v Holloway Co., La. App. 149 So. 167

it was evident that it was the same property, but it would not enlarge the former, as the latter act was of a larger tract. It would merely aid in identifying the property (1)·

A survey controls measurements and acreage (2) and boundaries unless it be too vague.

Boundaries: In determining boundaries, the law recognizes, (named in order of their importance) natural monuments, artificial monuments, distances, courses and quantity, but the controlling consideration is the intention of the parties (3).

Where owner of peninsular tract of land of about 4,000 acres conveyed, "what is known as the south one-half" thereof with a specified exception, and subsequently sold to another purchaser a tract described as bounded "on the south by the southern half of the land . . . containing approximately twenty-five hundred acres" intention was to convey half of such tract according to acreage, and first grantee obtained such half as fixed by a contemporaneous survey and occupied by first grantee (4).

It is impossible in one chapter such as this to give a full list of every instance in which the principles outlined above have been applied in litigated cases, and in fact were this to be done, it would avail the examiner little, because most of the decisions have their basis not on a general rule of law, applicable to all cases, but on the facts developed by each case and on what the courts have found the intention of the parties to have been in each case. Nor has it been found advisable or necessary to discuss the law and jurisprudence governing actions of boundary, for

1—Bender v Chew, 129 L.849
2—Maginnis Land Co. v Marcello, 168 L.997
3—Meyer v Commagere, 147 L.851; Tulane Ed. Fund v Stair, 148 L.11
4—Dufrene v Bernstein, 190 L.66

the reason that the examiner is not called upon to and will not decide more, in each title examined, than the location, identity and quantity of the property involved, as set out in the deed and as disclosed by the survey and the established fences and other boundaries.

However, an endeavor has been made, in the preceding pages and those to follow, to set up guide posts which will assist the examiner in deciding whether the description, as given in the link under examination, meets, within reasonable limits, the requirements as to the identity, location, measurements and quantity of land conveyed in that link and which is to be conveyed to the new purchaser, or to be mortgaged as the case may be, with substantial assurance that the link in question is fairly safe against attack in that respect, or if not, wherein it fails to be so.

Among the factors which have a bearing of importance in questions hereinabove discussed, is the survey. In general an official plat or survey becomes part of the deed and controls as to notes, lines, description and landmarks (1). However, there are circumstances or conditions in which this is not true, as for instance, where the map is incomplete, or contains an error, or where the map is used merely as a means of identification, but not of quantity or measurement (2). For example: A description may read: "a certain tract of land. etc., measuring 250 feet front on the highway by a depth, between equal and parallel lines. of 1250 feet and designate dby the letter X on a plan made by John Doe, Surveyor, a copy of which is annexed hereto." The map or plan as annexed to the act show that Lot X measures 250 feet on the high-

1—Police Jury v Marceaux. 13 La. App. 332
2—Bender v Chew. 129 L.849

way, 1250 feet on the east side line and 1350 feet on the other side line and 312 feet ten inches on the rear line. In this case the map would not govern as to the quantity sold, as it is evident that the parties contemplated a sale of the smaller quantity out of the whole. Again, a description may refer to natural or fixed boundaries, such as water courses, hills and trees, whereas the map attached and referred to may show artificial guides such as courses, distances and quantity fixed and ascertained by human agencies. Where there is a conflict, the former prevails over the latter where the attention of the parties is not otherwise disclosed (1).

A patent from the State, if in conflict with grant from United States, as shown by the United States survey must yield to such survey as it is part of the grant from the United States (2).

When the description as shown on the conveyance records conflicts with the description as shown on map, the map controls (3). Where parties had a plat, with notes, lines, description and landmarks before them and grant refers to such plat, the plat controls, whether a survey has been made or not (4).

Another factor of importance in certain circumstances is what is known as the "meander line." In general meander lines are not run as boundaries of the surveyed land, but for the purpose of defining the sinuosities of the banks of the stream or other body of water and as a further means of ascertaining

1—Nattin v Glassel. 156 L.423; Mahaffey v Miller, 159 L.610; Barker v Houssiere-Latrielle Oil Co, 160 L.52; Sullivan v N. O. & N. E. R. R., 9 La. App, 162
2—Richard v Poitevent & Farve Lbr. Co.. 10 L. App. 608
3—Sou. La. Fair Assn. v Robert. 3 La. App. 505
4—Acadia-Vermillion Rice Irr. Co. v Miller. 178 L.954

the quantity of land included in the survey. The stream and not the meander line as actually run is the boundary, unless otherwise shown (1). A meander line supposed to show shore line of a body of water, must conform to and approach the shore line, otherwise deed given according to such survey does not give title to water's edge, but only to line laid out (2). When two contiguous owners own on opposite sides of a non-navigable stream which is designated in their title as boundary, center of such stream is to be considered the dividing line, unless a different intention is evident (3). While it has been held that a body of water is the true boundary line and not the meander line, this does not hold true where real shore line is distant from the supposed shore line and large tracts of land exist between supposed shore line as shown on plat and actual shore line (4).

A patent of land described as outside White Lake, conveyed land down to actual shore line, where survey filed in General Land Office showed no meander line on plat of such survey; hence subsequent patent to land between shore and meander lines conveyed no title thereto (5).

Surveys

An examiner should never approve or accept a description until he has an opportunity of checking it with an official plat of survey.

If such is not available, either as annexed to the act under examination, or to another link in the chain, he should require that one be made. This is

1—Palmer v Wilkinson. 141 L.874. This should be read for its full discussion of the subject
2—Brunning v N. O., 165 L.511
3—Nattin v Glassell, 156 L.423
4—Acadia-Vermillion Rice Irr. Co. v Miller, 178 L.954
5—Ibid

also true where the date of the survey is so old as to suggest possible changes or encroachments, at least in municipalities. This is also true where the map or plan does not show location of improvements and fences or where the property is not tied in with the corner of the square in cities and subdivisions or with well established starting points in the case of rural property. In all cases, outside of the City of New Orleans, the survey should have been or should 'be officially recorded in the parish where property is situated (1).

The examiner should familiarize himself with the rectangular system of land measures, adopted by the United States in 1785, which, with some amendments, none of which is important here, except the one made in 1896, which will be referred to hereafter·

By this system prime or principal meridians are established along the true meridian. A base line is established at some point in the principal meridian, extending east and west from the principal meridian along a true parallel line of latitude. Standard parallel or correctional lines are extended east and west from the principal meridian at intervals of twenty-four miles north and south of base line. Guide meridians are extended north and south from the base line at intervals of twenty- four miles east and west from the principal meridian. These form quadrangles and embrace sixteen townships.

Lines are then formed north and south parallel with the principal meridian six miles apart called ranges. These strips or ranges are numbered east and west from the principal meridian. Cross lines are then run six miles apart dividing the ranges into squares six miles each way, constituting townships.

1—Act 151, 1930; 182, 1912; 201, 1932

The first township above the base line is numbered one north, the second two north etc. South of the base line the first township is number one south, the second township is number two south, etc.

Each township is divided into thirty-six sections, each, one mile square. The thirty-six sections in each township are numbered consecutively, beginning wtih the one in the northeast section and proceeding west and east alternatively through the township with progressive numbers until the thirty-six sections are completed.

Prior to 1896 the section numbers ran from the number one in the southeast corner and ran from south to north in each tier.

In Louisiana there are two principal meridians, the 91st west of the Mississippi river and the 90th east of the Mississippi river, or as it is called the St. Helena Meridian.

One base line transects the State about the center thereof.

The examiner should also learn to read maps and should familiarize himself with the use of the protractor, as without it it would be impossible to check descriptions in country titles without a map.

As few lawyers are familiar with reading maps and with the proper terminology in the confecting of a description therefrom, it is suggested that whenever a new survey be made (in connection with the act for which the examination is made) the surveyor be requested or required to draw up a proper description in the margin of his survey to be used in the act, as this would insure full and complete conformity of the description with the map.

The French having originally settled Louisiana,

French terminology and French measurements appear in old titles, particularly in the settlements along the Mississippi river and for the convenience of such examiners as are not familiar with such terms and measurements, they are here given, with their American equivalent.

"Arpent" is rated as 0.85.07 of an acre or 5/6 of an acre.

Surveyors in southern Louisiana approximate an acre as being 208.56 feet square and an arpent as being 192 feet square.

A French foot is computed as the equivalent of 1.066American foot.

There is also a Spanish measurement which is occasionally found in Louisiana titles, called the "toise" or 6.39 plus feet.

N

			T5N					
ST ANDARD				PAR ALLE L				
			T4N					
			T3N			N		
			T2N					
BASE			T1N	LIN E				
R3W	R2W	R1W	R1E	R2E	R3E	R4E	R5E	
			T1S					
			T2S					
			T3S					

S

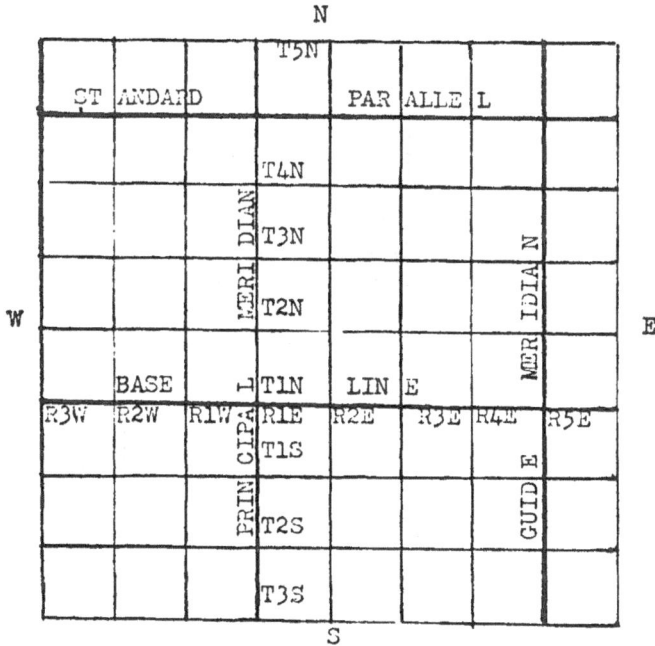

The above figure shows the division of a tract
of land into Townships and the standard parallel,
base line, principal meridian and guide meridian and
the system of numbering the townships and ranges
in accordance with the principles of the rectangular
system of land surveys.

N

36	31	32	33	34	35	36	31
1	6	5	4	3	2	1	6
12	7	8	9	10	11	12	7
13	18	17	16	15	14	13	18
24	19	20	21	22	23	24	19
25	30	29	28	27	26	25	30
36	31	32	33	34	35	36	31
1	6	5	4	3	2	1	6

W (left)   E (right)

S

The above figure illustrates the numbering of sections contained in a township and the position of
adjoining sections in other townships.

N

		NW¼ NW¼ NE¼	NE¼ NW¼ NE¼	NE¼ NE¼
N½ NW¼ 80 ACRES		SW¼ NW¼ NE¼	SE¼ NW¼ NE¼	40 ACRES
S½ NW¼ 80 ACRES		SW¼ NE¼	N½ NE¼ 20 Acres	
			A 2½	10 Acre
			5 Ac	
NW¼ SW¼ 40 ACRES	E½ SW¼ 80 ACRES	SE¼ 160 ACRES		
SW¼ SW¼ 40 ACRE				

W   E

S

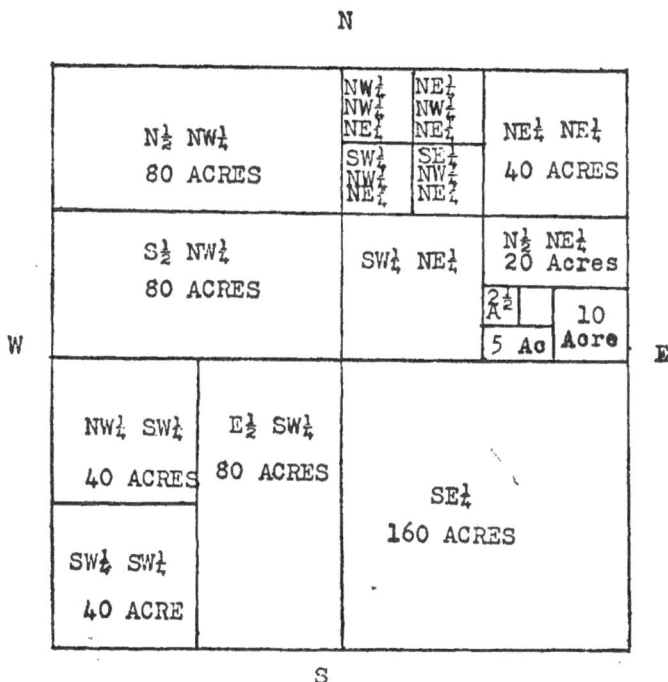

The above figure illustrates a section which is usually divided first into quarter sections, viz: N. E. ¼; N. W. ¼; S. E. ¼; and S. W. ¼. Each quarter is divided in like manner, the division bearing the same relation to the quarter that the quarter bears to the section. Each smaller division follows the same order. The section and the quarters may also be divided into halves.

Every such division is designated by the words or letters which indicate its position in the section and in the quarter, thus: The north ½ of the Northeast quarter of Section 10, or the N. E. ¼ of the N.E.¼ of Section 10 etc.

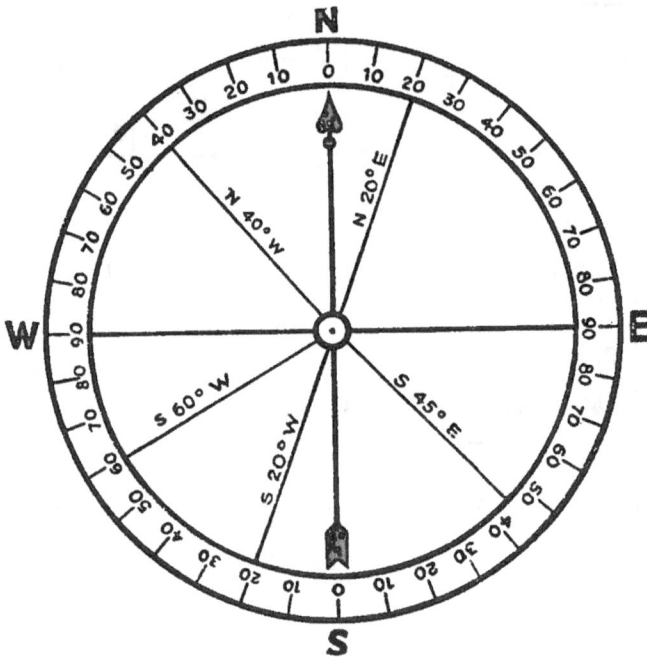

The above figure illustrates a circle and the designation of the courses of any given tract of land whether square, or irregular.

CHAPTER XLI

Clerks of Courts

As the examiner is interested in the powers which Clerks of Courts have in the exercise of quasi judicial functions which may affect a title, the law and the jurisprudence in re same are here set forth.

All of the constitutions of the state contained articles on the subject of clerks of court and their powers, with the exception of that of 1812 (1)

The language used in the Constitution of 1921 is substantially the same as was used in all other constitutions, with the exception of that of 1812: The legislature shall have power to vest in clerks of court authority to grant such orders and to do such acts as may be deemed necessary for the furtherance of the administration of justice; and in all cases the powers thus vested shall be specified and determined (2).

The Revised Statutes of 1870 (3) granted the clerks of courts power to issue all writs and orders in probate proceedings not required by law to be issued by the parish judge. These powers were not specifically set out by the statutes, but gradually specially enumerated and enlarged by acts of the Legislature, in 1880; 1882; 1884; 1888; 1894; 1921 and 1924 (4). The latter provides that clerks of the courts outside of Orleans parish shall have power to grant orders for writs of arrest, attachment, sequestration and fix the amount of the bond thereof, except where it is fixed by law; to allow interventions, grant orders of third opposition, appoint special tutor or tutors

1—Art. 79, 1845; 76, 1852; 81, 1864; 133, 1868; 122, 1879; 123, 1898; 123, 1913; Sec. 66 Art. 7, 1921
2—Sec. 66 Art. 7, 1921
3—Sec 484 Rev. Stat. 1870
4—Act 106, 1880; 43, 1882; 75, 1884; 137, 1888; 13, 1894; 41, 1921 204, 1924

ad hoc to minors, appoint curators and curators ad hoc, to appoint attorneys for absentees, grant orders for sale of succession property upon application of the administrator, tutor or curator, provided that the application be accompanied by a statement of the debts of the succession, to appoint attorneys for absent heirs, to appoint and confirm tutors, under tutors, dative testamentary executors, administrators, curators of vacant successions after giving the notice prescribed by law, provided no opposition be filed thereto, to take bonds required of tutors, dative executors, administrators, curators, syndics and to homologate their proceedings when not opposed, to issue orders for the advertisement of the filing of accounts of tutors, executors, administrators, curators and syndics, to order family meetings and meetings of creditors, to order execution of wills and to confirm testamentary executors provided no opposition is made thereto, and to issue orders for executory process . . .

The constitutionality of the foregoing act has been upheld under Article 2, SS 1, 2 and Section 66 Article 7, par 2 Constitution 1921 (1).

The clerks have these powers whether the judge be present or absent from the parish, though previously he could not issue such orders or exercise the powers unless the judge was absent from the parish (2), which fact had to be proved by the affidavits of the applicant for the order, but the absence of such proof could not be made the basis of an attack collaterally (3).

An act of 1924 (4) forbade the deputy clerk to exercise such powers as are therein or thereafter

1—McCoy v Hunter, 167 L.1032
2—Gates v Gaiter, 46 A.298
3—Hibernia Bank & Trust Co. v Whitney, 122 L.890
4—Act 204 of 1924

granted to clerks, pursuant to Section 37, (sic) of Article 7 of the Constitution of 1921, but the authority of the deputy clerk cannot be inquired into collaterally (1). The Chief Deputy Clerk may issue executory process, but not an ordinary deputy clerk (2).

In successions of less than five hundred dollars, where they are not under administration, the clerk had the duty of acting as administrator but by a subsequent act, any party at interest could apply for appointment as such administrator (3). The clerk did not have to give bond.

1—Wilder v Jackson, 150 L.864; Cole v Richmond, 156 L.262;
        Succ. Boyd, 12 A.611; Bankston v Cypress, 117L.1053;
        Hibernia Bank & Trust Co. v Whitney, 122 L.890
2—Denham v Kelly, La. App., 142 So. 292
3—R. C. C. 1190; Act 153, 1900; 70, 1906

CHAPTER XLII

Community of Acquets and Gains

Marriage in Louisiana superinduces of right, partnership or community of acquets and gains, if there be no stipulation to the contrary (1).

This community consists of all the profits of all the effects of which the husband has the administration and enjoyment, (this includes the revenues and profits derived from the separate property of the husband and of the separate property of the wife, if she has given the administration thereof to the husband (3)) ; of the produce of the reciprocal industry and labor of both husband and wife, and of the estate which they may acquire during the marriage either by donations made jointly to them both, or by purchase, or in any other similar way, even although the purchase be only in the name of one of the two and not of both (4).

The husband is head and master of the community and may alienate them by an onerous title without the consent and permission of the wife (5) ; and where it is in his name alone it is presumed that it is community property (6).

A sale by the wife as agent of the husband is valid (7) ; and a deed made by husband during the community not recorded until after the death of wife, is binding on her heirs (8), though the property was purchased with the separate funds of the

1—R. C. C. 2399; Succ. Dill. 155 L.47; Hardee v McGaga.
 8 La. App. 794
2—Glenn v Elam, 3 A.611
3—Courrege v Colgin. 51 A.1069; Falconer v Falconer, 167 L.595
4—R. C. C. 2402
5—R. C. C. 2404
6—Tourne v His Creditors, 6 La. 459; Guice v Lawrence, 2 A.226;
 Simon v Merux, 143 L.760; Bywatter v Enderle, 175 L.1098
7—Succ. Brown, Mann, Unreported Cases
8—Porterfield v Parker, 189 L.720

wife, it is still community property, the wife being relegated to a claim against his heirs (1).

Property in name of both husband and wife, or in the name of the wife alone is also presumed to be community property (2) but when it stands in the name of the wife alone it becomes a matter of proof and if sold by the husband without the written consent of the wife the purchaser takes it at his risk because the wife, or her heirs may prove it to be her separate or paraphernal property by evidence dehors the record, even oral testimony, this forming an exception to the general rule that titles to real estate can not be proved or contradicted by parol evidence (3).

On the other hand, a sale by the wife, even if property stands in her name is open to attack by husband's creditors or heirs, because of the presumption under Article 2402 of the Civil Code, unless she is joined by her husband in the sale (4).

Problems and doubts arising in such cases are due to the difficulty of establishing in a satisfactory manner, the community or separate character of the property. This dificulty may be further increased by the mixed character of the property which may be in part separate and in part community.

The jurisprudence of the State present numerous cases which were decided on facts as varied as the number of cases litigated and which facts could have been developed only on trial.

A husband who joins in an act wherein there appears a declaration by the wife that it is purchased with her separate and paraphernal funds, is bound by

1—Clark v Norwood, 12 A.598
2—Burns v Thompson, 39 A.377
3—Succ. Burke, 107 L.83; Newhauser v Burthe, 110 L.825
4—Durruty v Musacchia, 42 A.357

such a declaration (1), but not his creditors or heirs (2).

An examiner when confronted by these problems may solve them to his satisfaction by the facts and circumstances which clearly indicate the property's character. For instance the property may have been inherited, or in a deceased spouse's succession his heirs may have bound themselves as to its character by their judicial admission.

Again, once the character of a property has been established, it does not lose that character, even where community funds have been used in developing, or repairing it, or building upon it, or has gone through a Building and Loan Association, in which event there is usually a sale and resale (3). Should separate funds be used for the benefit of the property, the owner of that fund merely has a claim against the community, or vice versa.

A judicial separation puts an end to the community, even though a reconciliation has occurred (4) and no divorce has followed. In such a case the husband is no longer head of the community and may not sell the property without the consent of his wife, unless there has been a settlement of the community in which event each spouse is the separate owner of whichever property falls to his or her lot·

A case illustrative of the difficulty sometimes presented in these cases, is that of the homesteader, who entered a homestead during his first marriage, but only made final proof after his second marriage. At his death, the case went up on appeal and the

1—Firemens Ins. Co., 140 L.638
2—Maguire v Maguire, 40 A.580; Succ. of Belland, 42 A.241
3—Succ. LeBesque, 137 L.567
4—R. C. C. 155

courts decided that the land belonged to the second community (1).

Again where the wife died prior to completion of proof of homestead has been made, the land homesteaded is not part of the community existing between the husband and wife (2).

1—Gibson v Pickens. 187 L.867
2—Wadkins v Producers Oil Co., 130 L.308

CHAPTER XLIII
Corporations

The Civil Code defines corporations, their rights, powers and restrictions in general and the legislature has enacted special laws which cover the rights, powers, obligations and limitations in detail. Corporations are divided into corporation for profit (which include Banks, Buildings and Loan Associations, Insurance, Pipe Line and Public Utilities. Railroads and general business and trading); and corporations not for profits (which include Religious, Literary, Social, Medical Associations, Fraternal, Professional and Co-operative Marketing and in general all such associations as are not for business or trading).

The validity of titles to real estate acquired or alienated by corporations is tested by the following factors:

Validity of incorporation, purposes and powers, correct procedure in acquiring and alienating.

The validity of all corporations organized or attempted to be organized prior to 1904, was set at rest by the provisions of an act of the legislature in that year (1); and it would seem that the act covers all classes of incorporation (2), but it does not cover those cases where there has been no organization, no incorporation, no recordation and no subscription to stock (3).

The validity of a corporation organized for business depends upon compliance with the following requirements:

An authentic act of incorporation signed by not

1—Act 120, 1904
2—Miller v Marks, 158 L.377
3—Provident Bank v Saxon, 116 L.408; Nat'l Bank v Henderson, 116 L.413

less than three incorporators of full age; recordation in mortgage office ;issuance of a certificate of incorporation signed by the Secretary of State.

Corporations for all lawful businesses, except banking, homesteads, and insurance, must be organized under the Act of 1928 (1).

That Act repealed all former acts on the subject (2).

The incorporation of banking business, insurance, homestead associations and non-profit corporations, are governed by special laws, banking under the acts of 1902 (3), 1912 (4) and 1924 (5); insurance corporations by acts of 1898 and 1914 (6) and 1916 (7); and building and loan associations by acts 1932 (8), 1928 (9), 1888 (10), 1910 (11) and 1912 (12). All former Acts were repealed by the Act of 1932, except those of 1888, 1928, 1910 and 1912, which were expressly excepted.

Non-trading corporations: Are to be or are organized under the provisions of the Act of 1914 (13), and 1924 (14). These acts repeals all the articles of the Civil Code and Code of Practice and sections of the Revised Statues on the subject and the acts of 1882 (15), 1890 (16) and 1902 (17).

1—Act 250, 1928
2—Act 158, 1884; 267, 1914, except as to foreign corporations;
     259, 1916; 152, 1918; Sec. 1 Subdiv. 5 Act 179, 1918;
     96, 1924; 148, 1926; 257, 1926
3—Act 179, 1902
4—Act 96, 1912
5—Act 229, 1924
6—105, 1898; Act 255, 1914
7—Act 266, 1916
8—Act 140, 1932
9—Act 340, 1928; Act 151, 1888; Act 180, 1910; 215, 1912
     Repealed Acts 120, 1902; 280, 1916; 292, 1910; 244, 1912;
     159, 1910; 214, 1910; 278, 1928; 122, 1920; 281, 1928; 185,
     1924; 128, 1926; 282, 1928
10—Act 151, 1888
11—Act 180, 1910
12—Act 215, 1912
13—Act 254, 1914
14—Act 190, 1924
15—Rev. Stat., Sects 677, 678, 679; Act 112, 1882
16—Act 50, 1890   17—Act 153, 1902

The validity of the incorporation of the above named corporations are governed by the several provisions of each act authorizing the incorporating of each particular class of corporations, but want of space prevents enumeration of these provisions.

Purposes and powers: This factor is of importance in determining the right and power of a corporation to acquire and convey property. The purposes and powers of each corporation are defined and limited by the charter provisions of each corporation and by the particular law under which it is organized.

Corporations organized for the buying and selling of real estate need only a resolution of their boards of directors. All other corporations may buy and sell real estate required for the purpose of their business by action of their boards of directors· Banks are limited to those authorized by the acts under which they are created.

But sales in globo of all property including real estate by other corporations not authorized by law and their charters to make such sales, must be by consent of a majority of their stockholders.

Correct procedure in acquiring and alienating real estate: In all cases the purchase or sale of property must be authorized by resolution of the board of directors, and / or the stockholders as the case may be adopted at a meeting regularly called, at which a quorum was present and which resolution should contain a correct description, the price and terms and the name of the officer or agent authorized to execute the act.

Consolidations and liquidations: The Act of 1928 (1) specifically and minutely provides for consolidations of business corporations, viz; There must be an

1—Act 250, 1928

agreement signed by the directors of each corporation, which agreement must be approved by the stockholders of each corporation, in accordance with the provisions of their respective charters, the vote of the stockholders to be certified on the agreement by the Secretary of each meeting, and signed by the president or vice president of each corporation. The agreement so certified and acknowledged shall be sent to the Secretary of State and a copy certified by him recorded in the mortgage office of the parishes in which both corporations have their domiciles, and in the conveyance offices of each parish in which each corporation has immovable property.

New articles of incorporation must then be executed by authentic act in which both corporations appear as the incorporators of the new corporation, signed by the president or vice-president and secretary or assistant secretary of each of said corporations and acknowledged by the officers signing the articles which must state the manner in which the shares of each corporation are to be converted into the shares or obligations of the new corporation. The article should then be filed and recorded in the mortgage office and a certificate of incorporation issued by the Secretary of State as in the case of new corporations.

These consolidations should be made by a majority of not less than two-thirds of the stockholders present or represented at the meetings.

A formal and specific transfer of the immovable property of each corporation should be made to the new corporation and registered in the conveyance office·

The liquidation of any corporation may be done

either voluntary or in court. If voluntary it must be in accordance with the provisions of the statute under which it was organized and the charter provisions not contrary thereto.

The voluntary liquidation must conform to the following requirements. The liquidation must be voted by a two-third vote of the stockholders and notice thereof published in a newspaper at least one time; a copy of such advertisement, accompanied by a certificate executed by the publisher of the newspaper in which it appeared must be filed with the Secretary of State. One copy of the resolutions adopted must be signed by at least one of the stockholders authorized by the meeting to sign it, or by a majority, must be sent to the Secretary of State. If the liquidation is authorized by all of the stockholders without a meeting, all the stockholders must sign the agreement, and a copy thereof, acknowledged by at least one of the stockholders, must be filed with the Secretary of State. The liquidators should be appointed by a majority of the stockholders and should give bond. The liquidator or liquidators, on final liquidation in voluntary liquidations, must file with the Secretary of State a certificate of that fact and that official's certificate that the corporation has been liquidated filed in the mortgage office of the parish where the corporation had its domicile.

Liquidations through court proceedings has been treated in another chapter hence will not be repeated here.

It has occurred in the past in the case of small corporations with only a few stockholders, such stockholders have joined in a transfer of the property of the corporation without appointment of a liquidator or where the liquidator or liquidators have failed to qualify or to act. Such a transfer is valid, provided that all debts have been paid and that all the actual stockholders are parties to the act, but necessarily both such facts are left open to doubt. It has been held that if all the stockholders sign an agreement and the Secretary of State certifies that all of the signers constitute all of the stockholders, any action under such agreement is a corporate act (1).

1—Renauld v Marine Spec. and Mill Co., 172 L.835

CHAPTER XLIV

Divorce

Divorce and/or separation proceedings are of importance in title examinations from three standpoints: Validity of the divorce or separation; date of the judgment; subsequent marriage if any.

The validity or invalidity of the divorce or separation proceedings determines whether or not subsequent acquisition of property belongs to the first community or to the second community, if there is one. The date of the judgment of divorce or separation, if valid, determines whether or not, the property is the separate property of the vendor, or belongs to the second community, if there has been a second marriage. If there has been a subsequent marriage and the divorce proceedings are invalid, all property acquired during the second marriage belongs to both wives or to the children. In such a case, if the second wife is in good faith, it is a putative marriage and she or her heirs have an interest in all community property acquired since the second marriage (1). If she is not in good faith, no civil effects will follow and neither she nor her heirs can claim any interest (2). In putative marriages the heirs of both wives inherit (3).

The proceedings for a divorce or separation involve checking of the following elements: Jurisdiction of the court; Matrimonial domicile; Cause of Action; Marriage; Citation; Judgment.

Jurisdiction: The rules applying to the jurisdic-

1—R. C. C. 117, 118; Smith v Smith, 43 A.1140; Jones v Squires, 137 L.888; Ray v Knox, 164 L.193; Johnson v Johnson, 167 L.861
2—Succ. Prieto, 165 L.710
3—Ray v Knox, 164 L.193

tion in other matters apply in these cases, with this exception; a court may not acquire jurisdiction by consent of the defendant (1).

Matrimonial Domicile: The matrimonial domicile must have been established in this State, either originally or where the parties have married outside the State and removed here.

The courts of Louisiana will not grant a divorce where the parties never had a domicile in this State, or for a cause which arose in another state before a domicile was acquired here (2); but where the matrimonial domicile was established here, though marriage was contracted in another state and the wife never resided here, our courts will take jurisdiction (3). In general the domicile of the husband is the domicile of the wife and suit for divorce or separation from bed and board may be brought against him or her, though absent (4).

Cause of Action: An action for a divorce or separation on grounds which are not recognized as a cause of action under our statutes, would be a nullity, as would be a judgment founded on a petition in which the cause of action was the living separate and apart for the statutory period, in which the petition failed to state the length of time during which the separation existed, or which did not recite that the plaintiff had resided continuously in the state for statutory period (5); or did not allege or prove in a suit for a divorce founded on a previous judgment of separation, the fact of that judgment (6).

1—Weiss v N. O. Board Trade, 125 L.1010
2—Smither v Smither, 145 L.752; Mann v Mann, 170 L.958;
    Mathews v Mathews, 157 L.930
3—Stevens v Allen, 139 L.658
4—Claude v Peat, 43 A.161... Lamarque v Lamarque, 40 A.457;
    Butler v Dudley, 11 L.1096
5—Laplace v Brierre, 152 L.235
6—Nicholas v Maddox, 52 A.1493

Citation: Must conform to the rules prescribed for that process. In domicilary service it is sufficient to make service at the domicile which the husband has abandoned, although he may have acquired another since his departure (1). Substituted service may be resorted to in the case of an absentee spouse, but the fact of absence must be alleged and proved (2).

Marriage: The marriage must be alleged and proved, as of course there can be no divorce without marriage.

Judgment: The judgment must be rendered and signed in open court. Foreign judgments are entitled to the same force and effect as the judgments of our own courts, but the examiner should require a copy, certified by the clerk of court which rendered it, and a statement that the time for an appeal under the law of the state had expired.

1—Spangenburg v Carter, 151 L.1038
2—Cormier v DeValcourt, 33 A.1168; Clarcor v Lane, 5 A.499;
    Whitney v Finnegan, 129 L.572

CHAPTER XLV

Emancipation of Minors.

There are three kinds of emancipations: Emancipation conferring the power of administration; emancipation by marriage; and the emancipation relieving the minor from the time prescribed by law for attaining the age of majority (1).

In the first kind of emancipation the minor has no power of alienating his property and hence such alineation must be made in accordance with laws governing such alienations in the case of unemancipated minors (2).

In the second kind of emancipation, the minor, whether male or female, is emancipated by right of marriage (3), but he or she must have reached the age of eighteen years in order to be fully emancipated. (4).

The third kind of emancipation is known as the judicial emancipation and the minor who has attained the full age of eighteen years, may present a petition to the court having jurisdiction wherein he shall set forth the reasons therefor and also the amount of his estate. This petition must be accompanied by the written consent of the tutor, if there be any, otherwise by that of a special tutor appointed for that purpose; and this consent shall contain a specific declaration that the minor is fully capable of managing his own affairs. If the tutor refuses his assent, or shall refuse to appear by way of answer to the application of the minor, he shall be cited, according to law, to show cause why the minor should not be emancipated (5).

1—R. C. C. 365
2—R. C. C. 373
3—R. C. C. 379
4—R. C. C. 382
5—R. C. C. 385

If the minor has a father or mother living, the consent of the father or mother, or both shall be necessary to authorize the judge to act, but such consent shall not be necessary if the application be made on the ground of ill treatment, refusal to support, or corrupt examples (1).

The word cruelty means that of a living and present parent and not merely an absent parent (2).

Both parents must consent to emancipation (3).

The exact procedure to be followed where a minor seeks emancipation under the authority of article 378 of the Code is not clear, but it would seem that a rule should be taken on the recalcitrant parent or parents to show cause why the minor should not be emancipated. A judgment of emancipation without the consent of the parent or parents or of the tutor whether regular or special is an absolute nullity (4).

The jurisdiction of the court pronouncing the emancipation is determined by the domicile of the parents, or of the tutor if there be one but it has been decided that the district court of the parish where the minor over eighteen was working had jurisdiction to emancipate the minor where parents' consent was given (5). This raises the question as to what court had jurisdiction where a minor had neither parents or tutor but had his domicile at a certain place, or rather was residing there. Would the court of the place of residence of the minor have jurisdiction? The jurisprudence is silent on the subject, but from the above cited case, it would seem that it would.

1—R. C. C. 387
2—Gaston v Rainich, 141 L.162
3—State ex rel v Sacred Heart Orphan Asylum. 154 L.883
4—Gaston v Rainich. 141 L.162
5—False v Hanagriff, 14 La. App. 249

A married woman who is above the age of eighteen years is sui juris and may mortgage and alienate realty and prescription begins to run against her the same as if she is a femme sole and has attained the age of majority (1).

A party, defendant, married but only seventeen, when suit was filed, was fully emancipated when she became eighteen years of age and then was relieved from all disabilities attaching to minors, hence suit commenced more than two years after she became eignteen, to set aside sheriff's sale of property sold under judgment rendered in original suit at which time she was 17, was barred as to her (2).

An emancipation carried on without the assent of a duly appointed and qualified tutor, or a special tutor, is void (3). In the case cited, the minor had neither parents nor tutor and no tutor was appointed, but where both parents are living, or where one parent is living but has not qualified regularly as tutor of the minor, a different situation is presented. With both parents living the father is tutor of his minor child without any necessity of qualifying. If one parent has died, or where the parents are divorced, the courts have held by inference at least, that the survivor or the parent to whom the custody of the child has been awarded in divorce proceedings, should qualify regularly as tutor of the minor for the purpose of emancipating him, or her. This conclusion has been reached because of a decision reported in the 188 La. Reports (4). In that case, a bank had been appointed tutor of the minor and the mother given the custody of the person of the minor. The bank went

1—R. C. C. 362; Murray v Hardee, 189 So.376
2—Ibid
3—In re Tutorship Webster, 188 L.678
4—Ibid

into the hands of a receiver and its successor continued to act as tutor, though not qualified. The mother emancipated the minor without being regularly qualified. The minor sued the bank for an accounting. The bank attacked the validity of the emancipation and the court sustained the bank's defense (1).

A minor may not, however, attack the judgment of emancipation where he has, on the strength of that emancipation, dealt with third parties (2); and a judgment of emancipation cannot be attached collaterally (3).

1—Tutorship of Webster, 188 L.623
2—In re Sacred Heart Orphan Asylum, 154 L.883; Munday v
    Kaufman,, 48 A.592; Allison v Watson, 36 A.616
3—Wilson v Lyons Lbr. Co., 7 La. App. 169

CHAPTER XLVI

Escheat

A decision which is of importance but which fails to clearly set out the rights of the State in cases of escheat of vacant successions as against third parties who have acquired the property prior to the date on which the State took possession of the succession, is that reported in the 143 L. (1). In that case the litigation was not between the State and another, but between two private parties to an agreement of sale, in which the plaintiff sought to recover earnest money deposited on the ground that the defendant's title to the property in question was fatally defective.

The court held that the defendant's title was a valid one, but beyond declaring that the State is not seized of right in vacant successions, left completely unanswered the question as to how or why the State's rights were defeated by a tax sale. The court in this case declined to pass upon the pleas of prescription and estoppel urged as a defense.

A recent examination of a title disclosed a problem which is of interest to title examiners but which must remain unanswered in the absence of an jurisprudence thereon.

The property involved is in the possession of the descendants of a slave who acquired the property by purchase subsequent to his emancipation by his master. Dying within a year thereafter his children, in being at the time of their father's emancipation, but not themselves emancipated, took possession and these children and their descendants have remained in possession and occupied the property until the present without any interruption or interference.

1—Puyoulet v Gehrke, 143 L.315

Under the law as it then existed, the emancipation of the father did not result in the emancipation of his children, consequently at his death, they were still slaves and as such could not inherit.

Third parties are not involved as there have been no transfers, all taxes having been paid and no sales executed.

Thus it will be seen that the situation in this case is entirely different from that presented in the cited case. The present possessors are tresspassers. However, three defenses might be urged against the State's claim, if made at this time. First; Prescription acquirendi causa, doubtful to say the least, against the State. Second, estoppel, on the ground that the State has for all these years, assessed the property in the name of the possessors and collected taxes thereon. Third, the children of the emancipated slave, subsequently became emancipated by law (Lincoln's Proclamation) and hence may have thereby acquired the status of legitimate heirs.

No opinion of course may be expressed as to the force of any of such pleas. The problem has been mentioned as one of interest to examiners and is presented only here from that standpoint.

CHAPTER XLVII

ESTOPPELS

The question of estoppels enter into an examination of titles only when a defect appears that may or may not be remedied by an estoppel.

Estoppels may operate in various ways: by writing; by acts; by words; by law.

An estoppel is based upon equity and being such may not be urged unless the other party has been induced to act to his injury, or where the party estopped has gained some advantage to which he would not have been entitled.

Not only may the principal be estopped but his privies may be, such as his legatee and legal heirs, but creditors and his forced heirs are not (1). One may not contest the title of one under whom he holds (2).

A husband may not claim property as community where he has joined in the act whereby his wife acquired the property as her separate and paraphernal funds (3). A vendor who accepts and receipts for the purchase price of the property sold, in whole or in part, ratifies whatever his agent may have done in the sale of the property, though not authorized by the terms of the agency (4).

Where one stands by and permits his property to be sold as the property of another, or does not object legally when it is being sold illegally, he is estopped from disputing the title thus acquired (5).

1—Kerwin v Insurance Co., 85 A.35; Pfister v Casso, 1616 L.940
2—15 A.684; 34 A.634
3—Succ. Hostetter. 128 L.470; Brown v Stroud, 34 A.374
4—Wood Slayback & Co. v Rocchi, 32 A.212
5—Lippmans v McCranie, 30 A. 125; Bradford-Kennedy Co. v Brown, 152 L.38

Heirs who sue for or participate in a partition, thereby ratify a will made by the decedent in whose succession the partition is made (1). Parties to a fraud may not be heard for the purpose of avoiding the transaction (2).

This estoppel may occur in judicial pleadings (3); in partitions (4); in transfers (5) in which the party estopped has appeared as vendor or mortgagor (6); in matters of agency the act of the agent is the act of the principal and the principal may be estopped by reason of the authority given, if not ultra vires, or even in this case by his subsequent action or silence (7); it may occur through silence or acquiescence (8).

Res judicata also operates as an estoppel, but in this case the cause of action and the parties must be the same (9). Acquiescence in a judgment which may or may not be final estops the party acquiescing (10).

Ratification by any means is to be considered an estoppel.

1—Cook v Martin, 188 L.1063
2—Ackerman v Peters, 113 L.156; Ackerman v Larned, 116 L.101
3—Savings & Homestead Ass'n. v Chase, Teisser Orleans,
        App. Dig. 69
4—Mohawk Oil Co. v Layne, 147 L.895
5—Pritchard v McCraine, 160 L.605
6—Consol. Progressive Oil Co. v Standard Oil Co., 158 L.982
7—Succ. of Ferrill, 166 L.479
8—Childers v Adair, 5 L.App. 213
8—Liquidators Nicholson Pub. Co. v Upton Printing Co., 152 L.270
9—Wakefield State Bank v Baker Wakefield, 4 La. App. 452
10 Gallagher v Conner, 138 L.633; Lockbaum v Southern
        Box Co., 121 L.176

CHAPTER XLVIII
Execution of Judgments.

This discussion covers executions of money judgments, whether under writs of fieri facias, or of seizure and sale, but does not touch upon judgments which require something to be given or done. The rules governing executions of judgments are to be found in general in the Code of Practice (1). Where an article does not apply to writs of seizure and sale, or because of certain conditions, this fact will be noted.

The execution of judgments belong to the court of first instance whether or not the case has been appealed (2), but if appealed, it can not be executed until it has been entered upon the records of the appellate court and in the records of the inferior court. (3). However, a bidder who is a party to the suit who permits the execution to go forward though the decree of the appellate court has not been recorded in the district court, cannot claim that sale was premature (4). The Appellate court must send its judgment to the inferior court in order that it may be executed (5). The fact that the writ of fieri facias directs the execution of the district court instead of the judgment of the Supreme Court has no effect on the validity of the execution (6). The judgment of the appellate court need not be recorded in the minutes of the lower court (7), but it cannot be executed until it has been recorded in the records of the lower court, which recording shall be directed to be made

1—C. P. Arts., 617 to 723
2—C. P. Art. 617
3—Thomas v Goodwin. 120 L.504: State ex rel Monroe, 133 L.1045
4—Gentilly Dev. Co. v Carbajal, 168 L.786
5—C. P. Art. 618, 915
6—Weil v Merz. 23 A.392
7—Amet v Boyer, 42 A.831

by the party in whose favor the judgment is rendered and the clerks have the power to receive and record all judgments of the higher courts, and to issue all legal processes therein (1).

All of the foregoing applies to the Circuit Courts of Appeal but not to appeals from Justices of the Peace, Municipal or City Courts where the suit is tried de novo by the appellate court.

If the judgment has been rendered where no appeal lies, or on confession of one of the parties, its execution may be prosecuted immediately; if the judgment has become final, if appealed, the execution may be prayed for as soon as it has been recorded in the lower court (2); in regard to judgments subject to appeal, they can only be executed ten days after the party cast has been notified, where notice is requested, if he has not appealed or if he has appealed, has failed to furnish the necessary security for a suspensive appeal, provided that where a defendant has appeared in court and filed his answer, the signing of judgment by the judge shall operate as a notice to the party cast.

None of the above apply to the executory process. In the executory process and hypothecary action service of the notice of seizure is a notice of judgment (3).

A sale prematurely made under a writ prematurely issued is not of itself a sufficient ground of annullment (4). It would certainly be a cause for an injunction.

When the judgment orders the payment of a sum of money, the party in whose favor it is rendered

1—C. P. Arts., 619, 620
2—C. P. Art., 623
3—Lomas v Robichaux. 14 A.105; State v Judge 2nd Dist.
       Court. 16 A.390
4—Alfano v Franek, 159 L.498

may apply to the clerk of court and obtain from him a writ of fieri facias (1). This article does not apply to executory process and hypothecary actions.

Whatever order or writ is issued by the clerk of court it should be signed by him and the seal of the court should be affixed (2). The seal of the court is essential as without it the sheriff has no authority to act (3). This writ is directed to the sheriff and orders him to seize and sell the property belonging to the party cast, and all such writs must be made returnable by the sheriff in not less than thirty days nor more than seventy days (4). In all cases, except in the parish of Orleans, where the sheriff has made a seizure under the writ but is not able to sell the property seized before the return day of the writ, he shall nevertheless make due return of the writ, but he shall make and retain a copy of the writ which he shall certify, and shall proceed under such certified copy of the writ in the same manner as though the original writ was in his hands and shall make a due return thereon; and in the parish of Orleans, the clerk of court shall make a duly certified copy of the writ, instead of the sheriff making it and he shall proceed as provided for above (5).

A fieri facias may issue to a sheriff where defendant's property is situated though out the jurisdiction of the court (6) issuing the writ.

Though a new seizure could not be made two years after a writ of fieri facias was issued, yet a seizure made within seventy days is effective for the

1—C. P. Art., 641
2—C. P. Art., 626
3—Fink v Lallande. 16 L.547; Bonin v Durand, 2 A.776; King v Baker, 7 A.570
4—C. P. Art. 642
5—C. P. Art. 642'
6—Lafon v Smith. 3 L.473, 475

purposes of a sale of the property (1); and property seized within seventy days after the date of the issuance of the writ can be sold after seventy days under the original writ (2). Where a writ of fieri facias has been issued further writs may not be issued until final return is made on the first writ (3).

Though the sheriff fails to return the original writ to the clerk's office before the return day, a sale under the certified copy made by him before the return day is not nullified for that reason (4).

Writs of seizure and sale (executory and hypothecary actions) are not returnable within a fixed delay but remain in the hands of the sheriff until satisfied, or ordered returned (5).

On receipt of the writ the sheriff must execute it without delay by seizing the property of the debtor in the parish, except that exempt by law (6). This exemption includes 160 acres of land, buildings etc., thereon, to the value of two thousand dollars, provided that the debtor owns the land and resides thereon and has a family or is the head of family; and provided that his wife does not own in her own right and in actual enjoyment thereof, of property to the value of more than one thousand dollars; no property is exempt for nonpayment of taxes or assessments levied according to law, nor for the purchase price thereof (7).

The debtor has the right of pointing out what property he wishes to be seized and sold first, and

1—Union Nat'l Bank v Hyams, 50 A.1110
2—Siess v Couvillion, 5 La. App. 464
3—Marine Bank v Schaffer, 166 L. 164
4—Smith v Lenahan Lbr. Co., 139 L.898
5—Stackhouse v Zuntz, 41 A. 415
6—C. P. Art. 643
7—C. P. 644

provided that this property is within the parish (1),
but he shall have no right to point out this property
if the judgment creditor has a privilege or mortgage
on a part of his property (2). The debtor also loses
the right of pointing out such property if he allows
the sheriff to execute the writ and advertise the
property seized without exercising that right (3). The
code further provides for the right of the debtor to
point out what portions of the land is to be sold,
the amount and to reduce excessive property and for
the appointment of appraisers, but as those rights
must be exercised prior to the sale and therefore does
not affect the validity of the sale if made, they
are not copied here.

As soon as the writ is executed the sheriff must
give notice thereof in writing to the debtor and annex
thereto a list of the property seized which he shall
deliver to him in person or leave at his place of ordinary residence, and if the property seized be lands
he shall notify the defendant to have the lands so
seized divided into lots (4). A sheriff is not bound
to give any notice previous to seizure (5). Three days
after this notice the sheriff shall advertise the sale
of the property seized, in the manner and form directed in the following articles (6). These articles
(7) provide for the possession of the sheriff, but
in the City of New Orleans it is sufficient for the
sheriff to record in the mortgage office the writ of
seizure containing a full description of the property
and the proper reference to the proceedings under
which the seizure was made. In the country the

1—C. P. Art. 646
2—C. P. Art 648
3—C. P. Art. 649
4—C. P. Art. 654
5—Tompkins v Stroud, 16 L.274
6—C. P. Art. 655
7—C. P. Arts. 656, 7, 8, 9, 660

sheriff takes physical possession of the property and retains same else the seizure is void (1).

The sale of the property must be made by the sheriff at the seat of justice for the parish where the seizure is made (2); except that if the property is situated in more than one parish, when the sale may be made in either parish (3). In the country the sale may be made on the plantations which are to be sold, if the debtor requires it, but in this case notice must be given of the fact in the advertisement of sale (4).

Three days after the sheriff shall have given the notice to the debtor he must advertise the sale at the day, place and hour which he shall designate. Every such sale must be announced by public advertisement composed in English only (5). These advertisements must be inserted in the official journals according to special laws (6), which contain full and specific regulations as to judicial advertisements but are too lengthy to be inserted here. All sales of immovables must be only after thirty days advertisement (7). Thirty clear days should elapse between the first day of advertisement and the day of sale (8), but sale on thirtieth day after advertisement thereof was legal but it has been decided that the first day of advertisement and day of sale must be excluded from the computation period of advertisement (9).

The same delay and formalities must be observed

1—Act 189, 1857; R. S. 3625; Majer v Hewes, 135 L.354; Conte v Hardy. 34 A.862
2—C. P. Art. 664
3—Act 8, 1926
4—C. P. Art. 667
5—C. P. 668
6—Acts 49, 1877; 82, 1900; 270, 1914; 33, 1916; 75, 1933
7—C. P. Art. 670
8—McDonough v Gravier, 9 L.531
9—Zibilich v Rousseo, 157 L.936

in executing writs of seizure and sale against mortgaged property (1).

Judicial sales will not be set aside for mere informalities or irregularities, unless injury therefrom is shown (2).

It is vital, however, that the advertisements appear once a week in each calendar week, though it is of no important as to what particular day in the week, or that more than seven days intervene (3).

In parishes where no papers are published it suffices that the advertisements be posted in front of the courthouse and two other public places (4).

Ten days before the sale the sheriff must notify the defendant to appear at a given time and place for the purpose of appointing appraisers to appraise the property to be sold (provided that appraisement has not been waived by the debtor), which appraisers are to be appointed in accordance with the procedure laid down by the Code of Practice (5) which are too long to be inserted here.

A mortgage debtor may waive appraisement in the act of mortgage (6). The appraisers when appointed must be sworn and they shall reduce their appraisement in writing and deliver it to the sheriff (7). On the day and hour appointed for the sale, the sheriff or his deputy shall proceed to cry the property, after having read the advertisement declaring the nature of the sale and a description of the property (8).

1—Grant v Walden. 6 L.623
2—Stockmeyer v Tobin, 139 U. S. 176. 35 L.ed 123
3—Succ. Valenti, 172 L.290
4—Act 75. 1938
5—C. P. Art.. 671, 673
6—Stockmeyer v Tobin, 139. U. S. 176; 35 L. Ed. 123; Broadwell v
      Rodriguez, 18 A.68
7—C. P. Art, 673
8—C. P. Art. 677

In all sales of immovable property the sheriff must obtain and read out before crying, a mortgage certificate from the Recorder of Mortgages; and in addition in the parish of Orleans, the sheriff of that parish must obtain and read out a certificate of the Register of Conveyance (1). Where parish records have been destroyed as in case of fire, that fact must be stated by the sheriff and the extent of the destruction (2).

Where there are mortgages and privileges which because of rank prime the judgment under which the writ of fieri facias was issued, the property must bring an amount sufficient to pay off the superior claims (3); and if the bid does not reach two-thirds of the appraisement (4), the sale shall be postponed for fifteen days, re-advertised and re-cried and sold for whatever it will bring on twelve months credit, provided it brings a sufficient amount to pay off privilege and mortgages which prime that of the seizing creditor (5).

These rules refer to general mortgages and not special mortgages (6). If the priming mortgages belong to the seizing creditor, the sale is valid though for less amount than is sufficient to pay them off.

If the seizing creditor's claim primes those of other creditors he may require that the property be sold for any amount in order to pay him (7). A sale for cash under an order which does not specifically call for a sale on terms but only requires the purchaser to assume payment of the mortgage notes al-

1—C. P. 678
2—Act 69. 1910
3—C. P. 679
4—C. P. 680
5—C. P. 680, 681, 682, 684
6—Pasley v McConnell, 38 A.470
7—C. P. 685. Wolff v Lowry, 10 A.272; Marsh v Foster, 11 A.181, 16 A.163

ready due, is valid (1). The property passes to the purchaser burdened with any real charges that have been imposed upon the land, such as usufruct, use, habitation, servitudes or others, provided that they have been imposed prior to the date of the judgment, or mortgages, or privilege (2). Either the judgment creditor or the judgment debtor may bid (3).

If the bidder fails to comply with his bid, the sheriff shall re-auction the property and adjudge it to another person (4), and he is not obliged to wait three days for the bidder to find security and he may immediately offer it for sale the same day (5). It is not necessary to put the adjudicatee in default (6)·

The validity of title is not affected, even though the purchaser was the judgment creditor, by a reduction in the amount of the judgment by the appellate court (7), and a delay in the execution of the sale does not annul the adjudication (8).

The sheriff must make a return of the original writ to the clerk of the court and a report of the sale he has made, including in this report, a description of the object seized, the amount for which it was sold and the terms and conditions of the sale (9).

1—Keenan v Ahern, 34 A.885
2—C. P. Art. 687
3—C. P. Art. 688
4—C. P. Art. 689
5—Lafon v Smith. 3 L.473; Walker v Allen. 19 L.307
6—Branner v Hardy, 18 A.537; Losee v Sauton. 24 A.370
7—Pasley v McConnell, 38 A.470
8—Interdiction Onorato, 46 A.73
9—C. P. Art. 700, 702

CHAPTER XLIX

Family Meetings

Since the Act of 1920, as amended in 1926, 1934 and 1935 (1), family meetings have not been a factor in title examinations, except in those cases which have been pointed out 'and in those links which are based upon an alienation of a minor's or interdict's property prior to that year, and though the legislature has passed several quieting acts in cure of certain irregularities, such acts do not cover irregularities not mentioned in those acts. Formerly family meetings were required where several relatives claimed the right to be appointed (2); sale or mortgage of minor's property (3); to authorize tutors to sue for a partition (4); to purchase for minors at partition sales of ancestor's property (5); to fix terms of succession sales in which minors were interested (6); to authorize tutor to dispose of land of minor residing in another state (7); to fix dowry of child of interdicted person (8); to authorize husband to give special mortgage in place of legal mortgage in favor of wife (9); to adjudicate minor's interest in property to parent (10); to authorize tutor to give special mortgage (11).

In effect it has been held that no action on behalf of a minor was valid unless approved by a family meeting (12).

1—Acts 110, 1920; 319, 1926; 47, 1934; 18, 1935
        2 E. S.
2—R. C. C. 267
3—R. C. C. 339
4—R. C. C. 1312
5—R. C. C. 1344
6—R. C. C. 1341
7—Bailey v Morrison. 4 A.523
8—R. C. C. 415, 416
9—R. C. C. 3339
10R. C. C. 344
11—R. C. C. 325
12—Elder v Elder, 142 L.95

Irregularities in the appointment and-or composition of family meetings are generally not vital, as innocent third parties need not inquire into such irregularities, but there are certain requisites of which the purchaser must take notice, such as the proper minimum of members; that all members were notified of the meeting or waived notice thereof; that they took the required oath, that the under tutor is present at the meeting and either approves or does not approve (1); that, where there were not a sufficient number of relatives living within the circle prescribed by law, no more than a sufficient number of friends to complete the minimum numbers of five members be present and vote in the meeting (2); that the recommendations of the family meeting be approved and homologated (3).

1—Succ. Marinovich, 105 L.106; Doucet v Fenelon 120 L.18
2—Succ. Marinovich. 105 L.106; Succ. Fried, 106 L.276; Succ. Carbajal, 111 L.944
3—Hecker v Brown, 104 L.524

CHAPTER L

Interdicts

The interdiction of a person can only be pronounced after formal proceedings which must be strictly observed (1). The examiner is therefore obliged to inquire into those proceedings and satisfy himself that they have been conducted in strict compliance with the law.

Every interdiction must be instituted by a petition and may be brought by any relative or husband or wife (2), or even by a stranger under certain conditions, and even by a corporation which is a creditor of the alleged insane person, as also defendants in a suit wherein the insane person was plaintiff, as having sufficient interest to sue for the interdiction of such a person (3). Judgment must be pronounced by the judge of the place where the person had his domicile or residence (4). The alleged interdict must be cited as in other suits (5). If he fails to answer within the usual period of delay for answer, the judge must appoint an attorney at law to represent him who must also be served and the defendant be cited through him, as the attorney at law cannot accept service on behalf of the defendant (6).

After trial and judgment which must be published, the court must appoint a curator and under curator in accordance with the rules governing appointment of tutors (7).

The examiner must check these appointments

1—State ex rel v Ford. 164 L.149
2—R. C. C. 391
3—Inter. Giacona. 158 L.148
4—R. C. C. 392
5—State v Kern, 153 L.829; Segur v Pellerini, 16 L.63;
  Vance v Ellerbe, 150 L.403
6—Segur v Pellerini. 16 L.63
7—R. C. C. 398, 404

and ascertain to his satisfaction that they have been made according to law.

Not only insane persons but persons who, owing to any infirmity are incapable of taking care of their persons and administering their estate may be interdicted (1).

The interdiction takes effect from the date of the filing of the petition and all acts done by the interdict between that date and the date of the judgment on same are null and void (2).

Where the party is notoriously insane his acts may be annulled but as this requires proof beyond the record, the examiner is not generally in a position to decide such a question, unless he is in possession of facts which justifies his refusal of the title.

Curators of interdicts are appointed in the manner and according to the same rules as tutors (3).

Curators like tutors may not dispose of their wards' property except on orders of court (4).

Interdictions proceedings when held contradictorily with an attorney appointed by the court are not exparte (5).

A judgment against alleged insane people, based on service of petition and citation on curator appointed without compliance with mandatory codal provisions, is an absolute nullity (6).

1—R. C. C. 422
2—R. C. C. 400, 401
3—R. C. C. 415
4—R. C. C. 415
5—Inter. Grevenig, 164 L.1026
6—Collins v Jones, La. App., 152, So: 802; State v Ford, 164 L.149; Vance v Ellerbe, 150 L.388

CHAPTER LI
Judgment by Default

Where there is involved, in an examination of title, consideration of a judicial proceeding of any kind, founded on citation, the examiner need only consider whether or not the appropriate prescription has run. (See chapter on prescriptions).

Questions of Jurisdiction, both over the person of the defendant and ratione materiea, are foreclosed by the judgment (where the defendant has been cited) and prescription has run. Where there has been no citation or service on the defendant and the court had no jurisdiction, the nullity of the judgment can be urged at any time (1), unless the defendant who was domiciled in the parish, permitted the plaintiff to execute the judgment (2).

Where, however, prescription has not run, it is, of course necessary to inquire into the validity and effectiveness of the judgment. And here the question of citation and service becomes of importance.

The articles of the Code of Practice, as amended, and interpreted by the courts, prevailed on this question until 1918 when the legislature enacted a comprehensive statue (3), detailing the manner of service on individuals (both sui juris and otherwise), partnerships, corporations and other legal entities, public officers and boards. In the main the act referred to made few changes in the articles of the Code of Practice but gave recognition to the jurisprudence on the subject and the change in the status of married women.

In all cases, except where special laws fix the time

1—C. P. Art. 612; Whitney Central Bank v Alfred, 136 L.230;
    Elmore v Johnson, 121 L.277
2—C. P. Art. 612
3—Act 179, 1918; as amended by Act 48, 1932

and conditions for appeal and the effectiveness of the judgment, no notice of judgment need be given where there has been personal service on the defendant, or he has answered in person or through counsel (1).

Where the judgment is by default based on domiciliary service in cases of money judgments, or where the judgment orders the delivery of personal property, or real estate which produces revenue, etc., notice of judgment must be given the defendant before the period of suspensive appeal runs or the judgment becomes executory (2).

No notice need be given in divorce actions as they are controlled by special laws (3).

Entry of default: An entry of default is absolutely necessary as without it no issue is joined and a confirmation without such a default is null and void (4). In city courts no preliminary default is required (5).

Confirmation: The default may be confirmed three days (judicial or otherwise but not on Holidays or Sundays) (6) but plaintiff must prove his demand (7).

The judgment of course must be signed in open court after the three days delay as in other cases.

1—C. P. Art 575
2—Shipp v Shipp, 182 L.1019; C. P. Art. 573
3—C. P. Art. 573
4—C. P. Art. 311; Cavanaugh v Youngblood, 10 La. App. 117;
        Hart v Nixon, 25 A.417; Johnson v Boyle, 14 L.268
5—State v Judge, 46 A.629; Goldman v Thompson, 3 La. App. 469
6—C. P. Art. 612; amended Act 31, 1890, 90, 1904
7—Saenger Amusement Co. v Masur, 158 L.745

CHAPTER LII
LEASES, SERVITUDES AND RESTRICTIONS.
Leases

Mineral leases and land leases constitute clouds on the title to the extent that they deprive the owner of the full enjoyment of the property, but the examiner is not called upon to do more than point out the existence of the cloud, so no further comment is needed here.

Servitudes

A servitude is likewise a cloud on a title for the same reasons given above and for the same reason require no extensive discussion, especially the subject occupies an entire chapter of the Civil Code (1) and it would serve no good purpose to set out here even a summary of the articles or of the jurisprudence.

Restrictions

The usual restrictions to be found today in titles constitute more than a mere interference in the full ownership of the property because any violations thereof gives rise to the right of disolving the original sale. However, such an eventuality is hardly to be looked for in most cases, although such a condition in a title may do much to reduce its merchantability.

Again the prescription of two years applicable under the act of 1938 (2) has the effect of putting at rest any doubt where there has been a violation of the conditional sale.

1—Chapter 4, R. C. C. Arts. 646 to 822
2—Act 328, 1938

CHAPTER LIII

Liens and Mortgages

It is only in certain phases of the subject that liens and mortgages and other encumbrances are of interest to the examiner as the mortgage certificate will ordinarily show just what encumbrances are re-corded against the property involved, but where a title is based upon a foreclosure proceedings, it is part of the routine examination to check the validity of the instrument upon which the proceedings and sale is founded, hence it has been found advisable to present here certain facts as bearing upon such validity.

Liens, privileges and mortgages are stricti juris; can be created only by law, cannot be extended by implication or from reasons of equity, nor by covenant (1).

The Constitutions of the State, since 1868 have variously provided for recordation of liens, privileges and mortgages and the effect thereof as against third persons, the Constitution of 1921 as amended, reading as follows (2):

No mortgage, or privilege on immovable property, or debt for which preference may be granted by law, shall affect third persons unless recorded or registered in the parish where the proverty is situated, in the manner, and within the time prescribed by law, except privileges for expenses of last illness, privileges arising upon the death of the owner of the property affected, and privileges for taxes, State, Parish and Municipal . . . . (3)

1—Boylan Detective Agcy. v Brown, 157 L.325; American Creosote
    Works v Natchitoches, 182 L.641
2—Arts. 123 Const. 1868; 176, 177, 1879;186, 187, 1898;
    186, 187. 1913; Sec. 19; Art. 19, 1921
3—Sec. 19, Art. 19, 1921

The Revised Civil Code and the Code of Practice contain articles covering the recordation and registration of liens, privileges and mortgages, but in view of the above constitutional provisions further expounding of the subject is not required, except as to the manner and the time prescribed by those articles which will be discussed from the standpoint of a judicial sale based on a foreclosure proceeding.

Until the year 1910 mortgages were without effect as to third parties until actually inscribed on the record (not merely filed) (1) but in that year an act was passed (2) which placed mortgages on the same footing with conveyances which did have effect from the time of their filing (3) so that such instruments became effective from the date, hour and minute of their filing as the act requires the recorder of mortgages to immediately indorse on the mortgage or lien on receipt, the date, hour and minute of depositing in his office, which data must be recorded with the document (4).

In connection with the subject of inscription it may be well to refer to the subject of re-inscription and its effect on the rights of the mortgagee, mortgagor and of third parties. To preserve the preference granted by law to recorded mortgages over mortgages and liens recorded subsequent to the mortgage first recorded, it must be re-inscribed in the mortgage office not later than ten years after its first inscription (5), though it is not necessary to re-inscribe it as between the parties to the instrument, or to record it originally, as it is the effect of the inscription and not

1—Charrier v Greenlaw Truck & Tractor Co., 2 La. App. 622
2—Act 215, 1910
3—Godchaux Sugars Co. v Boudreaux, 153 L.685
4—Act 215, 1910
5—R. C. C. 3333 (now 3369)

of the mortgage that ceases or has effect against third parties from the original inscription (1). In other words recordation is not required as between a mortgagor and a mortgagee to give effect to the mortgage, and therefore it follows that re-inscription is not required or necessary as between the same parties.

In certain classes of mortgages re-inscription is not required such as mortgages given in favor of the Poydras Legacy Commission (2) and where the debt secured by the mortgage is payable in installments running over a period of nine years, prescription against the mortgage does not begin to run until six years after the maturity of the last installments, hence re-inscription is not necessary until that time has elapsed and may be extended by written agreement duly recorded, for six years beyond the extension of last installment (3).

A special form of rural mortgages and bonds was established in 1914 by the legislature, the details of which are too numerous to be recited here, but the essential features of which act are that the Trustee, to be appointed under the act, and the mortgage itself, is irrevocably the agent and representative of the holders of the bonds or notes of the corporation making the mortgage, to act in their behalf to effect enforcement of the mortgage; and that the property mortgaged may not be sold under foreclosure unless a certain per cent of the bond or note holders request same (4). A bondholder can not enforce his rights via ordinaria (5).

1—Schurtzman v Doborowlski, 191 L.791; Hite v Charbonnet, 193 L.581
2—R. C. C. 3333 (now 3369)
3—R. C. C. 3369; Act 227,1918; 52, 1924; 322, 1938; 247, 1940
4—Act. 176, 1914; 23, 1917, E. S.
5—Rowe v La. Agri. Corp. 155 L.241

A mortgage granted by an insolvent within three months of his surrendering his property in bankruptcy is null and void (1).

A discrepancy between the note and mortgage may be corrected prior to suing out of the executory process (2).

The courts have established a line of jurisprudence which determines either the validity or the non-validity of a title acquired through foreclosure proceedings, on the ground that certain irregularities which may exist are not sufficient to strike the sale with nullity, or that other defects are fatal.

Where community property was about to be foreclosed upon and the court authorized the confection of a new mortgage, upon the petition of the natural tutrix, for the purpose of satisfying an old existing mortgage and directed that the interventing tacit mortgage in favor of the minors be ineffective insofar as new mortgage was concerned, intention was to subordinate tacit mortgage to new mortgage (3).

Where recorded authentic act of sale showed a consideration upon its face and there were no prima facie evidence of fraud, innocent purchaser of vendee's mortgage for value received before maturity, was protected by public records (4).

The holder of a conventional mortgage need not foreclose against all property covered by the mortgage, but may proceed against distinct tract included therein, but he cannot proceed against an indivisible portion of the mortgaged premises in disregard of the rights of mortgagor (5).

1—R. C. C. 3359
2—Act 118, 1934
3—Gumpert v Signal, La. App. 152 So. 403
4—Jefferson v Childers, 189 L.46
5—Continental Sec. v Wetherbee, 187 L.773

The lack of authentic evidence to support an order of foreclosure by executory process must be raised by appeal from order of seizure and sale and not by a rule for injunction (1). To prevent the sale it would seem a suspensive appeal must be taken.

A mortgage taken in good faith from record owner was valid, regardless whether or not mortgagor was real owner (2).

Purchaser of a mortgaged property which mortgage contained the pact de nonalienando occupies no better position than mortgagor and can not set up defenses which the latter could not (3).

Purchasers of different parts of mortgaged premises, though acquiring property under single transaction and assuming to pay same mortgage debt, were debtors in solido as regards entire mortgage (4).

An erroneous cancellation of the inscription of a mortgage does not effect the mortgage; the inscription remains unimpaired even as against an innocent purchaser with a clear mortgage certificate (5).

Cancellation of mortgage by recorder on presentation to him of duplicate note, without mortgagee's consent, did not deprive mortgagee of security even with regard to third party dealing with property on his faith in public record (6).

No title can be conveyed to an adjudicatee on the foreclosure of a mortgage note that has been paid. He acquires no title (7).

1—Coreil v Vidrine, 188 L.343
2—Terral v Jones, La. App., 160, So. 315
3—Bass v Biggs, 167 L.126
4—Simon v McNeel, 167 L.243
5—Mulling v Jones, 7 La. App. 184; Freeland v Carmouche, 177 L. 395
6—Freeland v Carmouche, 177 L.395; Zimmer v Fryer, 190 L.814
7—Jefferson Savings Bank v Keller Tessier's Orleans App. Dig. 155; R. C. C. 3284-5; State ex rel. Landry v Broussand 177 So. 403

Though property sold was covered by mortgage act, where in foreclosure proceedings via ordinaria, the petition and fieri facias referred only to sheriff's return and deed omitted such tract, it was not included in the foreclosure sale (1).

Where husband of owner of land sold it as owner and not as agent for his wife, to one who granted a mortgage thereon, which was foreclosed, such a sale did not convey a valid title and the foreclosure purchaser acquired none (2).

Where family meeting proceedings were regular, widow and minor children received benefit of monies lent and there has been a subordination of minors' general mortgage and extract of inventory, to new mortgage, the widow and children were estopped to question priority of new mortgage (3).

A prospective mortgagee or purchaser need not interview the occupants of the land sought to be mortgaged, or sold by record owner to determine if there are any latent rights or equities (4). In effect mortgagor or purchaser need not look beyond the public record, or judicial notice.

An adjudication at a public sale under executory process for an amount less than sufficient to discharge paving liens affecting property is not void for that reason; tax privileges and liens not being contemplated in codal provision concerning execution sales where price offered is not sufficient to satisfy privileges and mortgages existing on property (5)· This simply means that purchaser takes property subject to such paving liens and tax privileges.

1—Greening v Natalie Oil Co., 152 L.467
2—Acme Land Co. v Brignac. 154 L.856
3—Wallace v Cassiere, 192 L.581
4—Bell v Canal Bank & Trust Co., 193 L.142
5—Morris v Foster, 192 L.996

An adjudication of mortgaged property, together with deed, to mortgagee where adjudicatee at second sale (adjudicatee at first sale did not comply with adjudication) failed to pay the price, and sheriff failed to make re-seizure or give notice of seizure, is void (1).

The service of process addressed to person appointed to represent defendant, individually, instead of being addressed to defendant, through such representative is a formality cured by the prescription of five years (now two) in judicial sales (2).

Neither recordation nor re-inscription of mortgage or vendor's lien, is necessary as between the parties thereto (3).

Tax sales cancel judicial and conventional mortgages but do not cancel vendor's liens or paving liens. or other liens and privileges (4).

Mortgage foreclosure proceedings under executory process where attorney was appointed to represent succession mortgage debtor and notice of demand for payment and seizure were served on the attorney only, whereas debtor was not dead, were null (5). Therefore proper evidence, in fact authentic evidence, should have been filed in the proceedings.

Sale of a property on which a vendor's lien has been retained may be rescinded for non-payment of purchase price any time within ten years after obligation becomes due or matures, even if note was prescribed (6) or even a suit for amount of the note

1—Williams v Simpson, 192 L.1022
2—R. C. C. 3543; Morris v Foster, 192 L.996
3—Schurtzman v Doborowlski, 191 L.791
4—Conservative Home. Ass'n. v Conery, 169 L.573; Conservative Home Ass'n. v Flynn, 178 L.17; McKeller v Dixie Inv. Co., La. App. 159 So. 195
5—Reid v Federal Land Bank. 193 L.1017
6—Meeb v Codifer & Bonnabel, 162 L.139; R. C. C. 2045-46

has failed (1). However this right is personal to the original vendor and can not be exercised by a transferee of the note (2). In such a case the property returns to the vendor free of all encumbrances subsequently placed thereon and not withstanding any alienation thereof (3).

Where a purchaser purchases a number of pieces of property, on one or more of which there are recorded mortgages, and he assumes payment of such mortgage or mortgages, the entire property collectively and individually becomes mortgaged for the payment of the assumed mortgages, unless contrary stipulations are entered into (4)·

The Constitution (5) provides that privileges for state, parish and municipal taxes prescribe in three years from the 31st day of December of the year in which they are due whether recorded now or hereafter (making the prescription retroactive) and all taxes and licenses, other than real property taxes, shall prescribe in three years from 31st day of December of the year in which they are due. But this prescription is not retroactive (6).

Paving liens, it has been decided are not taxes and therefore are not included in the provisions of the above cited constitutional provision (7).

Ordinary state, parish and municipal taxes are disclosed in an examination of title by the usual researches, but other taxes such as corporate franchise taxes, income taxes and social security taxes and

1—Ragsdale v Ragsdale, 105 L.409
2—Castle v Floyd, 38 A.583
3—Prudential Sav. & Home. Ass'n v Langermann, 156 L.76
4—Citizens Bank v Cuny, 32 A.360; Scionnaux vWaguespack, 32 A.283
5—Sect. 19, Article 19, Const. 1921, as amended by Act 35, 1938
6—International Shoe Co. v Picard & Geismer. 30 Fed. Supp. 570
7—Grasser Paving Co. v Richardson, 144 L.933

severance taxes being taxes imposed by the State, do not have to be recorded and therefore proper evidence of payment should be required.

The attention of the examiner is called to the chapter on sales between persons sui juris and the paragraph therein regarding tax researches.

The mortgage act upon which foreclosure proceedings are based should be examined and checked for proper confection in respect to authenticity of act, signatures, certificates, security clauses etc.

CHAPTER LIV

Minors and Their Tutors
(Interdicts and Their Curators)

There are four kinds of tutorships; the tutorship by nature; the tutorship by will; the tutorship by effect of law; and the tutorship by appointment of the court (1).

Tutorships by nature takes place of right; every other kind of tutorship must either be confirmed or given by the judge (2).

Upon the death of either parent the tutorship belongs of right to the other. Upon divorce or judicial separation from bed and board of parents, the tutorship of each minor child belongs of right to the parent in whose care he or she has been placed or to whose care he or she has been entrusted (3).

The tutorship of natural children, not acknoledged by the father belongs of right to the mother; after the death of the mother the tutorship belongs by right to the father of the minor acknowledged by him alone. The natural child acknowledged by both parents have for a tutor, first the father, in default of him, the mother (4), but where an adopting mother dies and appoints a testamentary tutor for him, the mother of the natural child may not be appointed tutrix, as of course (5).

The father or mother who is entitled to the tutorship of the natural child may choose a tutor for him, but the appointment must be approved by the judge (6).

The right of appointing a tutor belongs exclu-

1—R. C. C. 246
2—R. C. C. 248
3—R. C. C. 250; Acts 72 and 196, 1924
4—R. C. C. 256
5—Succ. Haley 49 A.709
6—R. C. C. 261

sively to the father or mother dying last (1). This is the tutorship by will.

Where a tutor has not been appointed by the parent dying last, or if the tutor so appointed has not been confirmed or is excused, then the judge ought to appoint to the tutorship the nearest ascendant in the direct line of the minor (2).

The articles of the Code following the foregoing provide the order in which the ascendants are to be preferred, the male being preferred, and declare that the grandmother is the only woman who has a right to claim the tutorship by effect of law (3), but it would seem that this has been abrogated by the statute placing women on the same footing with men.

The tutorship shall be given to the nearest kin in the collateral line and if there are more than one in that line the tutor shall be appointed on the advice of a family meeting (4).

The dative tutor is appointed where there is no tutor appointed by the parent dying last, or where the relatives cannot act, or where there are none (5). He is to be appointed upon the advice of family meeting.

All the above mentioned tutors, except the natural tutor or the one appointed under article 271 must give bond or surety, and in the latter cases the inventory must be recorded in the mortgage office (6).

An inventory must be taken in every case of tutorship (7). Every kind of tutor may give a special mortgage or a surety bond (8).

1—R. C. C. 257
2—R. C. C. 263
3—R. C. C. 264, 265, 266
4—R. C. C. 267
5—R. C. C. 270, 271
6—R. C. C. 270, 271
7—R. C. C. 316
8—R. C. C. 318, Act 254, 1916; 68, 1924

Letters of tutorship must be issued (1); and an oath must be taken by every tutor (2).

An undertutor must be appointed in every tutorship (3) and he must take an oath (4). It is his duty to act for the minor whenever the interest of the minor is in opposition to the interest of the tutor (5), but he cannot represent the minor in place of the tutor (6). He must be present at family meetings (7).

Innocent third parties need not look beyond the appointment of a tutor, except that where a father is alive, he cannot decline the appointment and must qualify unless he is barred for the reason laid down in the code (8), so that the foregoing exposition of the codal provisions is unnecessary but they are given as a matter of reference.

There are certain prerequisites, however, which must be observed in all tutorships and which should be checked by the examiner. These prerequisites and formalities are:

Jurisdiction of the court, hence the authority of the court to appoint.

The appointment, recognition or confirmation of tutors must be made by the judge of the parish where the minor has his domicile, if he has a domicile in the State, or if he has no domicile in the State, by the judge of the parish where the principal estate of the minor is situated (9). If the father and mother of the minor be dead, the appointment shall be made by the judge of probate of their last place of domicile,

1—R. C. C. 335
2—R. C. C. 334
3—R. C. C. 273
4—R. C. C 274
5—R. C. C. 275
6—In re Fortier. 31 A.50; Netter v Sullivan. 137 L.7
7—Stafford v Villian 10 A.319
8—R. C. C. 430
9—R. C. C. 307

or if they had no domicile, of that of the minor's nearest relations (1).

If the father and mother of the minor reside out of the state and are not represented in it, and the minor be also absent, he may be provided with a tutor or curator by the judge of probate of the place where he has interests to assert or defend (2).

However, a tutor regularly appointed in another state may sue for and take possession of property situated in Louisiana and will be recognized here without confirmation by the courts of this state (3), but a decree of the court of another state appointing guardian for minors for special purpose is not evidence of general authority to sue for property of succession due the minor here and to compel administrator to account (4).

A tutor appointed under Code of Practice Article 946 is a tutor ad bona and is an exception to Code of Practice Artice 944 (the appointment of a tutor or curator to a minor belongs to the judge of probate of the place of domicile or usual residence of the father or mother of such minor, if they are either of them living). If a minor be absent the judge with the advice of a family meeting, or of friends if he has no relatives, shall appoint for such minor, a tutor and undertutor as above provided (5).

Interdicts

All the rules of tutorship apply to Curators. The person interdicted is, in every respect, like the minor who is under a tutor, both as respects his person and estate; and the rules respecting the tutor-

1—C. P. Art. 945 Succ. Winn 3 Rob. 303
2—C. P. Art. 946
3—In re Chiappella 8 L.84; Vick v Volz, 49 A.42; Act 251, 1920
4—Douglas v Edwards 9 L.234
5—C. P. Art. 959; Act 209, 1932

ship of the minor, concerning the oath, the inventory and the security, the recording of the legal mortgage, the mode of administering, the sale of the estate, the commission on the revenues, the excuses, the exclusion or deprivation of the tutorship, the mode of rendering the account.

A widow who has adopted a minor under act 31 of 1872, cannot appoint a testamentary tutor for such minor to the exclusion of the natural mother (1).

Prior to 1924 neither father or mother could qualify as tutor to their children where both were alive, notwithstanding divorce from each other (2), but since then the parent in whose custody the minor was entrusted may be so appointed (3).

Mother appointed natural tutrix after passage of statute giving women the same rights as men, did not forfeit tutorship by remarrying without convocation of family meeting (4).

Orders convoking family meeting appointing tutors and homologating proceedings of family meeting may be signed in chambers (5).

The appointment of a tutor whether a relation or a stranger belongs exclusively to the father or mother dying last (6).

Natural tutrix may substitue a bond for the general or special mortgage given by her (7).

An interesting change in the laws governing the adoption of minors has occurred not only in the respective rights of the minor and of the adopting parents in their respective estates and rights of inherit-

1—In re Pelham. 155 L.1021
2—Walder v Walder 159 L. 231
3—R. C. C. 250 as amended by Acts 72 and 196, 1924
4—Hedecker v Fidelity & Casualty Co., N. Y. La. App. 152 So. 35
5—Cole v Richmond 156 L.262
6—Heitkamp v Ragan 142 L.81
7—In re Lee's Tutorship 147 L.231; Act 254 1916

ing from each other, as evidenced by recent legislation, but in their relations with each other, notably the right of an adopting parent to be appointed tutor (or tutrix) to such a minor, with preference over all others, provided that such a minor has no parent living in the State (1).

A tutor may not acquire an adverse interest in a property belonging to his ward, that is, should there be an outstanding interest or claim or to his ward's property the tutor cannot acquire that interest or claim adversely to his ward (2).

1—Act 243, 1926
2—Ingram v Hintz 112 L. 496

CHAPTER LV

Monition Proccedings

The purchasers of property at sheriffs' sales, those made by authority of court, those made by the syndics of insolvent estates, and finally those of any description which are made by the authority of justice, and all subsequent purchasers by a regular chain of titles, may protect themselves from eviction of the property so purchased or from any responsibility as possessors of same by pursuing the rules hereinafter prescribed (1). To so protect themselves they must publish a monition calling upon all persons who can set up any right to the property in consequence of any informality or illegality in the appraisement and advertisement in time or manner of sale or for any defect whatsoever, to show cause within thirty days from the day the monition is first inserted in the public papers, why the sale so made should not be confirmed and homologated (2). The advertisement called for in the case of property situated in New Orleans, to be published three times, or if in the country outside of Orleans parish, must be published in accordance with the manner required for judicial proceedings, which is once a week for four weeks.

The advertisement must refer to the judicial authority under which the sale was made, a description of the property purchased as contained in the conveyance to the buyer and the price at which it was bought (3).

The judge of the court from which the orders or judgments were issued shall grant his monition in the name of the State and affix its seal (4).

1—R. S. 2370
2—R. S. 2371
3—R. S. 2372
4—R. S. 2373

At the expiration of thirty days, the party obtaining the monition may apply to the judge and it shall be the duty of the judge to confirm and homologate the sale in case no cause is shown against the prayer for the monition, but he must be satisfied that the requirements above set forth shall have been complied with. In case of opposition he shall, if the sale was made contrary to the law, annul the sale (1).

The judgment on the monition shall be conclusive evidence that the monition has been regularly made and duly advertised nor shall any evidence be received thereafter to contradict same or to prove an irregularity in the proceeding (2).

The judgment shall be res judicata against all persons, including minors whether present or absent (3).

A mortgage creditor has sufficient interest to oppose a monition of the sale of a mortgaged property (4).

A judgment of monition showing that land was sold for taxes but without sufficient description to show what land was meant, is void (5). The monition does not bar a mortgagee's exercise of a right he had no opportunity to oppose to plaintiff's in execution (6). Judgment in monition proceedings confirming title through sale of property of succession held res judicata as to heir who assisted in securing appointment of administrator (7).

In view of the fact that these proceedings have been held not to be binding on a former owner of

1—R. S. Art 2374
2—R. S. 2375
3—R. S. Art. 2376
4—Fortier v Zimpel 5 Rob. 189
5—Cooper v Falk 109 L.474
6—Moore v Knapp 7 A. 21
7—Gravet v Gonsolin, 10 L. App. 553

the property where the defect was such as to render
the proceedings ab initio null and void, such as want
of citation etc., it may be considered that the prescription provided by Article 3543 of the Civil Code would
be just as effective, unless suit was initiated prior to
the time of prescription provided by that article.

CHAPTER LVI

Prescription

The jurisprudence of the State on the point of prescription is so well established and is so uniform in principle that it has added greatly to the stability of our land titles and enables the examiner when otherwise perplexed and uncertain on other points, to arrive at a decision which permits him to approve and recommend many titles which he would perforce be obliged to reject.

The two prescriptions chiefly relied upon by title examiners to cure otherwise serious defects in titles are the thirty and ten years prescription, which when supported by the requirements of law, constitute a defense which is beyond attack.

Thirty Years Prescription: The elements necessary to a prescriptive title of this character are few in number but they must be present in every case and in strict accordance with the law.

These elements are: Intent to possess as owner (1) and not under some other tenure ,such as tenant, usufructuary, depositary, but it is not necessary that the claimant be in good faith, or under any color of title (2).

Adverse possession: Must be continuous, uninterrupted, public and unequivocal (3). This possession when it has commenced by the corporeal possession of the thing, may, if it has not been interrupted, be preserved by external and public signs, announcing the intention of the possessor's intention to preserve the possession of the thing, such as keeping up roads

1—R. C. C. 3500
2—R. C. C. 3499; Croom v Noel, 143 L.189; Lawrence v Young 144 L.1
3—R. C. C. 3500; Wilson v Marshall, 10 A.327; Johnson v Congregation Daughters of the Cross 162 L.657

and levees, payment of taxes and other similar acts
(1).

,What constitutes public, unequivocal, uninterrupted possession is sometimes difficult to decide,
but in the main, it is such possession as would lead
the public in general to recognize the claimant as
owner. Such acts as constructing buildings on the
property, cultivating, paying taxes, living on the place,
enclosing the property with a fence would be acts evidencing intention to preserve possession and would
constitute corporeal possession (2), but whatever the
character of possession it will be confined to the exact
amount of land possessed as evidenced by the facts
(3). On the contrary, there are other acts which do
not, especially when unaccompanied with sufficient
number of other acts as above, evidence or constitute
corporeal actual possession. The grazing of cattle on
unfenced land or the cutting of timber is not sufficient to support the prescription (4). When the possession is interrupted such as where fences once sur-
rounded land claimed by thirty years prescription
were allowed to decay and to disappear, it would defeat the claim (5).

In those cases where the land is "swamp" or
wild land, the problem becomes exceedingly difficult
and while the courts have relaxed somewhat the rules
applied to land where actual physical possession is
more possible, no set rule is possible. It has been
held that timbered swamp lands may be actually possessed by the construction of roads and canals, especially when accompanied by the felling of trees (6).

1—R. C. C. 3501; Ramos Lumber Co. v Sanders 117 L. 615
2—R. C. C. 3501
3—R. C. C. 3503; Opdenweyer v Brown, 155 L.617
4—Harang v Gheens, 155 L.68; Pierson v Shepherd 6 La. App. 333
5—Tillery v Sample 190 L.586
6—Albert Hanson Lumber Co. v Miller, 126 L.347

In view of the rule that the prescription is confined to the amount of land actually possessed, it becomes difficult to understand how the above mentioned acts would support the claim, unless the canal, or a ditch has been dug to establish boundary, though proof must be made that such a canal or ditch was dug with that intention (1).

Payment of taxes alone is very poor evidence of intent to possess in either swamp lands or other lands susceptible of actual possesion (2) and has only cummulative value where other acts evidencing possession can be shown (3). There are, however, physical acts of ownership performed by owner in cutting logs, cultivating land and preventing encroachments which constitute sufficient possession to establish title by thirty years prescription (4). Enclosures unquestionably constitute possession which is sufficient to support the plea of thirty years (5). This prescription is limited to acreage which had with certainty been enclosed, or such other barriers as would give definite notice to the public of character and extent of such possession, and possession of larger tract which had been enclosed could not be deemed to include a non-contiguous tract (6).

In general a claim of thirty years prescription must be based upon and commences only from the time actual possession begins, notwithstanding claimant may have another form of title, such as tax title, where he did not have possession under that title

1—Aubrey v Diggs, La. 165 S.719
2—Jackson v Gordon. La. App. 186 So. 399
3—Zahn v Ahrensberg 154 L. 70; Plum v Hammonds Lands Inc., 16 La. App. 668 W. W. Duson v Hunsicker 10 La. App. 657
4—Pfister v St. Bernard Cypress Co. 155 L.575
5—Holmes v Hendricks. 4 La. App. 1; Johnson v Daughters of the Holy Cross 162 L. 657; Wheat and Baer v Thayer Hard Co., 15 L. App. 806
6—Peters v Crawford, 185 So. 716; Jackson v Gordon, 186 So. 399

and although the constitutional prescriptive period of three years has run (1). Nor will a deed which is not a deed translative of property support such a claim where there has been no possession under that title. Nor could possession under such a deed which contained an inaccurate description form a basis for the thirty years possession. of the tract intended to be conveyed by the deed.

In order to acquire possession, under thirty years prescription it is not necessary that the land be fenced to fix the boundaries of the land possessed if the limits thereof are fixed by natural boundaries such as a river, sea shore, etc., but there must be evidence that there is actual possession, such as cultivation, etc (2).

In General

A statute providing that where parties acquire property from a common proprietor, preference shall be given to him whose title is most ancient, unless adverse possession alters the situation, contemplates thirty years prescription and not ten years (3).

Husband and wife cannot prescribe against each other, and this prescription in case of a divorced wife's claim against her husband for paraphernal effects does not begin to run from a decree of separation from him, but from the date of divorce (4)·

An action for partition is imprescriptible but an action for partition and liquidation of a partnership is prescribed in thirty years (5); and the faculty of accepting or renouncing a succession becomes barred

1—Crawford, Jenkins & Booth v Wills 189 L.366
2—Continental Land & Fur Co. v Lacoste 192 L.561
3—Dufrene v Bernstein 190 L.66
4—R. C. C. 3523; Succ. McCloskey 144 L.438
5—R. C. C. 1304; King v Wartelle 14 A.740

by thirty years (1), but an heir does not lose the faculty of accepting so long as the property has not been acquired by others. This applies to the legal or forced heir, who is seized of right on the death of the ancestor (2). A claim to an estate is barred by lapse of thirty years (3). If an heir has enjoyed the whole or part of the succession separately, or all of the heirs have possessed separately each a portion of the hereditary effects, each acquires by thirty years prescription notwithstanding that the action of partition is imprescriptible (4). If one of the heirs has possessed part of the estate alone and all the other heirs have possessed in common, there can be no prescription (as regards partition) as to the heirs so holding in common (5).

It has been held that one who is in uninterrupted possession for over thirty years, since the date another purchased for him, though transfer was not made until a time which was within the thirty years, acquired title by prescription (6).

Prescription cannot accrue against the revocation of a donation by a person of all of his property without reservation of enough for his subsistence, though donee agreed to support the donor for life (7).

Thirty years prescription is suspended during minority or interdiction (8), but it is merely suspended but not preempted (9). Prior to 1908, a minor who had arrived at the age of eighteen years, though eman-

1—R. C. C. 1030
2—Dew v Hammond 150 L.1094; Bendernagel v Foret 145 L. 115
3—R. C. C. 78
4—R. C. C. 1305
5—R. C. C. 1306; King v Wartelle, 14 A.740
6—Bremer v Lang, 172 L.261
7—Ackerman v Larner, 116 L.101; Welch v Forest Lbr. Co. 151 L.960
8—R. C. C. 322; 54
9—Smith v Escoubas 43 A. 932

cipated, could not be prescribed against until he had reached the full age of majority (1), but since Article 382 R. C. C. was amended in that year (2), it has been held to the contrary (3).

Where authors in title were in fact without a deed translative of property, their successors will not be allowed to add period of time authors in title had possession, to their own (4), but where both are in good faith purchaser may so add his vendor's possession to his own (5). It also been held that where a vendor has acquired beyond his title, or rather has perfected his title by thirty years prescription, including in these years the prescription of former owners, he could tack on his possession to that of his predecessor because of privity of contract between them (6).

Where a purchaser has acquired a tract described as bounded on the north by the line X and another purchaser buys the adjoining tract as bounded on the south by the same line X, and then the first purchaser erects a fence 22 feet beyond line X and on land of the second purchaser and then after 25 years sells to a third purchaser, describing the land as bounded on the north by the land of the second purchaser and the third purchaser goes into possession of the whole tract up to the fence erected by his vendor, thirty years prescription runs against an action of boundary. This because there was a privity of con-

1—Barrow v Wilson, 39 A.403; Succ. Mitchell 33 A.356
2—Act 224, 1908
3—Arrington v Gray 161 L.413; Succ. Hecker 101 L.302; Roe v Caldwell 145 L.853; Bostick v Thompson 149 L.152
4—Bullard v Davis 185 L.255; Lewis v King 157 L.718
5—Tremont Lumber Co. v Powers & Critchett Lbr. Co. 173 L.937; Barnett v Botany Bay Lbr. Co. 172 L.205; R. C. C. 3493
6—Opdenweyer v Meyer 155 L.617; Emmer v Rector 175 L.82

tract between the first and third purchasers (1). On the other hand if A takes possession of a whole tract belonging to B and keeps it for 25 years, thereafter selling the north half thereof to C, the latter cannot at the end of another five years acquire the whole tract on thirty years prescription because if he takes possession of only the north half he cannot acquire the south half and thus the whole tract, because he has had possession of the south half for only five years, because neither A nor C were his authors in title as to the south half (2).

Prescription of any kind does not run against the United States Government or the State, where land has been served, or no survey made to segregate it from the public domain (3), nor against property dedicated to public use (4).

Where a vendor sells property but remains in possession he can not prescribe against vendee, unless he does some act or makes known to him his intention to possess adversely to him (5).

Prescription begins to run from the date that a patent issued to patentee or his heirs, and as soon as property is severed from the public domain (6).

Land held by educational institution, after expiration of charter is not alienable or subject to sale, except by the legislature and cannot be acquired by prescription as that cannot run against state (7). Though the grantee and those to whom he conveyed

1—Opdenweyer v Brown, 155 L.617
2—Ibid
3—Welch v Forest Lbr. Co., 151 L.960; Martin v La. Central Lbr. Co. 157 L.538; Evans v Jackson 165 L.737; Cocke v Spangler, 159 L.409
4—Kemp v Independence La. App. 156 So.56
5—Roberts v Phillips La. App. 394
6—Rutledge v Harrell, 6 La. App. 172; Security Trust Co. v Rockett 6 La. App. 833; Evans v Jackson 165 L.737
7—Martin v La. Central Lumber Co. 157 L.538

did not pay therefor, the grantor could not acquire title thereto in less than thirty years, by merely resuming possession and paying taxes without any reconveyance and without knowledge or consent of grantee or his successor in title (1).

Of even greater importance to the validity of titles than the prescription of thirty years, is the prescription of ten years which, though subject to requirements not found in the former prescription, gives security to titles within a much shorter period and which requirements are considerably more liberal, though more numerous, than the thirty years prescription.

The prescription is founded on an article of the Revised Civil Code (2) which has been amended by two acts of the legislature (3) and as amended now reads:

He who acquires an immovable in good faith and by a just title prescribes for it in ten years. This prescription shall run against interdicts, married women, absentees and all others now excepted by law; and as to minors this prescription shall accrue and apply in twenty-two years from the date of the birth of said minor; provided that this prescription once it has begun to run against a party shall not be interrupted in favor of any minor heirs of said party.

Prior to the enactment of the aforesaid acts the suspension of the prescription in favor of minors and interdicts, was a source of doubt and uncertainty in the minds of all title examiners, but more than sixteen years having elapsed since the last amendment to the article, all questions arising out of defects in titles

1—Chornos Land Co. v Chrichton, 156 L.963
2—R. C. C. 3478
3—Act 161, 1920; 64, 1924

executed prior to 1924 have been set at rest, with very few exceptions, provided that such titles meet the requirements of a title translative of property as laid down by the Revised Civil Code in the article following the above mentioned article (1), the former reading:

To acquire the ownership of immovables by the species of prescription which forms the subject of the present paragraph, four conditions must occur:

1. Good faith on the part of the possessor.
2. A title which shall be legal and sufficient to transfer the property.
3. Possession during the time required by law, which possession must be accompanied by the incidents hereafter required.
4. And finally an object which may be acquired by prescription.

The good faith spoken of in the preceding article is defined in the chapter which treats of possession (2). It is sufficient if the possession commences in good faith; and if afterwards the possession should be in bad faith, that shall not prevent prescription (3). To be able to acquire by the species of prescription mentioned in this paragraph a legal and transferable title of ownership in the possessor is necessary; this is what is called a just title (4). By the term just title, in case of prescription, we do not understand that which the possessor may have derived from the true owner, for then no true prescription would be necessary, but a title which the possessor may have received from any person whom he honestly believed to be the real owner, provided the

1—R. C. C. 3479
2—R. C. C. 3480
3—R. C. C. 3482
4—R. C. C. 3483

title were such as to transfer the ownership of the property (1).

Good faith: Good faith in a purchaser means not only moral good faith which would prevent the doing of a wrong, but it means a legal good faith. In other words, a purchaser must intend to purchase and does purchase for himself as owner and not to conceal a fraud or to assist in perpetrating a fraud. It also means that the deed or other conveyance is not defective because of facts the knowledge of which is imputed to him by law as being illegal and void, such as purchases made by sheriffs, auctioneers, and other offices of court, sales by minors, or interdicts, by married women of community property without consent of their husbands. An acquisition given in an act of sale by which it is clearly shown that the vendor was not the owner of the property conveyed, would clearly defeat a claim of good faith on the part of the purchaser. A registry of a lis pendens would equally bar such a claim (2). It has been held in the following instances that the defects mentioned appearing in the deed destroyed any claims of good faith. Disclosure of judgment in favor of claimants of the property (3); Ignorance of law that title was defective when title deed on its face is defective is not possession in good faith (4). A deed which describes a tract different from the one claimed is not a title in good faith (5). Acts of partition are not titles translative of property, hence vendee is not in good faith (6); Where vendor sells only his right, title

1—R. C. C. 3484
2—Southwestern Gas Co. v Nowlin, 164 L. 1044; Montgomery v Whitfield, 41 A.649
3—Fellman v Interstate Land Co., 163 L.529
4—Jackson v Harris, 18 La. App. 484
5—Salmen B. & Lbr. Co. v Weston Lbr. Co., 144 L.186
6—Ramsey v Beck, 151 L.190

and interest and declines to warrant title and sets out and shows what kind of title he has, vendee is not in good faith (1).

There are other facts, the knowledge of which the courts have declared destroys a vendee's claim of good faith, which facts are only ascertainable dehors the deed, and hence are usually unknown to the examiner, are included here because of the jurisprudence established.

A purchaser at a tax sale made with knowledge of vendee for the purpose of defeating a mortgage, is in bad faith (2). A perpetrator of a fraud cannot plead ten years prescription (3).

One who without authority joins minors in suit, knowing them to be such, is not a purchaser in good faith (4). Where purchaser because of his family relation with vendor was chargeable with knowledge that other members of family had an interest in the property purchased by him (5).

Vendee of a vendor who acquired in bad faith, but is himself in good faith, may plead the prescription of ten years (6), but if the period has not run, he would not be much helped by that principle.

Vendee who acquired only the right, title and interest of vendors, where he knew at time of purchase that property was community property and that wife was dead at the time of sale, is not protected by the prescription of ten years (7).

A vendee's good faith may not be impugned because, if he had examined the record, it might have

1—Clayton v Rickerson, 160 L.771
2—11 L. App. 27
3—Industrial Lumber Co. v Farque, 162 L.793
4—Scaife v Jones, L.5
5—Roberson v Reed, 190 So. 153; Rocque v Lebesque, 110 L.306
6—Vance v Ellerbee, 150 L.388
7—Victoria Lbr. Co. v Dawson, 189 L.848

disclosed the defect, if as a matter of fact he did know of such a defect (1). A declaration in title that grantor was married, was not sufficient notice of claims of grantor's divorced wife's children to half interest in land, to put grantee on inquiry, in absence of any thing in deed recognizing any rights of others nor is he required to examine title thoroughly in order to be purchaser in good faith, in lack of proof that he knew of the defect (2).

A purchaser is none the less in good faith though he could have obviated or discovered error into which he fell, had he employed a competent engineer (3). Recital in deed that grantor was widow, was not sufficient to impute to grantee knowledge of her want of ownership (4). A deed from father to son for one dollar and valuable services rendered, apparently obtained in good faith sufficient for a title translative of property (5). A purchaser in good faith having corporeal possession more than ten years after purchase, has better title than record title (6). A tax purchaser whose deed is prima facie valid, though in fact invalid, is in good faith and it is not essential that he should investigate the assessment rolls or verify the recitals of the tax deed (7). Stipulation against waranty by vendor is no indication that purchaser did not believe he had good title (8). That vendor retained possession of usufruct to property did not

1—Keller v Summers. 192 L.103; Tyson v Spearman, 190 L.871; Coleman v Pollock, 191 L.813; Act 122, 1908; Frank v Brown, Orleans Court of appeal, decided Nov. 17, 1941
2—Keller v Summers, 192 L.103; Tyson v Spearman, 190 L.871; Land Dev. Co. v Schulz, 169 L.1
3—Peters v Crawford. 185 So. 716
4—Johnson v Sugar, 163 L.785
5—Morris v Monroe Sand & Gravel Co., 166 L.656; Tremont Lbr. Co. v Powers & Critchett Lbr. Co., 173 L.937
6—West v Green. 10 La. App. 216
7—Eivers v Rankin, 150 L.4
8—Cherami v Cantrelle. 174 L.995; Land Dev. Co. v Schulz, 169 L.9; Gaskins v Marshall Tessier Orleans Dig. 119

show bad faith on part of purchaser (1). Possession under just title must be considered good faith, unless there is reference in deed which destroys such good faith (2). Lack of knowledge on elements necessary to make title defective will sustain good faith (3). Possession is deemed to be in good or bad faith according to belief in validity of title to part of which possession is vicious or defective (4). When community property is sold after death of wife and there is nothing of record to show death of wife, possessor is in good faith (5). Honest belief that purchaser is buying from real owner, constitutes good faith (6).

Title Translative of Property: Such a title is a title that is valid in form sufficient to transfer ownership if the vendor was the real owner and which discloses no defect on its face (7). Tax deed is a title translative of property where valid on its face (8). A patent from the State is a title translative of property when properly executed (9).

An act which in effect is a partition, is not a title translative of property (10); nor is an act of exchange in which vendor declared he grants bargains and sells and quit claims all of his right, title and interest (11); nor a testamentary disposition in favor of a designated class of persons collectively to any particular or designated members of the class (12).

1—Land Dev. Co. v Schulz, 169 L.9
2—Blumson v Knighton, La. App. 140 So. 302
3—Scott v Dickson, 148 L.907
4—Mereaux & Nunez v Gaidry, 171 L.852
5—Bennet v Calmes, 116 L.600
6—R. C. C. 3484; Brewster v Hewe, 113 L.51; Knight v Berwick Lumber Co., 130 L.234; Beer v Leonard, 40 A.485
7—Franks v Scott, 191 So. 175, La. App.; Smith v King, 192 L.346; Keller v Summers, 192 L.103; Nugent v Urania Lbr. Co., 16 La. App., 78
8—Land Dev. Co. v Schulz, 169 L.1; Tillery v Fuller, 190 L.586
9—Rutledge v Harrell, 6 La. App. 172
10—Tillery v Fuller, 190 L.586; Ramsey v Beck, 151 L.190
11—Succ. Bonnette, 188 L.297
12—Tyler v Lewis, 143 L.228

Description as affecting title translative of property: Recourse may be had to another public record, such as a plat of survey, where description in deed is uncertain and insufficient (1). A deed which describes property different from one in controversy can not form basis of prescription (2). Deed which expressly excludes land in dispute is not translative of property quo ad that land (3), nor is a tax deed in which description is defective or absent (4); nor one in which the land could be included only by inference (5).

Possession: Actual corporeal possession is necessary for ten years prescription (6), but once commenced civil possession is sufficient to complete the possession (7); and possession of part is possession of the whole; sale of right of way to railroad which was only a servitude, does not make two tracts of the original whole and non contiguous; and possession of one side of the right of way is possession of the whole (8). Where, however, two tracts are held by different titles possession of one does not amount to possession of the other; and possession of the front part of a tract is not possession of the rear or swamp part, where they were acquired by different titles (9).

1—Continental Land & Fur. Co. v Lacoste, 192 L.561; Leader
      Realty Co. v Taylor, 147 L.115
2—Salmen Brick & Lumber Co. v H. Weston Lbr. Co., 144 L.186;
      Cont. Land & Fur. Co. v Lacoste, 192 L.561
3—Callier v Profito, 171 L.693; Harvey v Bowie Lbr. Co., 145 L.96;
      Futrell v Holloway, La. App. 149 So. 167
4—McHugh v Albert Hanson Lbr. Co., 145 L.421
5—Bendernagel v Foret, 145 L.115
6—Bruton v Braselton, 157 L.65
7—Pardee Co. v Bodcaw Lbr. Co., 3 La. App. 169; Earnest Realty
      Co., 189 L.379; R. C. C. 382; Bussey v Barrileaux, 172 L.264
8—Railsback v Keith, 142 L.747; Leader Realty Co. v Taylor, 147 L.256
9—Haas v Currie, 169 L.1041; Perkins v Wisner, 171 L.898;
      Screen v Taylor, 172 L.51; Kees v La. Cent. Lbr. Co.,
      183 L.111

Civil possession, after physical possession, is only maintained by external and public signs (1); it may be retained sufficiently to prescribe so long as there remains on it a vestige of the works erected by him, as for example the ruins of a house (2), but the possession must be open and not clandestine (3). Physical acts of ownership such as cutting logs, cultivating land and preventing encroachments is sufficient possession to maintain possession (4).

An owner does not lose his title by prescription by being out of possession, unless there has been adverse possession long enough to defeat his ownership by prescription (5). The sale by co-owner by authentic act which is not defective on its face, transfers the whole and the prescription of ten years applies, even though the other co-owner did not authorize sale, where there has been actual possession (6). Purchasers of forty acres, out of which vendor had sold three acres but included same in sale of the forty acres, prescribed by ten years where owner of three acres did not take possession of the three acres, but purchasers of the larger tract did (7).

Tacking on possession: Possession in good faith is sufficient to maintain subsequent right to plead prescription, even though intermediate possessors were in bad faith (8). The possessor is allowed to make the sum of possession necessary to prescribe by adding his own possession to that of his author, in whatever manner he has succeeded him, whether by universal or particular, lucrative or onerous title (9).

1—Roussel v Grant. 14 Orleans App. 57
2—R .C. C. 3502
3—Moore v Morgan. L. & T. R. 126 L.898
4—Pfister v St. Bernard Cypress Co., 155 L.575
5—Thibodaux v Bonnabel Land Co., 171 L.639
6—Varnado v Meyer & Neugas, 16 L.APP. 686
7—Lewis v Standard Oil Co.. 154 L.1048
8—Wheat & Baer v Thayer Hard Lbr. Co., 15 La. App., 306
9—R. C.C. 3493

The possession of the author should also be in good faith (1). If the author was in bad faith it continues with universal legatee, but it is otherwise of donations and particular legacies (2).

As illustrative of the principle that a deed which shows no defect on its face, is a title translative of property, it has been held that such a deed signed by one who really did not have the authority to sign is sufficient to support a plea of ten years prescription (3). And supporting the statement that the bad faith of a testator does not attach to a particular legatee, the courts have held that a bequest of a property fully described made in a testament and which has been duly probated and executed, forms the basis of a title translative of property (4).

Prescription Liberandi

Under this classification is to be included, not only statutes which specifically provide for the prescription of this character, but those statutes which in effect are quieting enactments, enactments rendered necessary, in the main, by practices indulged in by the profession in a mistaken sense and comprehension of the law in certain procedures, and contain, as a necessary corrolary a prescription period from date of the statute, varying from three months to six months.

From the standpoint of the title examiner, the most important of the legislation providing for prescriptions liberandi, are those of two and five years, this because of their wide reaching effect in land titles.

1—Innis v Miller, 10 Mar. 289
2—Griffin v Blanc, 12 A.6
3—Bowers v Langston, 156 J..188
4—Howell v Noah, 6 La. App. 538

Five years: Chief among these statutes are the article of the Revised Civil Code on the subject of sheriff's sales (1) and several amendments thereto (2). Under this article and amendments, all informalities and irregularities in public sales are cured by the prescription of five years as against claims of minors, married women and interdicts, and, as amended by act of 1924 (3), of two years as against those of the age of majority. The jurisprudence of the State has defined just what informalities and irregularities are cured by this prescription in a long line of decisions and have included therein defects which might be classed as nullities.

The courts have held: Failure of Sheriff to actually seize property (4); sale by executor was not advertised; that inventory of estate was not completed before sale; that it was partly made by appraisers appointed by the executor, or that it was signed by only one appraiser (5); waiver of notice of order of seizure and sale by administrator of succession; that adjudication was for less than the appraisement (6); a defective and insufficient description of the property sold, in the sheriff's advertisement (7); informalities in the appointment of undertutor; in the composition of the family meeting recommending a sale of the succession to pay ancestor's debts and in which minor's have a residuary interest, in the method of proving the existence of debts of the deceased, and all other irregularities in proceedings antecedent to and resulting in the probate sale (8); objections to a succession sale

1—R. C. C. 3543
2—R. C. C. 3478; Act 161, 1920; Act 64, 1924
3—Act R. C. C. 3478
4—Pike v Evans, 94, U. S. 6, 24 L.ed. 40
5—Davis v Gaines, 104 U. S. 386, 26 L.ed.757
6—Munhold v Scott, 33 A.1043
7—Walling v Morefield, 3 A3.770
8—Webb v Keller, 39 A.55

in conformity to an order of court, for the reason that no tutor was appointed for the minor heirs who were unrepresented at the making of the inventory; that inventory was not taken within the time provided by law, that the property was inventoried at less than its value, and that no list of debts was furnished as a foundation o fthe order of sale (1) ; are all informalities cured by this prescription.

If the judge was absent and clerk failed to require affidavit as to his absence (at that period necessary for the appointment by the clerk) (2), failure of court to designate place of sale in order authorizing tutor to sell property of minors (3) ; informalities connected with or growing out of probate sale under an order of court, made at public auction (4) ; designation of attorney appointed to represent absent mortgagor in a foreclosure proceeding as curator ad hoc instead of attorney for absentee (5) ; that no copy of advertisement appeared in record (6) ; that one of the members of a family meeting which accepted an offer of compromise in a partition suit, was a minor (7); that sale of succession property was by the sheriff and not by administrator, or failure to notify Italian Consul of death of native of Italy (8).

While the jurisprudence of the state has extended the scope of the informalities or irregularities which are within the effect of the article, matters which are the essence of contracts or are substantial rights of the parties, are not affected by it, such as a sale where there was no mortgage (9) ;

1—Thibodaux v Barrow, 129 L.395
2—Hibernia Bank & Trust Co. v Whitney, 130 L.817
3—Cole v Richmond, 156 L.262
4—Linman v Riggins, 40 A.761
5—Richardson v McDonald, 139 L.651
6—Samuels v Parsons, 146 L.262
7—Wright v Calhoun, 151 L.908
8—Rizzotto v Grima 164 L.1
9—Pons v YazooR. Co., 122 L. 156 ; Thibodaux v Thibodaux, 142 L.906

where lands appraised at $600.00 are sold under court order, at their first offering, for $55.00 (1).

This prescription does not apply to sale of property not belonging to defendant in execution, nor to minors or interdicts, but it does where owner knew of the sale, and the purchaser or his successors went into possession and remained in actual possession for five years and purchaser paid the consideration (2).

In addition to the foregoing prescription, which applies not only to sheriff's sales, but to all public sales made under order of court, the following irregularities, informalities or defects are barred by the prescription of five years; in partition from date thereof and in case of error or fraud from the date of discovery (3). This prescription does not run against minors except from date of their majority (4); in case of lesion it runs against minors if partition has been judicilly made (5); in favor of heirs of deceased person from date of opening of succession against tax liens (6); in sale of land owned by foreign corporation sold by sheriff (7); probate of will null for defects of form, though made ex parte, is sufficient basis for prescription against an action to set aside for nullity (8); but this does not apply to a suit filed for the purpose of proving that will was never signed and that the X was never affixed by the putative author (9), or that signature was a

1—Lacroix v Crane, 133 L.227
2—Act 6. 1928
3—R. C. C. 1413; Hamilton v Hamilton, 130 L.302; Doucet v Fenelon. 120 L.18
4—Sewell v Hebert, 37 A.155
5—R. C. C. 141
6—Act 82, 1924
7—Act 192, 1932
8—Provost v Provost, 13 A.574; Fuentes v Gaines. 25 A.85; Miller v Miller, 32 A.437
9—Cox v Lea, 110 L.1030

forgery. It does apply to any suit to set aside a will for fraud brought after five years from date of discovery of fraud (1); in actions or reduction of excessive donations (2); rescissions of partitions; nullity or rescissions of contracts, testaments or other acts (3). An action to dissolve a sale for non-payment of price, is not technically one for nullity or rescission and is prescribed only by ten years (4). This article applies to a suit by a wife to set aside a sale to enforce a mortgage given by her during husband's life time, to secure her husband's debts (5).

Six years prescription: Applies to suits to set aside patents issued by the State of Louisiana (6).

Four years prescription: Applies to a suit by a minor to rescind a judgment against him on the ground that he was not properly defended or that he has been aggrieved by said judgment; runs four years after his majority (7). Also to minor in suits against his tutor (8), but this refers to acts which the tutor had authority to do if legally done, but not the sale of property as his own which belonged to the minor.

Lesion: Action of lesion is prescribed in four years in case of majority and from date of their majority in case of minors (9). It runs with, and is not suspended by that granted for redemption (10).

Three years prescription: The constitutional provision (11) reads: . . . provided that such tax liens,

1—Calais v Semere. 10 A.684: Bissell v Bodcaw Lbr. Co.. 134 L.839
2—Cox v Ahlefeldt, 105 L.543; Succ. Williams, 132 L.862
3—R. C. C. 3542
4—George v Lewis, 11 A.654
5—Colgin v Courrege, 106 L.684
6—Act 62, 1912
7—C. P. 615
8—R. C. C. 362
9—R. C. C. 2595
10—R. C. C. 2596
11—Sec. 19, Art. 19, Const. 1921, Act 35, 1938.

mortgages and privileges shall lapse in three years from the 31st day of December in the year in which the taxes are due, and whether such liens are now or hereafter be recorded; and provided further that all taxes and licenses other than real property taxes shall prescribe in three years from the 31st day of December in the year in which such taxes or licenses are due. Prior to the amendment of 1938 of this section, there was no prescription as to corporate license tax and the amendment was not retroactive (1), hence any license taxes due prior to said amendment are not prescribed.

In view of the constitutional provision, other legislative acts are of little import, as the said provision is clear and unambiguous.

Any suit to set aside a sale by executory process against the estate of a deceased debtor when such proceedings were theretofore conducted and carried on against the administrator or executor as such is prescribed (2).

Two years prescription: Against a suit to review a judgment rendered in rem against an absentee (3). Against a suit to set aside a sale made by an auctioneer, sheriff or other person under order of court, for informalities or irregularities in the legal procedure (4). Against a suit arising out of a violation of restrictions contained in a deed to real estate (5).Must be brought within four months from date of act if violation existed at time of act for two years prior thereto.

Prescription of one year: The action of a creditor

1—International Shoe Co. v Picard & Geismer, 30 Fed. Supp. 570
2—Act 147, 1920
3—C. P. 267; 614; Keith v Renard 18 A.734
4—R. C. C. 3543; Act 213, 1932
5—Act 328, 1938

to annul transfer of property by his debtor, is prescribed by one year (1).

Interruption of prescription: A redemption from the State of property sold for taxes, after redemption period has expired, interrupts prescription (2).

Servitudes: Servitudes may be both acquired and lost by prescription, thus the right to use a portion of ground occupied by a post supporting a guy wire, is acquired by ten years (3), while prescription for non-usage for discontinuous servitudes may be acquired from the day they cease to be used, and for continuous servitudes from the day any act is committed which is contrary to the terms of the servitudes (4). This prescription in ten years. A servitude or drip or of drainage is acquired by the same period of prescription (5).

The public may acquire use of a road by open and public possession through the parish, after the road has been declared a public highway by the police jury (6).

Acts Quieting Titles

These acts were passed for the purpose principally of preventing confusion and uncertainty in titles. Of such a nature are the acts of 1916 (7) and of 1928 (8) in reference to alienations of minors' interest. Also an act of 1926 and 1912 (9) as well as an act of 1938 (10). Another act of like character is that of 1926, quieting titles derived from sales to effect a

1—R. C. C. 1994
2—Home Land Co., v Bryant. 6 La. App. 130; Act 310, 1936
3—Viering v N. K. Fairbanks Co. 156 L.592
4—Thompson v Meyer, 34 A.65
5—Vincent v Michel 7, A.52; Guenard v Bird, 33 A.796
6—R. C. C. 765
7—Act 3. 1916
8—Act 17. 1928
9—Act 243, 1926; Act 53, 1912
10—Act 406, 1938

partition where the sole ground of the action was that the partition was made by roots and not by subdivisions there of between individual coproprietors claiming under same root (1). Of like character was an act passed in 1928 for the purpose of quieting titles incorrectly executed under the provisions of Act 149 of 1924, divesting minors' interest (2). An act passed in 1924 (3) was required under the peculiar fact that a minor, whose interest had been incorrectly divested was interdicted before his majority.

In General

A power of attorney attached to an act, authorizing president and secretary to sign, though president only signed, is prescribed by ten years (4); a deed need not be recorded to form a basis for prescription (5); tax assessment and sale not made in accordance with statute not such absolute nullities as to bar 10 years prescription (6); a deed which fails to describe by legal subdivision by which property was intended to be sold, or made no reference to any deed, map, plat, patent or survey, or boundary by which description might be ascertained, is void as to third parties for want of description and cannot serve as basis of 10 years prescription (7); a deed conveying property to wife, which deed recited that husband was present and consented to wife's purchase not signed by either husband or wife, but which showed on its fact that it was community property, will serve as basis of ten years prescription where parties sold parts thereof (8)

1—Act 406, 1938
2—Act 77, 1928
3—Act 131, 1924
4—Rutledge v Harrel, 6 La. App. 172
5—Douglas v Fos, 14 Orleans App. 322
6—Morris v Hankins, 192 L.504
7—McCluskey v Meraux & Nunez, 188 So.669
8—Franks v Scott, 191 So.175

Lack of possession of land sold by son by warrantly deed, which land belonged to father who survived son, defeats 10 years prescription (1). Ten years prescription runs against claimants to lands once owned by a non-trading corporation, and transferred by it to another non-trading corporation, formed by same members forming owning corporation and which new corporation succeeded old corporation (2).

The City of New Orleans in order to prevent running of prescription against its property, must record a declaration that said property is public property (3).

Title cannot be perfected by prescription where suit is pending for possession (4).

Where deed of mortgagor is defective in description at foreclosure and in title of purchaser's successors, prescription does not run (5).

Title to the property belonging to foreign corporation, sold by agent without proper authority, quieted by ten years prescription (6). Third persons purchasing from community widow with no title to husband's half of the community, or no more right than usufructuary, prescribed against husband and heirs in 10 years (7).

It must not be presumed that the lengthy synopsis of the law and jurisprudence covering prescription given in the preceding pages, is based upon the idea that recourse to them will be required by an examiner of necessity or even frequently. The summary was made simply with the idea that should he be con-

1—Mims v Sample, 191 L.677
2—Act 19, 1918. E. S. Act 115, 1920
3—Act 169. 1926
4—In re Amite Land Co., 147 L.672
5—Tircuit v Burton Swartz Lbr. Co., 162 L.319
6—Act 40, 1930
7—Jordan v Richards, 114 L.329

fronted with a problem requiring further study during the course of his examination, he would have at hand, for ready reference, citations which might enable him to solve questions otherwise requiring tedious research.

A deed, for instance, involving a title translative of property, presents three questions: First, is it valid in form; second, was the purchaser in good faith; third, was there possession? The first factor will present itself and be solved on the face of the instrument, that is, the instrument will show wherein it is defective or that it is not so defective. The second factor, good faith, seldom presents itself to the examiner and does not often constitute a problem, as it is based upon facts dehors the record and he is not compelled to go beyond that record, unless in the course of the examination of the title, he becomes aware of conditions which puts him on notice of lack of good faith, were it only legal good faith.

The third factor, possession, invokes responsibility on the part of the examiner, for the checking of the point where circumstances indicate the need thereof.

In the event that any of these problems present themselves it is hoped that the law and jurisprudence herein cited, will prove of value to the examiner.

CHAPTER LVII

Registration

While the subject of registration (and this includes recordation of liens, privileges and mortgages) requires no extended discussion, yet it is of vital importance in titles from two standpoints, positive in that registration is notice to the world and binds everyone, and negative because, unless there has been registration, no one is bound, except the parties to the act (1).

There are some phases of the matter, however, which call for attention such as sufficiency of registration, which in turn involves names, description of property. The registration of the true name of the vendor, though the act was signed in another name erroneously is notice to third parties. A registration of an act under private signature is sufficient notice (3).

The law governing registration and recordation are found in the Constitution (4) and in the Civil Code (5).

One exception to the principles ennunciated, were to be found in the matter of succession, it having been held that judgments of courts did not have to be registered or recorded (6), but in view of the amendment of article 2265 of the Civil Code, this is no longer true.

1—Smith v Routon. La. App. 181 So.684; Schultze v Frost Johnson Lbr. Co., 132 L.366
2—Agurs v Belcher, 111 L.378
3—Rawles v Thomas, 3 La. App. 484; Stallcup v Pyron. 33 A.1249
4—Sec. 19. Art. 19. Const., 1921; Arts. 2246; 2264, 2265. 2266
5—Arts. 2246. 2264. 2265, 2266
6—Brewer v Bright, 130 L.491; Greig v A. Hansen Lbr. Co., 151 L.353

CHAPTER LVIII

Slaves

A link which is seldom encountered in a chain of title, but which may be of vital importance, is that one which involves slaves and this importance arises from several factors. First, marriage; second, legitimacy of the children. The second factor is largely dependent upon the first factor. For a clearer appreciation of the points involved it is necessary to review the status of the slave and his children prior to the Civil War. Slaves had no civil rights, could enter into no contracts, could not bind themselves in marriage, receive no donations nor inherit from any one.

However there frequently occurred among the slaves a union which when entered into with the consent of the master or respective masters of the parties, possessed all of the force of marriage but none of the civil effects and of which unions the courts have said: the civil effects of slave marriages which lay dormant during the condition of slavery, came into being as of the date the marriage was contracted, if on emancipation the parties continued to live together as husband and wife thereby confirming the marriage (1).

A child born of such a marriage, which marriage was followed by cohabitation and the living together as husband and wife after the emancipation of the parties, is the heir of those persons (2).

Another factor which may arise in connection with such a link is the effect of the manumission of a slave by his master on his children.

1—Succ. Young. 166 L.285
2—Wiley v Bowman, 144 L.181; Succ. Blackburn, 124 L.618

A child of a freed slave, born before the emancipation of the father, is a slave (1), and a child born of a slave who has acquired the right of being free after a certain time, is free becoming so at the time fixed for the enfranchisement (2).

The right of children to inherit from their parents after slavery was abolished, furnishes another angle in a link of this character. It has been shown that the children of a slave marriage were recognized as legitimate and therefore inherited as all other legitimate children, but in those cases where there had been no such marriage the laws in reference to acknowledgement or legitimating of a child varied from the laws covering the acknowledgement or legitimating of children of the white strain. Prior to 1870 such laws did not differ in their provisions as regards children of slaves (3); but in that year an act was passed (4) which permitted the parents of such children to acknowledge their natural children by a statement in the presence of two witnesses. The courts also have held that a child of a negro woman slave could prove his maternal descent by any legal evidence other than the notarial acknowledgement (5); and that the mother of a bastard child born in this state, need not prove that such child was legally acknowledged by her, so as to enable her to inherit from him (6).

1—Catin v Dorgenoy, 8 Mart. (O. S.) 218
2—Gaudet v Gourdain. 3 A.136; Henderson v Rost, 11 A.541
3—Thomassin v Raphael, 11 L.128
4—Act 68, 1870
5—Briggs v McLoughlin, 134 L.138
6—Neel v Hebert, 30 A. 808

CHAPTER LIX

Substituted Service

Generically speaking, all judicial appointments of temporary representatives, whether it be an attorney, counsel, curator ad hoc, tutor ad hoc, or the curator appointed under the provisions of Article 964 of the Code of Practice, may be classed as substituted service, since the defendant or party interested is not brought into court personally or directly, the representative appointed being substituted for him, but a distinction must be noted. Cases in which citation is required, such as divorces and separation from bed and board suits, executory process, hypothecary actions, partitions attachments and petitory actions and proceedings in rem, service on these judicial representatives, is real substituted service. In all other cases, such as absent heirs, where such appointments are made they are made solely for the purpose of protecting the interests of the parties and usually do not involve citation or other process.

All appointments of the above character made by the courts, are made only in case of the absence of the parties represented, or where their whereabouts are unknown (whether residing in the state or not), with the exception of those made under Article 964 of the Code of Practice and the articles of the Civil Code (1), where the minor or insane person is in the state, but are without a tutor or curator.

The tutor ad hoc or the curator ad hoc appointed in the latter cases occupy the same position and exercise the same powers as a regularly appointed and qualified tutor or curator, although it is only a temporary appointment and the powers and functions are

1—R. C. C. 313; C. P. 116

limited strictly to the specific suit or other action.

These appointees are and have been variously designated by the title, attorney for absentee, counsel for absent heirs and curators, and at one time the use of one title in place of another constituted an irregularity, but an act was passed which abolished the distinction and provided a six months prescription in all cases where the improper designation had been used in such. The act in question reads:

In judicial proceedings, where absentees, minors or persons interdicted, who are not represented, are interested and are necessary parties, the judge having jurisdiction over the proceedings shall appoint an attorney at law to represent said absentees, minors or persons interdicted, and the designation of such representative as special tutor, tutor ad hoc, curator ad hoc, or any other title shall not be required, and if incorrectly made shall be construed as the proper designation (1). Section two of the same act provides the prescription above referred to (2).

Following articles of the Civil Code, Code of Practice and statutes specify cases in which these appointments are to be or may be made; Curator in a suit against an absentee who has no known agent in the state, or whose estate is not under administration (3); in separation suits (4); where minor is in state but is without a tutor (5); where a tutor previously appointed dies or leaves the state without having appointed an attorney in fact (6); counsel to absent heirs in successions (7); qualifications and duties

1—Act 219, 1918 as amended by Act 133, 1926

2—Bienvenu v Factors. Ins., 23 A.209; Webster Bank v McDonald 137 L.574; Coves v Bertoulin, 44 A.683

3—R. C. C. 56

4—R. C. C. 141

5—R. C. C. 313

6—R. C. C. 314

7—R C. C. 1210

of the counsel appointed (1); duties and obligations
of such representatives (2); appointment of counsel
to absent heirs in testate successions and their duties
(3); unrepresented minors (4); in actions for annulment of marriages in certain cases (5); in claims
against a minor without a tutor and/or an insane
person not interdicted but committed to any asylum,
before a regular tutor or curator has been appointed
(6): in proceedings in rem (7): in executory and hypothecary actions (8); in partitions by licitation (9);
attorneys to represent absentees, minors and interdicts (10); appointment of tutors to minors who have
no tutor (11); appointment of tutor or curator in partition proceedings (12); in separation or divorce suits
(13); in action to quiet tax title (14).

There is a considerable amount of unnecessary
duplication in these acts and the statutes seem particularly to have been passed to fit special circumstances.

Duties, powers and obligations of an attorney,
tutor and curator: An attorney appointed under the
provisions of the various acts cited above has to be
a fully qualified attorney at law. He need not accept
in writing or take an oath, as such (15); nor give
bond, although he may be designated as curator ad
hoc (16). Prior to act of 1918 (17), all curators had

1—R. C. C. 1662
2—R. C. C. 1661, 1662
3—R. C. C. 1661
4—C. P. 116 as amended by Act 190 of 1904; 167, 1924
5—Act 150, 1906
6—C. P. 964
7—C. P. 294
8—C. P. 737 as amended by Act 130, 1920
9—Act 96, 1928
10—Art 219, 198, as amended by Act 133, 1926
11—Ibid
12—Act 209, 1932; Act 219, 1926
13—C. P. 1190 as amended by Act 296, 1910
14—Act 101, 1898
15—Saenger Amusement Co. v Masur, 158 L.745
16—Act 219, 1918 as amended by Act 133, 1926
17—Act 219, 1918

to take an oath, but as the office of curator ad hoc
has practically been abolished this is no longer true.
Tutors ad hoc must take an oath and give bond, except
the bond has been dispensed with in certain cases (1).

The validity of any transaction or transfer of ownership of real property in proceedings wherein there
is substituted service, is determined by these factors:
First, jurisdiction of the court making the appointment. This is entirely dependent upon the location of
the property or of the succession, or the domicile of
the minor or interdict not represented. Second, absence
from state, or circumstances which justify the presumption of absence, but not death, as substituted
service is not valid where principal is dead, although
it has been held that where a curator has been appointed to an absentee who is living, his subsequent death
does not vitiate the proceedings, provided his death
is not known to the court or the curator (2).

An absentee may be represented by substituted
service in a partition suit. The court having jurisdiction, the innocent purchaser is protected (3).

An absentee may be brought into court through
a curator ad hoc in an action to quiet title (4).

The appointment of a curator ad hoc will be made
conclusive only after proof has made it reasonably
certain that the defendant was absent (5). In cases of
substituted service on an absentee the record must
show that citation and copy of petition were served
on the regularly appointed curator ad hoc (6).

1—Act 209, 1932
2—Telle v Senac, 122 L.1040; Elmore v Johnson, 121 L.277
3—Ibid
4—Hobson v Peake, 44 A. 383; Bartels v Souchon 48 A.783; Clay-
        ton v Quaker Realty Co. 128 L.103
5—Whitney Central Bank & Trust Co. v Alfred, 11 Orleans App. 223
6—Lanan v Johnson, 140 L.863

The important point in these decisions is two fold:

1. There should be an allegation in the petition for the appointment, sufficient grounds to support the application and these allegations should be supported by at least affidavits; and

2. Citation and service should be made on the defendant through the curator.

Proceedings under these circumstances which fail to meet the foregoing requirements can only be cured by prescription.

CHAPTER LX

Third Persons

As has been said previously there are three classes of titles:

The first class is made up of those titles which are perfect because the formalities and requisites of the law have been complied with and they are proof against attack, even by minors, without the aid of prescription acquirendi or liberandi, or through the presumptions of law. Such titles are rare, though links in the chain may be and frequently are to be found which are of this description. Discussion of such titles or links is pretermitted here because they are not germain to the subject of the chapter.

The second class is made up of those titles in which defects exists, but which, by reason of the legislative enactments and the jurisprudence are not open to attack on the ground of such defects. Before a title, however, can be placed in that class, it must possess two attributes, or rather, meet two require-ments:

1. The purchaser must be in good faith.
2. It must be a title translative of property.

These requirements have been discussed in a previous chapter so there is no necessity of a repetition here. It suffices to summarize to this extent. It must be a title which shall be legal and sufficient to transfer the property (1) and must be valid in form. This definition applies to voluntary transfers or to transfers under order of court, but not inheritances, or partitions (2), for the reason that these changes of ownership are governed by different rules.

1—R. C. C. 3483
2—Succ. Lampton, 35 A.424; Anglin v Kilbourne, 131 L.186

A more nearly perfect title is required in this class of titles than is required in titles which are perfected or rather placed beyond attack by prescription.

Titles of this character are not dependent upon prescription for their validity but upon the law. This law is not to be sought in any single enactment, or statute, but is made up of a number of elements, such as rules of property, presumption of law and of fact and estopples.

The Supreme Court of the state has established the following rules of property which are applicable in these cases:

Unrecorded encumbrances or alienations have no effect against recorded transfers; and third persons need not look beyond the public records and no knowledge is imputed to them beyond that disclosed by such public records.

Third persons need not look beyond the jurisdiction of the court, the judgment thereof and the regularity in all sheriff's and other public sales.

In sales to pay debts in succession proceedings, receiverships, or other probate matters, the purchaser at such sales is protected against the claims of all, even minors, by the judgment of the court ordering such sales, provided it has jurisdiction ratione matereia and personem, and that the sale was conducted regularly and in conformity with the laws.

Heirs are bound by the written contracts of those from whom they derive, with the exception that forced heirs may sue to annul the simulated sales made in defraud of their rights.

Parol evidence will not be admitted to divest title to real property except by forced heirs in simulated transfers by their ancestors; and then only in cases where the ancestor has held title in himself and has executed a transfer to another in defraud of such forced heirs.

These rules of property are based upon a long line of decisions in which it has been held:

A third person can acquire a good title from the owner of record even though knowing this owner is not the true owner, since he is not affected by knowledge acquired outside the record (1). No claims against either the owner of the property, not recorded, affect the property (2). A purchaser from one who holds a deed sepcially reserving the right of redemption a long time after period for redemption has expired is not bound to institute an investigation beyond what appears in the record, to ascertain if property has been redeemed (3). A person who acquires from the record owner obtains a good title though he has knowledge that another holds an unrecorded deed to same land (4). Purchasers accepting deeds at their face value are not bound by secret equities between vendor and prior owners (5).

Where a purchaser at a sheriff's sale shows a judgment execution and sale, omnia recte acta will arise in his favor (6).

A purchaser at public sale of succession property made under order of court is protected by that order (7). In this case the sale was attacked on various grounds involving proceedings prior to sale

1—Tharp v Richardson, 179 L.829
2—Nilson v Brinkerhoft, 146 L.697; Jackson v Creswell, 147 L.914;
        Masters v Cleveland, 182 L.493; Cole v Richmond, 156
        L.262; Loranger v Citizens Nat'l. Bank, 162, L.1054; Miller v Bruges, 176 L.106
3—Coleman v Washington, 167 L.658
4—Howard v Coyle, 163 L.257
5—Beard v Nunn, 172 La. 155
6—Harmon v O'Moran, 18 L.526
7—Fissette v Taylor, 167 L.1110

The leading case of Cole v Richmond, et als (1), is of special interest in a discussion of these points, because of the defects existing in the title involved in that case and the emphasis laid by the court on the principles governing the good faith of an innocent third party. The prescription of ten years had not accrued in the case and that defense was not made.

The principal points of attack were the alienation of minors' interest and the irregularity and even fraudulent proceedings by which this was done. The court, after reviewing these grounds continued:

We have dealt with these particular grounds of attack made upon the public sale, as they are matters more or less of public record and defendants are third persons. The District Court of Evangeline parish was unquestionably vested with jurisdiction to order sale of property of these minors . . . The proceedings are regular and defendants as innocent third persons have purchased this property upon the faith of the deed to Mary L. Richmond (she had purchased at the public sale and then transferred to defendants), the adjudicatee at a public sale held under a decree of a court of competent jurisdiction. Said deed being valid on its face and duly recorded cannot be affected by any irregularities subsequently ascertained, nor are they bound to look beyond the decree recognizing its necessity. The truth of the record concerning matters within the jurisdiction of the court cannot be disputed. (Citing a number of cases (2)). The conveyance records are the only thing one dealing with real estate needs to look into,

---

1—Cole v Richmond, 156 L.262

2—Irwin v Flynn, 110 L.882; Nesom's heirs v Neisdale, 34 A.1810; Chaffe v Minden Lbr. Co., 118 L.753; Bell v Lafosse, 126 L.528

under the repeated decisions of this court. nor can innocent third persons purchasing upon the faith of the public records be bound by any knowledge, except such as is disclosed by such records (Citing a number of cases (1)).

Neither fraud, nor want of consideration, nor secret equities between the parties who have placed on the public records a title valid upon its face, can be urged against a bona fide purchaser for value who has acted on the faith of a recorded title. (citing various cases (2)).

The court then reviews the proceedings leading up to the sale and the grounds for the attack, and then held: All the attacks are made up on alleged facts dehors the public record and cannot affect innocent third parties.

In the same decree the court gave judgment against Mrs. Richmond who had retained in her own name a part of the property adjudicated to her, annulling the sale as to her, thus clearly on the ground that she was not an innocent purchaser.

The principles above enunciated hold good in all public sales, whether it be in execution of a money judgment, sales to pay succession debts, vacant successions, sales of minors' property, or to effect partition.

Co-owners, in partitions made at private sale as purchasers can not plead such a defense as such a title is not translative of property and they are not innocent third parties.

Partitions in kind, exparte putting in possession of legal heirs or even of universal legatees, not done

1—Baird v Atlas Oil Co., 146 L.1099; McDuffie v Walker, 125 L.167; Waller v Colvin, 151 L.772
2—Broussard v Broussard, 45 A.1095; Succ. of Guillory, 29 A.495; Chaffe v Ludeling, 34 A.967

contradictorily with forced heirs (1), do not give rise to a title translative of property, hence the purchaser must need be careful that all the formalities and requisites of the law have been fully complied with, to insure a good title, in such transaction.

The fact that a husband unduly influenced his wife to sell her paraphernal property cannot affect a bona fide purchaser without notice from vendee who had a legal title (2). A purchaser in good faith need not look beyond the order of sale made by a court having jurisdiction of the succession (3). The fraud by which an administrator buys succession property through a third party interposed, cannot affect a third person who without notice of such fraud buys the property in good faith from such interposed party or his vendee, even though the latter be the administrator himself (4). A more or less vague reference in a deed to a prior deed in a matter of description, is not necessarily notice of want of authority of the vendor or the vendor's vendor (5). A vague or uncertain description in a title deed will not amount to notice to a purchaser in good faith (6). But the description must not be one which fails utterly to identify the property. A sale by a married woman with the authorization of her husband, for a valid consideration and the subsequent sale by the vendee of the property to a third party, protects the latter, if he is in good faith, against any claim by the wife (7). A sells to B who fails to record but sells to C who does record. In the meantime A sells same property to D who records but sub-

1—Bourges v N. O. etc., R. R. 5 Orleans App. 239; Anglin v Betourney, 131 L.186; Tyson v Spears, 871
2—Blanchard v Castille, 19 L.362
3—Succ. Thomas I Orleans App. 124
4—Chaffe v Minden Lbr. Co., 118 L.753
5—Mendelsohn v Anushazy 52 A. 1300
6—Wilfert v Duson, 131 L.21
7—Colgin v Courrege, 106 L.684

sequently to C - C's title prevails over D (1). A widow (whose marriage to deceased was not of record) sold her community interest to her children but the transfer did not show that it was a partition between her and her children. A purchaser in good faith who relied upon the public record would be protected in such case against the claims of the widow (2). Notice or knowledge outside record is not equivalent to registry, in other words purchaser is not affected by such notice or knowledge (3). As differently expressed, fraud which of course is not a matter of record, does not vitiate sale by vendee to an innocent third party (4).

However firmly the principle that an innocent third party is protected by the record is established, he is put on notice by that record and may not plead ignorance of the laws or ignore matters of record which have been brought to his attention. Thus, it has been held that titles by descent need not be recorded in the usual conveyance records of a parish where property is situated and third persons are put on inquiry as to the nature and extent of such titles (5).In view of the statute which require all judgments of a court to be recorded to have effect against third parties (6), it would seem that this principle no longer applies (7). Although at law a purchaser is not required to examine previous titles beyond the deed which is tendered by his own vendor, yet he will be held to the knowledge of the defects in previous titles, if it appears that he has actually examined the

1—Phelan v Wilson, 114 L.813
2—Roque v Freeman, 125 L.60
3—Coyle v Allen, 168 L.504; Beard v Numa, 172 L.155; Westwego Canal & Ter. Co. v Pezani, 174 L.1068; Burgas v Stoutz 174 L.586; Coleman v Richmond, 156 L.262; Prater v Porter, 176 L.324
4—Chaffe v Minden Lbr. Co. 118 L.753
5—Brewer v Wright, 130 L.491 (1912)
6—R. C. C. 2265
7—Ibid

link in which such defects are apparent (1). Where there has been an error made in the recording of an act of sale, as under the law all original acts must be deposited in the recorder's office, the purchaser will not be protected by the record in conveyance book or mortgage book (2). Registration in parish records is not affected by incorporation of land concerned in a new parish, and no additional registration is necessary (3).

For a better appreciation of the principles enunciated in the foregoing, it is necessary that the difference between an alienation protected by the foregoing line of jurisdiction and one protected by prescription be noted. When it is said that an innocent third purchaser is protected by the record and need not look beyond that record, it is reference to sales alone, whether it be private sales, sales made under orders of court or public sale. It also means that un-recorded transfer, claims and equities are of no force or effect as against an innocent third party who is not involved in such claims or equities. The rule has no place in successions, partitions in kind or other change of ownership which do not constitute a title translative of property.

A title valid under such principles does not need the aid of prescription to perfect it.

A title which is perfected by prescription connotes an existing defect which is cured by the particular prescription applicable to the nature of the defect. Five years prescription applies to certain classes of defects and ten years prescription is all embracing and within certain limits validates any title which is translative of property.

1—Dohan v Murdock, 41 A.494
2—R. S. 2251
3—Parish Board v Edrington, 40 A.633

CHAPTER LXI

Defects and Their Cure

Theoretically a title examiner need do no more than examine and report on a title, it not being part of his employment to correct any errors, omissions or other defects which may exist, but in practice he is compelled, in the interest of his client, especially when that client is anxious to take title to the property, to take such measures as he deems necessary to place the title in proper shape to justify its acceptance.

He may even find it advisable to extend these efforts to the extent of "streamlining" the title, as it has been somewhat facetiously called. The term describes the supplying of omissions and correcting of defects which though more or less serious, have ceased to be of moment due to the elapse of time, or through other facts by which the possibility of a successful attack on the title, has been materially reduced to a point where acceptance, despite such defects, is ordinarily justified.

To some such streamlining may seem unnecessary and overly zealous, but a proper appreciation of an examiner's duty, should convince anyone to the contrary. In this day when the federal government and its numerous agencies, purchasing and otherwise, as well as other lending institutions such as insurance companies, who follow closely the requirements of the government in matters of titles, require as a prerequisite to the making of loans, just such streamlining as outlined above, under the penalty of a refusal to lend, it becomes clear that the merchantibility of a title of this character has been and is considerably impaired. The owner, though he might force a purchaser to accept such a title, can not force the lending institution, or the federal government to do so. At best he would be put to considerable expense and what is equally important, delay, which might have been avoided had the title been corrected in these respects before he acquired title.

In any event an examiner is interested in knowing wherein a defect exists, to what extent it is serious and how it may best be cured.

To that end a review of the jurisprudence in connection with such defects is given and the cure suggested where possible.

Prescription as a means of perfecting a title is omitted here as it is to be found in a separate chapter on the subject.

For convenience and ready reference each link set out in this work is followed here in the same order.

Patents

As a patent is conclusive when issued (1), unless attacked for error or fraud, factors which cannot appear on the face of the patent, and if regularly issued and properly describes and identifies the property, there is little room for doubt or question. This is true particularly of the United States' Patents but not so true of patents issued by the State, as in the latter case patents have been issued valid enough on their face, but contrary to or not in accordance with law, or because the state itself had not acquired the land patented. The state really stands in the position of a second owner in the chain of title and hence a divestiture by it is only as valid as its own acquisition. Thus a state patent under act March 25, 1844 No. 91 for land in the Houmas claim in the rear of the sur-

1—Bell v Hearne, 10 A.515; Slattery v Kellum, 114 L.282

vey of 1829, must yield to a United States patent under pre-emption Acts, May 29, 1830 (1). Again, no pre-emption claims could be acquired under Act 21 1886, on land in the Bossier District, after the passage of Act 89 1892, donating those lands to that district (2).

In effect, a patent from the State is subject to scrutiny both as to form and as to validity.

As duplicate patents have been issued by both the State and Federal governments, it would be well, in certain cases, to obtain from the Land Office at Baton Rouge, a check of the patents issued to insure that no dual or duplicate patents have been issued on the land involved.

In most patents, whichever patent was valid, operated as a divestiture of title from the government, and so possession and prescription would enter into the question, in which event, priority of issuance of patent would be of little importance.

A certificate issued by either the state or the federal government vests an equitable title in the purchaser, his heirs and assigns, but a patent, if not already applied for or issued, should be obtained and registered in the conveyance office of the parish in which land is located, though it has been held that a patent need not be recorded (3).

Neither entryman nor his heirs acquire any rights until final proof is made and certificate issues (4); entry made before marriage but perfected after marriage becomes community property (5); on the con-

1—Foley v Harrison, 5 A.75
2—Hall v Com. Bossier Levee Dist., 111 L.913; also 111 927
3—McQueen v Flasdick, Black Land Co., 135 L.698; Tear v Williams, 2 A.868
4—Brewer v Hill, 178 L.583; Doucet v Fontenot, 165 L.458; Ford v Edenborn, 142 L.927; (A. F. C. A. , Title, 43 SS164-171
5—Ford v Edenborn, 142 L.927; Doucet v Fortenot, 165 L.458

trary, entry made during marriage but perfected after death of entryman by widow is her separate property (1).

Patents issued by the United States to land owned by state by virtue of its sovereignty is wholly void and subject to collateral attack (2). Though a patent gives acreage patented as 160 acres, where field notes show a fractional section, a part of which had been cut off by previous patent, patentee takes only what is left (3).

Act 97 contemplates that the donation of land to the levee district should stand open indefinitely and is not affected by Act 215 of 1908 (4); and this applies equally to purchaser from the Levee Board, though conveyance of the land from State to Levee Board had not been executed (5).

Suit by State to recover bed of lake from innocent transferee of title granted by patents signed by Governor and Register of Land Office and recorded there, is barred by six years (6).

Act 94 of 1890 granting certain lands to levee district did not affect title of entryman whose application was recorded in land office previously (7). Patent from State which showed on its face that it was issued under Act 104 1888, was void where it did not show compliance with provisions of Act 215 1918 (8). Though original patentee entered 640 acres and did other acts wrongfully, such matters would not entitle state to recover from innocent third party who

1—Ford. v Edenborn, 142 L.927; Doucet v Fontenot, 165 L.458
2—State v Bozeman, 156 L.635
3—Gilmore v Lyon Lbr. Co. 159 L.18
4—Atchafalaya Basin Levee Dist. v Capdeville, 142 L.111
5—Atchafalaya Land Co. v Grace, 143 L.637
6—State v Sweetwater Land & Oil Co. 164 L.240
7—Ellis v La. Planting Co., 146 L.652
8—Albritton v Shaw, 148 L.427

was in good faith (1). A patent issued to A as legal representative of D and E is too indefinite and uncertain. It should have been issued to D and E for benefit of A (2).

Execution and proof of recordation of patent, with declaration that grant was made according to government survey, held presumption survey was actually on file prior to issuance of patent (3). Application under Act 75 of 1880, where there has been no survey, secures no right (4). Individuals cannot attack title of patentee on ground that it was issued for script and not cash. The State alone could bring such a suit (5). In the case of swamp and overflowed lands, certificate held to be valid as against patent issued subsequently (6). Sea marsh subject to tidal overflow are swamp lands within meaning of federal grant rather than lands within tide water of sea which belong to the state by virtue of its sovereignty and not subject to sale and private ownership (7). After creation of Bossier Levee District, private person could not acquire rights to lands within said levee district, under Act 21 of 1886 (8). Act 21 1886 was held to be applicable to land subject to entry as well as land which was for want of approval or survey, not open to entry. It did not require that one in possession should be an actual settler or resident on the land. The act prohibited the entry of such lands as were in possession of anyone who was improving or cultivating them (9). Prescription

1—State v Hackley. Hume & Joyce, 124 L.854
2—McQueen v Flasdick-Black. 130 L.1071
3—LaTerre   Co. v Billiots Shell Island Inc., 20 Fed. Supp. 106
4—Duggan v Crandall. 144 L.21
5—Frellsen v Crandall, 217 U. S. 71, 24 L.ed.670
6—Betz v I. C. R. R., 52 A.893
7—State v Sweetwater Land & Oil Co., 164 L.240
8—Act 89, 1892; Hall v Bd. Levee Comm. 111 L.913; West v Robert, 135 Fed.350
9—Act 21, 1886

against attack on patents issued by State, does not apply to suit by levee board to compel Register of Land Office to certify lands within grant made by certain acts (1).

The Act (2) confirmed sales and locations of land made by state from January 1, 1861 to October 14, 1864, shown by the records of the Register of the Land Office. This act fixed in a patentee, who recorded his title in the Land Office in 1862, a vested and irrevocable right (3). Claims based on receipt of Land Office in 1862 and recorded that year in the Land Office in Washington and not discovered until 1918, and patents issued thereon were invalid (4).

An act which conveyed to the levee districts all lands of state however acquired, did not restrict lands conveyed to grants from Congress and those sold to the state for taxes (5). An act passed in 1908 (6), which cancelled all applications on which patents or certificates had not issued was held not to apply to a case where entry was complete and the requirements of the law complied with prior to enactment of Act (7).

This act was repealed and applications reinstated by an act in 1914 (8). It was also held not to apply to grants to levee boards or their vendees though not actually conveyed to the boards, but it did not apply to lands not so granted (9).

An Act was passed in 1861 which repealed in

1—Hyams v Grave, 161 L.1039
2—Act 104, 1871
3—Garrison v Natalbany Lbr. Co., 4 La. App. 596
4—McQueen v Flasdick-Black Lbr. Co., 130 L.1071
5—Ellerbe v Ellerbe, 162 L.846
6—Act 215. 1908; Repealed Act 283, 1914
7—Armstead v Grace, 129 L.694
8—Act 283, 1914
9—Hartigan v Weaver, 126 L.492; Atchafalaya B. & L. Bd. v Capdevielle, 142 L.111; Board Levee Com. v Hartner, 164 L.632

part Act 197 of 1859 but it was declared that it did not repeal that part of the latter act which authorized the entry of lands subject to overflow at 25c an acre (1).

Sales made under contract by Levee Boards prior to the enactment of an act regulating sales of land by those boards, cannot be effected by such an act (2).

Where fraud has been committed by a patentee the government cannot recover from a bona fide purchaser (3).

The State by virtue of its inherent sovereignty, owns all tidal overflowed lands within its boundaries (4).

A description in a private land grant in 1765 which read, "with all the depth that may be found" was interpreted as extending the side lines back to the nearest watercourse in the rear (5).

Incomplete claims under grants from the French and Spanish governments, when not asserted in the time allowed, were properly ignored by the Land Department and the government could validly dispose of the lands as its legislative department saw fit (6).

Actual occupancy for more than 30 years of land within a short distance of New Orleans during the Spanish regime, brought to public attention by two notarial transfers, considered as a tacit if not express confirmation by the Spanish regime (7).

Failure of a successor of grantee under a private land grant made on June 25, 1776 by the French Government, to present his claim to the register and

1—In re Sulphur Mining Co. 110 L.699
2—Hartigan v Weaver, 126 L.492; Act 215, 1908
3—State v Hackley Hume Lbr. Co., 124 L.854
4—Board Levee Com. v Forest Fur Farms of America, 178 L.696
5—State v Bowie Lbr. Co., 148 L.581
6—Brott v N. O. Land Co., 151 L.134
7—State v N. O. Land Co., 143 L.868

receiver of the land office for registry and approval within two years after the passage of act of Congress February 6, 1835, was not an abandonment or forfeiture of his claim to the land (1).

Where swamp lands were not conveyed to State under swamp land grant, Congress could give those claiming under a Spanish grant another chance to have their title confirmed as was done by Act of Congress June 22, 1860 and June 10, 1872 and patent thereunder conveyed a valid title (2).

Inchoate rights to land in territory of Louisiana which were of imperfect obligation when confirmed by Congress, take legality and validity wholly from act of confirmation and elder confirmee had better right than junior confirmee, without reference to date of origin of their claims (3).

Where possessor of inchoate title did not confirm as required by law and it was never filed, he could not attack defendant's title confirmed in 1823 (4).

Grant of land made by Spanish had not been surveyed to ascertain its limits and when instrument refers to no line of boundaries it could create no right of private property in any particular parcel which could be maintained in a court of justice (5).

By the usages of the Spanish Government a double concession could only be in the rear of the front concession (6).

A grant to Baron Bastrop for the purpose of colonizing was for the benefit of the colonists and was not a grant to Bastrop personally (7).

Commandants of Posts under Spanish Regime,

1—State v Bowie Lbr. Co., 148 L.581
2—Smith v Albritton, 153 L.507
3—Carrerre v N. O., 162 L.981
4—N. O. v Union Lbr. Co., 145 L.476
5—U. S. v King, 3 Howard (U. S.) 772
6—Broussard v Gonsoulin, 12 Rob. 1
7—U. S. v Philadelphia and New Orleans, 12 How. (U. S.) 433

had power to grant inchoate titles to land within their jurisdiction (1).

France could not make grants of land between November 3, 1762 and October 1, 1800 (2).

Until October 22, 1798 the Governor of the Providence had the right to grant public lands, thereafter the power was vested in the Intendant (3).

The sovereignty of the United States dated from the Treaty of cession April 30, 1803 and the effect of its ratification reverted to that date. No grants of land made by either the French or Spanish government after April 30, 1803 was valid (4).

No authoritative answer can be given to the question as to whether or not a grant by the Spanish government of an area which included a navigable stream can be given, but a decision in which it was held that the Spanish Monarch could not alienate land dedicated to public use is persuasive in view of the fact that navigable streams have always been held by all nations as public property (5).

Colonial Grants and Concessions

The local Land Office (New Orleans) is not a judicial tribunal, hence its decision that sale by supreme council of Louisiana in 1760 was equivalent to patent is not controlling (6). An order or decree of the supreme council of the province of Louisiana in a succession of land is not binding as it had no authority to grant patents to public lands, while sitting as a judicial tribunal (7).

1—U. S. v Davenport, 15 How. (U. S.) 1
2—U. S. v Dauterive, 10 How. (U. S.) 600
3—Choppin v Michel, 5 Rob.233
4—U. S. v Reynes, 9 How. (U. S.) 127
5—New Orleans v U. S., 10 Pet. (U. S.) 662
6—Carrere v New Orleans, 162 L.981
7—New Orleans v Union Lbr. Co., 145 L.476

The regulations of O'Reilley were not binding on succeeding Spanish Governors of Louisiana (1); and the regulations of O'Reilley were not in force in upper Louisiana (2). Spanish grants recognized as valid by the United States cannot be subsequently declared vacant and subject to homestead by the General Land Office (3). Land not severed from the public domain by the French or Spanish authorities and set apart as private property, passed to the United States by the treaty (4).

The country between the Iberville and Perdido rivers formed part of the territory ceded by Spain to France; a grant within that tract by the Spanish government September 1, 1806, is void. (5). The issuing of a grant is not proof of the authority to make such a grant (6). A party not an inhabitant of Bellevue, is without a right to a grant, as the concession was made only to inhabitants thereof (7). The mere presentation of a petition to a Spanish intendant praying for a grant, on which no further action was taken at the time of the transfer of the territory to the United States, conferred no title (8).

The Spanish government recognized verbal grants and where the property was separated from the public domain and the settlers put in possession, which possession continued for years, title was valid (9).

The court will presume a written grant, where there has been continued possession for fifty years

1—Delassus v United States, 9 Peters (U. S.) 117
2—Mackey v United States, 10 Peters (U. S.) 340
3—Teddlie v McNeely, 104 L.603
4—Nixon v Houillon, 20 A.515; Board Directors v N. O. Land Co., 138 L.32
5—Foster v Neilson, 2 Peters (U. S.) 253
6—N. O. v United States, 10 Peters (U. S.) 662
7—Richard v Perrodin, 116 L.440
8—Blanc v Lafayette, 11 Howard (U. S.) 104
9—Landry v Martin, 15 L.1

and the archives of the province had been partially destroyed (1).

When a certain number of arpents is granted on a part of a bayou and where the quantity cannot be obtained unless by making such part of the watercourse a side line of the survey, it may be done, and where title calls for land on the east or west side of a watercourse, without specifying how much on each, it should be located in equal quantities on each side (2).

The Spanish provinces of Florida and Louisiana were under the jurisdiction of the Captain General of Cuba, but the Governor of Louisiana had authority over the Governor of West Florida (including the Florida parishes) and could grant lands in that province (3).

A confirmation by commissioners cannot avail against a complete Spanish title (4). One claiming under an order of survey must trace his title from the grantee of the order; it is not sufficient to trace it from the holder of the commissioner's certificate (5). Confirmation by Congress is but a relinquishment of its claim, but leaving subject to adverse claims under former government (6).

Acts of Sale.

Defects in an act of sale consists chiefly in omissions, such as the date (though this seldom occurs), witnesses, declarations as to marital statii, etc., and errors in names, indefinite or vague descriptions of the property, no certificates, failure of parties to

1—Landry v Martin 15 L.1
2—Holstein v Henderson, 12 Mart. (O. S.) 319
3—Murdock v Gurley, 5 Rob. 457; Choppin v Michel, 14 Rob. 233
4—White v Wells, 5 Martin (O. S.) 652
5—Rachal v Irwin, 8 Martin (N. S.) 331, 332
6—Murdock v Gurley, 5 Rob. 457; Kittredge v Hebert, 9 A.154

sign their names and failure to properly record.

Lack of a date may be supplied by the notary, or other officer before whom the act was passed, if alive. The date of registry would be sufficient to fix the approximate date, and establish the basis of a title translative of property (1). Though there be but one witness to an authentic act this fact will not invalidate the sale as it would operate as a sale under private signature (2).

Information as to the marital status should be in all cases supplied, if possible, in at least those acts the date of which does not bring them beyond the prescriptive period of twenty two years; and this information should be of the fullest. Proper affidavits by responsible parties should be attached to the act.

Errors in names, especially of vendors, bring into question the identity of the owner and requires that sufficient evidence be obtained to establish reasonably the identity of the vendor.

Descriptions which do not reasonably establish the identity and location of the property sold, should be supplemented by a survey and a check of prior sales. It is in this respect that a clear reference to the acquisition in the act itself may be the means of removing any doubts on the subject.

Where no certificates are attached to the act (that is mortgage and conveyance certificates and U. S. Court certificates, where deemed necessary) certificates should of course be obtained, or the records run by the examiner. Absence of such certificates does not justify rejection of title on that fact alone and consequently the vendor does not have to stand cost of their production (3).

1—Cole v Richmond, 156 L.262
2—Ely v Coreil, 166 L.153
3—Norton v Enos 158 L.428

Failure of vendor to sign the act undoubtedly would be a serious defect, but where it could be established that such a vendor had stood by and made no attempt to disavow the transfer where he was in, or had been, a position to have done so, but on the contrary dealt with the purchaser as the owner, he would be estopped (1). A written ratification of the sale by the vendor or his heirs would be the best action to be taken in such a case.

As an act under private signature may be, and can be a title translative of property, an authentic act which is defective in form does not necessarily invalidate a title, otherwise valid.

The lack of a proper authorization of an officer who signs on behalf of a corporation should always be supplied, if possible, but such a defect may be cured by estoppel or ratification, as for instance the sale of the same property, or if a sale by the corporation, its receipt of the consideration, whether cash or notes and failure to disavow the action of the officer within a reasonable time (2).

Powers of attorney are strictly construed and hence any defect can only be cured by estoppel or ratification. An act of procuration under private signature, or containing an incorrect description are some of the defects which would invalid a sale through agency. It does not acquire the character of an authentic act merely because it is attached to an authentic act (3).

Death of the principal necessarily terminates a mandate, but not if it is coupled with interest (4).

1—Chatman v Bundy, 180 L.158
2—J. P. Barnett Co. v Ludeau, 171 L.21; Tulane Educational Fund v Carbajal, 180 L.355
3—Denegre v Fairex, 52 A.1760
4—Succ. Tombs, 167 L.21

In all cases where the principal accepts the benefit of the act of the agent (1), or where, being in a position to object and disavow the agent's act, he does not do so, he is bound by that act (2).

Corporations: A defect may arise where, the corporation being either a purchaser or vendor, no proper authorization either by the board of directors or the stockholders as the case may be, was shown, but such a defect is more or less serious according as the corporation is a purchaser or a vendor. In the former case, like an individual, the corporation may by its action ratify the purchase, that is, for instance by selling the same property or other acts indicating ratification. Where it is the vendor, it may estop itself by accepting the purchase price, and collecting notes, etc (3). The validity of the incorporations organized prior to 1904, was confirmed and established by an act in 1904 (4), so the examiner is only concerned with that question where the corporation has been organized since that date. Sales made by a de facto corporation, unless it was of the entire assets thereof, could not be questioned, provided that there be only a lack of one or more formalities in organization which might, in other respects be the basis for an attack directly. In other words such an attack could not be made collaterally by anyone.

Where possible, however, a ratification should be obtained by those who might have the authority to seek to set aside the sale.

Married woman: A sale by a married woman can involve only one question, and that is whether or not the property sold was community or separate

1—Watson v Schmidt, 173 L.92
2—Jones v Sanford, 163 L.799
3—J. P. Barnnet Co. v Ludeau, 171 L.21; Tulane Educational Fund v Carbajal, 180 L.355
4—Act 120, 1904

property of the vendor. The appearance of the husband to authorize the wife to sell, is no longer necessary since 1916, though it is in acts prior to that date. If the husband is a party to the act in any capacity, he and his heirs are bound, though his creditors are not. Prescription, however, will in many cases, in fact most of the cases, effectually lay that doubt at rest.

Where judicial partition in kind is to be made, it must be divided into lots of equal, or nearly equal value and lots must be drawn by chance and not selected by the co-proprietors (1).

Sales by School Boards.

The sale of surveyed 16th sections made under Act 168, 1894, not invalid, because made without consent of inhabitants (2).

Public Sales.

The defects which may arise in such sales have been discussed in the chapter devoted to that subject and there are no cures for such defects, except prescription, estoppel and ratification, other than the jurisprudence which has declared what defects are not sufficient to invalidate the sale. Under "Execution" will be found a further discussion of the subject.

Executory Process

The identity of the notes sued on, must be established, though it may be by other means than the notarial paragraph and certificate (3). An administrator cannot obtain an order of executory process without authentic proof of his appointment (4). A

1—Jefferson Lake Oil Co. v Loughridge, 182 L.57
2—State v Joyce Lbr. Co., 261 Fed.128
3—Chambliss v Canik, 2 A.488
4—Landry v Landry, 12 A.167

sale made in executory process, under a fieri facias, instead of a writ of seizure and sale is not invalid where all defendants have been cited (1). An agent's authority to sue out executory process must be in authentic form (2). In an act by a corporation, the the authority of the officer acting must be part of the record. If lost, the loss cannot be proven by parol (3). A mortgagee having sold the property mortgaged, after the loss of the note, his authentic acknowledgment of the loss and consent that the writ issue, cannot authorize it (4).

Executory process on a prescribed note, is valid, where maker did not plead prescription until after the sale (5).

No demand or notice other than the three days notice is necessary (6), but a writ of seizure executed before the three days, is null (7). A note made payable to order and endorsed by the maker, requires no further proof of ownership (8).

Hypothecary Action.

Process against third possessor will be set aside unless mortgage has been recorded (9). Neither the contracting parties, nor their heirs, nor the witnesses to act can take advantage of the nonrecording of mortgage (10). Where there is no mortgage at time of seizure a sale thereunder is null, not being prescribed by five years (11).

1—Truxillo v DeLaune, 47 A.10
2—Crescent City Bank v Blanque, 32 A.264; Ardona v Hulse, 158 L.997
3—Bank of Leesville v Wingate, 123 L.386
4—Prevost v Pellerin, 105 L.589
5—Huber v Jennings-Heywood Oil Syndicate, 111 L.747
6—Rogers v St. Martin, 110 L.80
7—Billgery v Ferguson, 30 A.84
8—Franek v Brewster, 141 L.1031
9—Lobdell v Bank, 8 A.117
10—Brown v Sadler, 16 A.206
11—Pons v Y. & M. V. R. R., 122 L.156

Auction Sales.

The subject needs no amplification, because as it has been shown such sales generally result in an authentic act signed by the owners and hence estoppel or ratification occurs in all cases.

Dation En Paiement.

Any defects occurring in ordinary acts of sale may occur in a dation en paiement, so it is unnecessary to elaborate, however, it has been held, contrary to the general rule that a purchaser, in good faith, is protected against claims against the vendor, is not protected in a dation en paiement, where the debtor is insolvent, or acted through motives of fraud, even though the creditor had no knowledge of these facts (1).

Dedications.

Requires no further comment than is contained in the chapter on the subject.

Counter Letters.

The foregoing apply to this subject with equal force.

Exchange.

All that has been said in reference to sales applies to this class of transfers, so nothing further need be said.

Partitions in Kind.

Partitions in kind made by major co-owners by consent partake of the nature of exchange as well as of sale, so no more than what has been found necessary to say in respect to those two classes of transfers will be said here, except that it has been held that a partition of this character may be made, when

1—Bullard v Nattin, 18 L. App. 75

there are minor co-owners, when authorized by court (1).

Redemption of Property Sold for Taxes

The subject has been sufficiently covered in the chapter on redemption of tax sales and anything said here would be nothing more than repetition.

Renunciations.

Except as to defects in form, nothing not already set forth in the chapter on renunciations could be added here. As to defects in form there can be no other method of renouncing except by authentic act or by judicial pleadings.

Rescissions.

Require no comment other than has already been made on the subject.

Vente a Remere.

The reader is referred to the chapter on the subject.

Acquisitions and sales by the State and its Subdivisions

The subjects having been discussed fully in the chapter bearing on these acquisitions and alienations, nothing more can be added of value to the examiner, hence no attempt will be made to do so.

The foregoing includes all changes of ownership executed voluntarily and the following pertains to involuntary alienations.

These alienations, with the exception of tax sales, expropriations and sales by trustees under established trusts, are the results of an order or judgment of court.

The alienations made under order of court are those made by sheriffs, auctioneers and notaries.

1—Act 15, 1918; Washington v Smith, 156 L.902; Levy v Levy, 180 L.77

In all alienations made at sheriff's sale defects and informalities therein are cured by two years in the case of majors and five years in the case of minors. The Judgments of the courts themselves protect the innocent third parties, unless the defects thereof are of such a nature as to amount to nullities. The Code of Practice enumerate these nullities as follows:

1 Where rendered against a minor unrepresented in court.

2 Where rendered against the defendant without citation.

3 Where rendered by a court without jurisdiction.

4 Where though there has been citation, defendants fails to answer, but the matter has not been put to issue and no default taken in the case (1).

The foregoing nullities are not exclusive. Any fraud nullifies a judgment, provided it has resulted in grave injury to the party cast (2).

In view of those two rules of property, it might appear that the detailed discussion as to essentials of these links was unnecessary, but as the two and five year prescriptions do not protect any purchaser at sheriff's sale prior to the expiration of those prescriptive periods, the examiner should have at hand for reference the law and the jurisprudence governing these sales.

In the chapters on the various proceedings leading to such alienation both the law and the jurisprudence have been set out in full detail in regard to both defects and essentials, hence nothing further is required here, except in cases where the ju-

1—Tarver v Quinn, 149 L.368
2—Miller v Miller, 156 L.46; Spence v Spence, 158 L.961

risprudence has been omitted in the particular chapter.

In those judicial sales made by sheriffs it is inevitable that doubts arising from omissions and irregularities occurring in the proceedings leading up to and including the sale, must be created in the mind of the examiner and it is of the greatest importance that he should know, as far as is practical, just how serious such defects are and what weight is to be attached to them. It is only when the prescriptive period has elapsed in a link of that character that these doubts may be ignored.

Thus it has been held that a sale made pending a third opposition is null if appeal is sustained (1). A sheriff may not deviate from the terms of the judgment (2). Property not specifically described in the advertisement cannot form the basis of a sale (3). Thirty days must elapse between the first date of advertisement and the sale, exclusive of the day of advertisement and the day of sale (4), but a sale advertised to take place August 25, meets with all requirements of the law, if it is published for the first time on July 21 and last time on August 18 and appears once each week in that interval (5). Upon foreclosure of a materialman's lien, the sheriff can not adjudicate property for less than the full amount of a prior mortgage (6). Property advertised to be sold in lots of 10 to 50 acres cannot be sold in block, (7), though it has been held on the other hand that a party may not complain of a sheriff's sale of lots in

1—C. P. 400; Emanuel v Presb. Church, 112 L.348
2—Doucet v Fenelon, 120 L.18
3—Continental Sec. Corp. v Wetherbee, 187 L.73
4—McDonough v Gravier, 9 L.531
5—Schwan v Sanders, 121 L.461
6—Robinson Slagle Lbr. Co. v Riede, 156 L.174; Keller v Summers La. App. 159 So.198
7—Morrison v Flournoy, 25 A.545; Norton v Citizens Bank, 28 A.354

block, unless he alleges and proves that he protested in vain against the sale (1). Adjudication for less than prior special mortgage is but a relative nullity (2), but still it is a nullity.

A sale for a larger price than the total appraisement is not a nullity (3). The fact that on appeal the amount of the judgment was reduced does not have the effect on the adjudication (4).

While the Digests are full of decisions in which sheriff's sales have been set aside for irregularities and other causes, a large majority of them have been founded on facts dehors the record and only developed on trial, hence the examiner is little aided by such decisions, unless he is in possession of facts otherwise obtained than through the records.

Sales by Administrators, Executors, Receivers, Syndics, Tutors and Curators.

These alienations are alike in that they are made by fiduciary officers under an order or judgment of court and unless they are so made they are null and void and afford no protection to the purchaser of the of the property sold by them.   On the other hand when a sale is made under a judgment of a competent court, regularly issued, the acts of these officers are valid and are good against the world. No extended discussion is required here as the chapters devoted to these matters contain full expositions of the law and the jurisprudence.

Partition By Licitation.

A partition by licitation of property owned entirely by major co-owners no matter how defective

1—Taylor v Graham, 18 La. App. 656
2—White Land Co. v Graham. 9 A.216
3—DeLa Villa v Palmer, 21 A.11
4—McWaters v Smith, 25 A.515; Citizens Bank v Ballemy Lbr. Co. 140 L.

it may be as regards the formalities required in its completion insofar as the sale is concerned, may be and usually is cured by the signatures of all the parties in the execution of the actual deed of sale. Such parties would likewise be estopped from any attack where they have received and accepted the proceeds of the sale.

Where minors or interdicts are co-owners the situation is entirely different as there can be no estoppel or ratification on their part until majority has been reached by the minor, or recovery and removal of the interdiction has occurred in the case of an interdict. A strict compliance with the requisites of the law is the only protection in these cases. In regard to the proceedings leading up to the sale, jurisdiction and regularity of the issuance of the order of sale, are the only requirements necessary to the validity of the proceedings.

In all instances of these sales, they are made by public auction and all the formalities required in these sales are the same as in other public sales and lack of compliance with them produce the same defects which defects are no more nor less in their effect than other defects in other public sales.

Alienations and Changes in Ownership Effected by Acts Before Notaries Public by Order of Court.

These alienations occur in sales to pay debts, dations en paiements and partitions in kind. Dations en Paiements under order of court occurs only in cases of administration and successions and can only be effected by compliance with the provisions of the law. Failure to properly advertise or to follow strictly the formalities prescribed by the acts authorizing these alienations, would be fatal to the validity of the transfer.

This applies equally to private sales of the property of successions and of corporation in liquidations.

Enough has been written in connection with partitions of various nature to render unnecessary further discussion.

Alienations of Minors' and Interdicts' property.

The chapter on this subject covers the field minutely and hence nothing can be added here of value to the examiner.

Inheritance.

An attempt to give in detail possible defects in links involving change of ownership by inheritance is hopeless because the number of such defects is so great that want of space alone would forbid. In the case of formalities by which these changes are made the difficulty is not great, but in the main a recital of these defects would avail little, for the reason that if they are serious, only estoppel or ratification can rectify them and if not, a simple compliance, even though belated, is sufficient.

The sale of inherited property without the payment of the inheritance tax is not void, but the property remains subject to the tax (1) which does not prescribe unless the succession has been opened. The foregoing statement refers only to a sale which has been made without the succession having been opened and the heirs placed in possession.

Wills.

Defects in a will are incurable, except by prescription, estoppel and ratification, but the examiner is constantly called upon to decide whether the will under examination, is valid, the question being pre-

1—Prieto v Faure, 169 L.75; Barborich v Meyer, 154 L.325; Green v Bagley, 154 L.965

sented by reason of omissions, deviations from the customary expressions used in such wills by experienced notaries for years, or some language confusing as to meaning.

The courts have frequently been called upon to pass upon the validity of wills, but these decisions are of little interest to the examiner, unless they adjudicate some point presented by the language of the will. Thus the courts have decided that a will made by a testator not interdicted, during a lucid interval, is valid (1); that the presumption is always in favor of the validity of the will, insanity never being presumed (2); that incapacity to make a will must be shown at time of execution (3), but the examiner would find the decisions of little use at the time of his examination, because the will itself would not disclose any reason for questioning on those points and the probate proceedings would be equally silent, unless the will had been attacked, in which case the judgment would settle the doubt, either one way or the other.

Such decisions, however, to the effect that the lack of a declaration in the will that the depositions were dictated by testator and written down by the notary in the presence of the witnesses, was fatal (4); or that the declaration that the "testator being illiterate made his mark" is not sufficient for a valid will (5), but the declaration that "the testatrix declared that she could not write" is sufficient (6), establish a guide by which to judge the validity of similar language in other wills. The foregoing seem

1—Succ. Conner, 165 L.890; Succ. Mithoff, 168 L.624
2—Wilcox v Hanemann, 163 L.489; Succ. Edgar, 184 L.775
3—Succ. of Knight La. App. 151 So.230
4—Succ. Vidal. 44 A.41; Succ Wilson, 183 L.1087
5—Succ. Carroll, 28 A.388; Succ. Whittington, 26 A.89; Succ. Nelson, 163 L.463
6—Brand v Baumgarten, 24 A.89

to have been decided on the point that in the first case is a statement by the notary, not the testator. In the second case, the declaration was stated to have been made by the testator.

The notary taking the will may be appointed as attorney for the succession (1); and one of the subscribing witnesses may be named as executor of the will (2). These cases were decided upon the ground that such appointments did not constitute legacies or donations mortis causa, unless it appeared from the language of the act that such appointments were intended as legacies, or could be so construed, but even in that event, the legacies would fall, but the will would still be valid.

A nuncupative will by public act, defective in form may still be valid as a nuncupativee will, by private act, provided there were at least four witnesses to the will, the notary in that case acting as the fifth witness. (3).

Where a will is not dictated by testator or written by notary in presence of witnesses; where one of the witnesses did not understand the language in which the will was written, and where what was done, was not done without turning aside to other acts, the will is void (4).

The omission of the will to declare that it was written by notary (5); to state by whom the will was read to the testator, is fatal (6). Express mention must be made of the presence of the witnesses (7); but it is sufficient if it can be inferred from the language used in the will that they were present (8).

1—Succ. Feitel, 187 L.596
2—Davenport v Davenport. 116 L.1000; Ibid
3—Succ. Feitel, 187 L.596
4—Succ. Dauterive, 39 A.1094; Richard v Richard, 129 L.967
5—Miller v Schumaker, 42 A.398; Massey v Pierre, 6 Mart. (N. S.) 263
6—Succ. Key, 5 Rob. 482
7—Conner v Brashear, 25 A.663
8—Martin v Kissinger, 26 A.338

The expression "in the presence of the witnesses" in the concluding clause qualifies indiscriminately the preceding declaration that the will was dictated and was written by the notary (1), so the will was de-clared valid.

The failure to declare in the will that it was dic-tated to notary in the presence of three witnesses, re-siding in the place where will was executed or that it was read to testator in the presence of said witness-es renders the will invalid (2). The declarations as to dictations, etc., may be written ahead of disposi-tions (3). The dictation must be oral; the expression of "comme ca", "Comme Ca" referring to a memo-randum is fatal (4).

The use of language foreign to the confection of a will, such as "the parties dispense with the cer-tificate required by C. C. 3328 and release me, no-tary from all responsibility" renders such a will void (5).

If averments in will show, no matter, however couched, that all formalities have been complied with, it is sufficient for the validity of the will (6). Lack of formal declaration that all of the formalities have been complied with at one time and without turning aside to any other act does not nullify the will if they have been complied with (7).

Notary must state the facts which establishes that witnesses are competent. He is not the judge of their competency (8). If it appears from other reci-

1—Needer v McCarty, 7 A.484
2—Langley vLangley, 12 L.114
3—Stafford v Stafford, 12 L.439; Ducasse v Ducasse, 120 L.731
4—Hennessey v Woulfe, 49 A.1386; Succ. Theriot, 114 L.611
5—Succ. Gough, 5 Rob.503
6—Martin v Kissinger, 26 A.338
7—Martin v Kissinger, 26 A.338; Succ. Murray, 41 A.1109
8—Succ. Volmar, 40 A.493; Weintz v Kramer, 44 A.35

tals in the will that testator was not able to sign his name on account of physical disabilities, will is valid (1).

Notary is not obligated to write word for word the declarations and dispositions of testator (2), and where the language used by the testator is that of an uneducated person, notary may convert it into correct english, or where notary changed phraseology of testator, but not his exact meaning, will was not invalidated thereby (3).

Will must be received and written down by notary himself (not another) (4); but it may be written by the notary on a typewriter (5).

The certificate to a nuncupative will "before me, C. R., a Notary Public for the parish of Orleans" without words "duly commissioned" or "sworn" is sufficient to express official character of notary (6). Failure to declare that the notary was qualified is not fatal to will (7).

It has been held that a will dictated in French and written down in English (8), or where a witness was deaf (9), or did not understand (10), was invalid, but these facts are not likely to appear as part of the will.

The word "domicile" has been declared as equivalent to the word "residence" (11). A declaration

1—Frith v Pearce 105 L.186
2—Hamilton v Hamilton, 6 Mart. (N. S.) 143
3—Succ. Saux, 46 A.1423; Succ. Nelson, 163 L.458
4—Cotonio v Guglelmo, 176 L.421; Succ. Wilson, 177 L.119
5—Prudhomme v Savant, 150 L.256
6—Succ. Marqueze, 50 A.66
7—Rostrup v Succ. Spicer, 183 L.1067
8—DeBaillon v Fuselier, 159 L.1044; Gonzales v Gonzales, 13 A.104
9—Succ. Gauthreaux, 173 L.993
10—Latapie v Bandot, 152 L.177
11—Martin v Kissinger, 26, A.338

that "at moment of signing, testator declared that she did not know how to write" has been found sufficient (1).

A last will and testament falls upon the birth of a child after the date of its confection (2), but the provisions of that will may be reinstated by a subsequent will valid in form, without repeating all of the provisions of the previous will (3), provided of course, that the legitime of the forced heirs are not infringed upon.

Minors and Their Tutors.
(Interdicts and their Curators)

In a sale of a minor's property through proceedings which appear regularly correct and conducted contradictorily with the undertutor, the order of a competent court for the sale will protect the purchaser (4), but where in the proceedings the minor is not represented, such as in a partition sale, a purchaser will not be protected by the decree (5); and persons knowing facts which render the sale invalid, at the time of acquiring the property, may not assert title by prescription as they are not purchasers in good faith (6). A judgment in an action against minors for a partition and sale held thereunder, is void where there has been no citation (7).

Conditions and clauses in a mortgage, such as the pact non alienando, attorneys fees, etc., not contained in the judgment of court authorizing the execution of a mortgage on minor's behalf, do not bind the minor (8).

1—Succ. Nelson, 163 L.458
2—R. C. C. 1705; Lewis v Hare, 8 A.378; Buelow v Mandel, 28 A.697; Succ. Desina, 135 L.402
3—Succ. Ledet, 170 L.489
4—Gandy v Caldwell, 169 L.870
5—Crayton v Waters, 146 L.238
6—Fradella v Pumilia, 177 L.47
7—Spears v Spears, 173 L.294
8—Kling Mortgage Inv. Co. v Donovan, 178 L.119

A sale of a minor's property by conventional act, not by public sale and not for the purpose of a partition was declared null and void (decided in 1905).

On the other hand, minor irregularities such as error in date of the deed (which was dated the day before the sale) (1); and failure to designate place of sale in order of sale (2), have been held not to constitute nullities.

Purchasers are held to have a knowledge of the law (regarding sale of minor's property) when buying property of minors (3).

Any deviation from this mandate (Act 25, 1878) works absolute nullity of sale of minor's property (4), A sale made of minor's property without a family meeting does not convey title (5); and a purchaser of such property (minor's) is not in good faith (6). In these two cases, the decisions were rendered prior to the enactment of Act 209, 1932 and 319 of 1926 and 47 of 1934, but the principles enunciated therein have not changed and must constitute a warning to the profession to observe caution in proceedings to alienate a minor's property under present statutes.

Where a sale of a minor's property by a tutor was a nullity, as to the major heirs it was a nullity of the whole sale (7). Because of this principle after the decision in the Womens League case, it was found necessary to pass a quieting act covering those cases where there were major co-owners with the minors whose interests had been illegally divested (8).

In the preceding pages of this chapter an effort

1—Cole v Richmond, 156 L.262
2—Ibid.
3—Roque v Lebesque, 110 L.806
4—Succ. Posey, 143 L.924
5—Succ. Drysdale, 130 L.167; Succ. Loeb, 52 A.433
6—Succ. Drysdale, 130 L.167
7—Higginbotham v Daigle, 120 L.464
8—Act 17, 1928

has been made to list defects which may occur in a title and to indicate as far as possible, either their serious nature or what steps may be taken to effect a cure. This has proven to be difficult, because in so many cases the nature of the link precluded any hope of remedying the error or omission constituting the defect, as for instance, defects in a last will or testament.

Wherever possible the jurisprudence on each subject has been cited, establishing either that the error or fault is fatal to the validity of the link, or that it did not have such an effect.

The examiner will bear in mind this fact. Time, in itself, will prove of the greatest assistance in the validating of many links, otherwise at variance with the requirements of the law. Again the acts of those parties who may have been possessed of the right to attack a title, may in many instances put completely at rest any doubt which arise as to the validity of a title, those acts being those of acquiescence, ratification or constituting estoppel.

Time is of importance not alone from the standpoint of bringing about the curative effect of prescription, but also in the matter of the law and jurisprudence existing at the date on which was performed the change of ownership. The fact a married woman may sell her separate property without the authority of her husband, at the present time, would not avail in a case where the transfer occurred at a time when the law forbid. Prescription, estoppel, or ratification alone could cure such a defect.

idity of certain, 326; fraud-
ulant cancellation of, 327,
328; effect of recordation
between parties, 329; rural
mortgages, 325.

Mortgage certificates:
In re acts of sale and mortgages, 65, 67; names in,
liens and privileges on, 68;
issuance by recorder, 65;
obtaining by notaries, sheriffs, 67.

Mothers:
As heir when, 222; natural
child, 231; legitimate child,
222; husband, 233.

Municipalities:
Acquisitions by, 55, 113,
sales by, 118

Municipal courts:
Jurisdiction, 127.

N

Natural persons:
When they inherit, 400.

Notaries:
Duties of, 49, 51, 65, 67;
73; clerks of court ex officio, 52.

O

Orleans parish:
Recordation of transfers, 7,
8.

Owners:
Those never married, 53;
married, 52; acting through
agent, 58; rights affected
by death of spouse; right
and power of transferring,
24.

Ownership:
In re titles, 2; form of
changes by involuntary
transfers, 121; changes in
by order of court, 143, 208;
by sales, dation en paiement,
partitions, 170; public sales;
p u b l i c auction, private
sales to pay debts, in receiverships, 171; in alienation of minor's and interdict's property; formalities
of, 175; to effect a partition, dation en paiement,
public sales, rescissions,
specific performances, 143;
changes by acts before notaries; sales to pay debts,
dation en paiements, partitions in kind, 170; private
sales under act 83, 1924,
170, 171, 172; definition of,
19; acquisition by inheritance, by effect of obligation, by operation of law,
and by prescription, 20;
from sovereign, 20; by voluntary transfer, 21; involuntary, 21.

P

Pact de non alienando:
Effect of, 129.

Parents:
Donations by, 80; adjudication to, of minor's prop-
erty, 187; as an irregular
heir, 229; legal heirs, forced
heirs, 223, 224, 225.

Parishes:
Acquisitions by, 113; sales
by, 118.

statutes in re land acquired from state, 37.

Public sales:
Essentials of, 122 to 127; by sheriffs, 122, formalities of, 124.

R

Receivers:
Appointment of, 152; formalities of, 153; sales by, formalities of, 159; defects in sales, 402.

Recordation:
Effecting ownership, 2; notice, 7, 8; necessity of, 74.

Recorder:
Duties of, 7, 65, 70.

Redemption of property sold for taxes:
Requirements of, 95; from City of New Orleans, 96; legislation in re, 97; defects in 399.

Renunciations:
By widow, heir, 98; of real rights, 98; by authentic act, judicial, 99; as a donation,99; real right, 101; by widow and heirs in successions, 225; form of, revocation of, 81; defects of, 399.

Rescissions:
Essentials of, act 103; when it may be sued for, 103; de--fects in acts of, 399.

Registration:
Effect of, 3; of act, 7, 8, 9; necessity of, 74; exception to rule, 9; in certain succession judgments, 10; principles governing, 366.

Register land office:
As commissioner to decide colonial land claims, 29.

Rules of property:
In tax sales, in re prescription, constitutional evceptions, no corporeal possession, no assessment, 193; identity of property, not subject to taxation; no recordation of sale; 194, 195, 196, 197; quieting of tax titles, 197, 198, 199, 200; kind of tax titles, 200, 201; principles of, 374 to 381.

S

Sales:
By sheriff, 143 when vendee not bound in, 19; definition of, 45; of immovables, 45; prohibited when, 46; authentic acts by, 49; property of another, 47, 48; elements of, 48, 52; parties to 52; by married man, mar-married woman, 54, 55, 56; married status in, 57; purchasers, 59; warranty in, 61; acceptance of, 60; emancipated minor, 56; consideration for, 64; by agent, 58, 59; right of state to sell school lands, 40; rescission of 68; auctioneer, 74, 167; before notary, 168; by state, 108; by schools, 119; public sales by judgment of court, of minor's property, interdict's property, tax sales, eminent domain, by trustees, bank-

www.ingramcontent.com/pod-product-compliance
Lightning Source LLC
Chambersburg PA
CBHW060747220326
41598CB00022B/2352